D1251225

McDougal Littell
Wordskills

Blue Level

James E. Coomber
Concordia College
Moorhead, Minnesota

Howard D. Peet
North Dakota State University
Fargo, North Dakota

McDougal Littell
A HOUGHTON MIFFLIN COMPANY
Evanston, Illinois • Boston • Dallas

IMPORTANT: No part of this book may be reproduced or transmitted in any form or by any means, electronic or mechanical, including photo-copying, recording, or by any information storage and retrieval system, without permission in writing from the Publisher.

ISBN: 0-395-97986-2

Copyright © 2000 by McDougal, Littell & Company
Box 1667, Evanston, Illinois 60204
All rights reserved. Printed in the United States of America.

7 8 9 10–HWI–03

CONTENTS

Word's Worth: satire

Spelling and Wordplay
- *Crossword Puzzle*

Excerpt from An American Childhood
by Annie Dillard

Refining Your Understanding

To the Student

Why study vocabulary? Increasing the number of words that you know helps you read, write, and speak better. You'll understand more of what you read with less reliance on the dictionary, and you'll be able to express yourself more accurately. This doesn't mean using twenty-dollar words to amaze others. It just means using the right words to say exactly what you mean.

How to Use This Book

You may notice something unusual about this vocabulary book. Definitions are not given with the word lists. Instead, you are given something more powerful—strategies for determining the meanings of words yourself. You'll find this information in Strategies for Unlocking Word Meaning (pages 1-12). Then, in the following units, you will master new words using a five-step process:

1. First you will infer the word's meaning through context clues.
2. Second you will refine your understanding by studying the word's use in a reading selection.
3. Then your understanding will be reinforced through a variety of exercises.
4. Next you will relate the word to other words in the same family.
5. Finally you will use the word in writing and speaking.

The words in this book are ones you are likely to encounter in your reading. Some you may already know; others may be completely unfamiliar. As you study these words, try to move them into your "active vocabulary." This means that you understand the words well enough to use them in your speaking and writing.

A Personal Vocabulary-Building Program

You can apply the vocabulary skills in this book to learning any new words that you encounter. Here are several tips that will help you:

1. Keep a vocabulary notebook. Jot down the new words you encounter. Record the essential information for each word: correct spelling, part of speech, pronunciation, definition.
2. Review the words in your notebook. Take a few minutes each day to study them. Set a realistic goal of learning a certain number of new words per week.
3. Study the words actively. Active study means that you use as many senses as possible in studying the word. Say the word. Listen to yourself say it. See the word in your mind's eye. Then make sure you use the word as soon as possible in conversation or in writing. A rule of thumb is that if you use a word twice, it is yours.
4. Invent your own memory devices. Try to associate the word with other similar words you know. Create a mental image that relates to the word and helps you remember its meaning. One student remembered the meaning of the word *pretentious*, "showy, flaunting," by picturing a small boy playing make-believe, *pretending* to be a king.

There is one final reason for studying vocabulary, one that we hope you discover for yourself as you use this book: Words are fascinating! They are as surprising and alive and insightful as the people who use them.

Special Unit: Strategies for Unlocking Word Meaning

What happens when you encounter an unfamiliar word in your reading? If you have a dictionary at hand, you can look up the word. If you don't have a dictionary, you still have two excellent strategies that can help you make sense of the word: **context clues** and **word parts analysis.** You will be using these strategies in every unit of this book. With practice, you can master these strategies and improve your reading skills.

Part A Determining a Word's Meaning from Context

Skilled readers often use context clues to determine a word's meaning. **Context** refers to the words or sentences before or after a certain word that help clarify what the word means. There are several types of context clues you can look for, including **definition and restatement, example, comparison, contrast**, and **cause and effect**.

Definition and Restatement

Sometimes a writer will directly define a word, especially if the word is a technical term that may be unfamiliar to readers. Here is an example:

Future space shuttles to the moon will need to be timed so that the trips will occur when the moon is in *perigee*, the stage in its orbit when it is closest to the earth.

More often, a writer will restate the meaning of a word in a less precise form than a dictionary definition.

Jeanne trained herself to be an *ambidextrous* basketball player. In other words she could dribble, shoot, or pass with either hand.

The meaning of *ambidextrous*—"able to use both hands with equal ease"— becomes obvious through the use of the restatement—"could dribble, shoot, or pass with either hand." Definition and restatement are often signaled by punctuation (note the comma in the first example) and by certain key words and phrases.

Words Signaling Definition and Restatement		
which is	or	also known as
that is	in other words	also called

Example

The context in which a word appears may include one or more **examples** that unlock the meaning of an unfamiliar word, as in the following sentence:

The work of an *agronomist* includes the selective breeding of crop plants and the development of methods to preserve soil.

The word *includes*, followed by examples of two types of work, helps reveal the meaning of *agronomist*—"a person who studies crop production and the management of farmland." The following words often signal examples:

Words Signaling Examples		
like	for instance	this
including	especially	these
such as	other	these include
		for example

Comparison

Another type of context clue is **comparison.** With this clue the writer compares the word in question with other, more familiar words. By noting the similarities between the things described, you can get an idea of the meaning of the unfamiliar word.

Her *penchant* for unnecessary explanations, like her fondness for big words, either annoyed or amused her audience.

The comparison *like her fondness* clearly conveys the meaning of *penchant*—"a strong liking or fondness." Comparisons are often signaled by these key words:

Words Signaling Comparisons		
like	resembling	also
as	likewise	identical
in the same way	similarity	related
similar to		

Contrast

Context may also help reveal the meaning of a word through **contrast,** as in this example:

The *intrepid* child, unlike her more fearful playmates, never doubted her ability to climb to the top of the tree.

In this sentence the word *unlike* signals a contrast. Therefore, you can assume that *intrepid* means the opposite of *fearful*: "unafraid, bold, brave." The following key words and phrases signal contrasts:

Words Signaling Contrasts		
but	on the other hand	dissimilar
although	unlike	different
on the contrary	in contrast to	however

Cause and Effect

Another type of context clue is **cause and effect**. The cause of an action or event may be stated using an unfamiliar word. If, however, the effect of that action is stated in familiar terms, it can help you understand the unfamiliar word. Consider the following example:

Since both sides involved in the labor dispute were *intransigent* in their contract demands, a federal mediator had to be brought in to help reach an agreement.

In this sentence, the cause—intransigent contract demands—leads to the effect—bringing in a federal mediator. Therefore, *intransigent* must mean "refusing to compromise" or "refusing to come to an agreement." Certain key words and phrases may signal cause and effect:

Words Signaling Cause and Effect		
because	consequently	when
since	therefore	as a result

Inference from General Context

Often the clues to the meaning of an unfamiliar word are not in the same sentence nor are they as obvious as the preceding examples. In such cases, you will need to look at the sentences that surround the word and **infer**, or draw a conclusion about, the word's meaning. A single piece of information several sentences away from the unfamiliar word may unlock the meaning. Study the following example:

The doctor's efforts to calm the young boy *exacerbated* the boy's sensation of pain. At first, he had struggled bravely to resist his natural impulse to scream as the doctor slowly stitched the gash on his knee. Then the doctor said that the pain wouldn't last long, and the boy let out anguished screeches that could be heard throughout the emergency room. The doctor's talking about the pain succeeded only in intensifying it.

The clue to the meaning of *exacerbated* is found at the end of the paragraph. The detail *talking about the pain succeeded only in intensifying it* suggests that *exacerbated* means to be "intensified, irritated, or made worse."

Sometimes the supporting details in a paragraph must be examined together to help you infer the meaning of an unfamiliar word. Consider the example below:

Eileen had the misfortune of working with a *cantankerous* lab partner. He wore a perpetual scowl on his face, a sign of his impatient contempt for everyone around him. When she made a suggestion, he could always be counted on to disagree with it. Whatever she did, he would find something to criticize. Finally, she realized that he preferred strife to harmony, and she did her best to ignore him.

A series of descriptive details follows the unfamiliar word *cantankerous*. The details help you draw a conclusion about what a *cantankerous* person is—"a bad-tempered, quarrelsome person."

Determining Meaning from Context   Each of the sentences and paragraphs below contains an italicized word you may not know. Look for context clues to help you determine the meaning of the word, and write the definition in the blank.

1. The famous actress showed a surprising *diffidence* when interviewed. She seemed shy and reserved, in sharp contrast to her dramatic renditions of strong-willed women. She downplayed her accomplishments and admitted that she often feared failure, even though many regarded her as one of the finest actresses of her generation. When asked direct questions, she often hesitated, as if reluctant to assert her own opinion.

   _____

2. Dr. Bennett was skilled enough to cope with any *exigency*, including a patient's sudden heart attack.

   _____

3. When Elizabeth heard the news of the disaster, her face became a *stolid* mask, showing no expression and betraying no emotion.

   _____

4. Numerous phone calls from angry voters forced the mayor to *accede* to their wishes and scrap her plans for constructing a costly new municipal building.

   _____

5. A morning of gardening coupled with the noon heat produced a *lassitude* in Marie, making the hammock look more and more inviting.

   _____

6. When suspected criminals are freed on bail, some of them try to *abscond*. This action only compounds their problems. Every state has strict laws and punishments to guard against such attempts. Also, most suspects underestimate the difficulty of life on the run. The majority are either caught by authorities, or eventually they abandon their attempts to hide from the law and turn themselves in.

   _____

7. The *discord* between the teams was obvious; in the case of the last game they played, several times a referee was called in to resolve angry confrontations.

   _____

8. Unlike John, who could never forgive an insult, Jeff was a *magnanimous* person.

   _____

9. A *hemorrhage* occurs when a large quantity of blood escapes inside the body from a ruptured blood vessel.

   _____

10. The man had the *temerity* to laugh in the judge's face; to punish the man for his insolence, the judge fined him heavily.

   _____

11. One theory about the disappearance of ships in the Bermuda Triangle suggests that the ships may have encountered *maelstroms*, large dangerous whirlpools.

   _____

12. Because visitors refused to stop feeding the animals at the zoo, the sale of peanuts was *proscribed*.

   _____

13. By donning her swimsuit and heading for the beach, Terry *contravened* the doctor's order that she rest.

   _____

14. By the time he was fourteen, Ronald had developed a reputation for *ignominious* behavior; he lied, he picked fights for no reason, and he took a shameless pleasure in boasting about his misdeeds.

   _____

15. The summer heat made all of us feel unusually *torpid* that afternoon. First we considered going to the pool. Then we thought about going out for ice cream. Finally, our sluggishness won out; we just sat in the shade, unwilling to move. For the rest of the day, we were like tortoises basking lazily in the sun.

   _____

Number correct _____ (total 15)

Understanding Context Clues Write a sentence for each of the words below, using a different type of context clue for each sentence. After the sentence, label the method you used to define each word, choosing from one of the following ways: **definition and restatement, example, comparison, contrast,** and **cause and effect.**

augment   mandatory   robust   liability   rampant

1. _____
   _____

2. _____
   _____

3. _____
   _____

4. _____
   _____

5. _____
   _____

Number correct _____ (total 5)

Part B   Determining Meaning Through Word Analysis

Word analysis is another way to determine a new word's meaning. If you know what each part of a word means, you can often understand the complete word.

Prefix   a word part that is added to the beginning of another word or word part
Suffix   a word part that is added to the end of another word or word part
Base word   a complete word to which a prefix and/or a suffix may be added
Root   a word part to which a prefix and/or a suffix may be added. A root cannot stand alone.

The word *nonconformist* is made up of the prefix *non-*, the base word *conform*, and the suffix *-ist*. If you know the meanings of these parts, you can determine the meaning of the word:

non ("not") + conform ("to follow or accept customs or traditions without question") + ist ("a person who does, makes, or practices")

nonconformist = a person who does not follow accepted customs or traditions

Now look at a word with a root. *Incredulity* is made up of the prefix *in-* ("not"), the Latin root *cred* ("believe"), and the suffix *-ity* ("condition or state of"). *Incredulity* means "the state of unbelieving," or more precisely, "an unwillingness or inability to believe."

Prefixes

The following chart contains prefixes that have only one meaning.

Prefixes That Have a Single Meaning

Prefix	Meaning	Example
bene-	good	benefit
circum-	around	circumvent
col-, com-, con-	with, together	collect, compile, conduct
contra-	opposed	contradict
equi-	equal	equidistant
extra-	outside	extralegal
hemi-	half	hemisphere
hyper-	over, above	hypercritical
inter-	between, among	international
intra-	within	intracellular
intro-	into	introvert
mal-	bad	maltreat
mid-	halfway	midday
mis-	wrong	misspell
non-	not	nonworking
post-	after in time, space	postpone
pre-	before	predawn
retro-	backward, behind	retroactive
sub-	under, below	subzero

Some prefixes have more than one meaning. Study these common prefixes listed in the following chart.

Prefixes That Have More Than One Meaning

Prefix	Meaning	Example
a-, ab-	up, out	arise
	not	abnormal
	away	absent
ad-	motion toward	adopt
	nearness to	adjoin
ante-	before, prior to	antecedent
	in front of	anteroom
anti-	against	anticensorship
	prevents, cures	antidote
	opposite, reverse	antimatter
be-	around, by	beset
	about	bemoan
de-	away from, off	derail
	down	decline
	reverse action of	defrost
dis-	lack of	distrust
	not	dishonest
	away	dispatch
em-, en-	to get into, on	embark
	to make, cause	enfeeble
	in, into	enclose
il, im-, in-, ir-	not	immature
	in, into	investigate
pro-	in favor of	prolabor
	forward, ahead	propel
re-	again	replant
	back	repay
semi-	half	semicircle
	twice in a period	semiannual
	partly	semiconscious
super-	over and above	superhuman
	very large	supertanker
trans-	across	transatlantic
	beyond	transcend
un-	not	unhappy
	reverse of	unfasten

Suffixes

Like a prefix, a suffix has a meaning that can provide a strong clue to the definition of a whole word. Suffixes can also determine the part of speech of a word. Certain suffixes make words into nouns; others create adjectives, verbs, or adverbs.

Once you know suffixes and their meanings, you can form new words by attaching suffixes to base words or roots. For instance, the suffix *-ation* can be added to the base word *deprive* to create the word *deprivation*. Notice that the spelling of a base word may change when a suffix is added. In the preceding example, the *e* from *deprive* was dropped when the *-ation* was added. For information about spelling rules for adding suffixes, see the **Spelling Handbook,** pages 198-205.

Noun suffixes, when added to a base word or root, form nouns. Become familiar with the following common noun suffixes.

Noun Suffixes That Refer to Someone Who Does Something

Suffix	Examples
-ant	commandant, occupant
-eer	auctioneer
-er	manager
-ier	cavalier
-ician	beautician, statistician
-ist	geologist, somnambulist
-or	counselor

Noun Suffixes That Make Abstract Words

Suffix	Examples
-ance	vigilance
-ancy	vagrancy, vacancy
-ation	imagination
-cy	accuracy
-dom	freedom, kingdom
-ence	independence
-hood	womanhood, brotherhood
-ice	cowardice, prejudice
-ism	realism, federalism
-ity	sincerity
-ization	civilization
-ment	encouragement, commitment
-ness	kindness, fondness
-ship	ownership, worship
-sion	decision
-tude	gratitude, solitude
-ty	frailty

Adjective suffixes, when added to a base word or root, create adjectives—words that are used to modify nouns and pronouns.

Adjective Suffixes

Suffix	Meaning	Example
-able	able to	readable
-acious	full of	vivacious
-al	relating to	musical
-ant	relating to	triumphant
-ful	full of	harmful
-ible	able to	convertible
-ic	pertaining to or like	heroic
-ical	pertaining to	economical
-ish	pertaining to or like	foolish
-ive	pertaining to	descriptive
-less	without	senseless
-like	like	lifelike
-ly	like	scholarly
-most	at the extreme	topmost
-ous	full of	furious
-ular	pertaining to	cellular

Verb suffixes change base words to verbs. The following chart lists four common verb suffixes.

Verb Suffixes

Suffix	Meaning	Example
-ate	to make	activate
-en	to become	lengthen
-fy	to make	simplify
-ize	to become	crystallize

Adverb Suffixes change base words to adverbs—words that modify verbs, adjectives, and other adverbs. The following chart lists the most common adverb suffixes.

Adverb Suffixes

Suffix	Meaning	Example
-ily, -ly	manner	readily, quickly
-ward	toward	skyward
-wise	like	clockwise

Roots and Word Families

A word root cannot stand alone but must be combined with other word parts. A great many roots used in our language originally came from Greek or Latin. These roots generate whole families of English words. A **word family** is a group of words with a common root. For example, all of the words in the following word family are derived from the Latin root *chron*, which means "time."

anachronism   chronicler   crony
chronic   chronological   diachronic
chronicle   chronometer   synchronize

By learning word roots, you develop your vocabulary because you can recognize roots in many related words. The following two charts show some common Greek and Latin roots.

Useful Greek Roots

Root	Meaning	Examples
anthrop	human	anthropology
aster, astr	star	asterisk
auto	self, alone	automobile
bibl	book	bibliography
bi, bio	life	biology
chron	time	chronology
crac, crat	govern	democracy
dem	people	epidemic
gen	birth, race	generation
geo	earth	geoscience
gram	write	grammar
graph	write	paragraph
hydr	water	hydrogen
log	word, reason	dialogue
logy	study of	geology
meter, metr	measure	barometer
neo	new	neophyte
nom, nym	name, word, law	economic
ortho	straight, correct	orthodontist
pan	all, entire	panorama
phil	love	philosopher
phobia	fear	claustrophobia
phon	sound	phonograph
psych	mind, soul	psychology
scope	see	telescope
soph	wise, wisdom	sophisticated
tele	far, distant	television
theo	god	theology
therm	heat	thermometer

Useful Latin Roots

Root	Meaning	Examples
capt	take, hold, seize	capture
cede, ceed, cess	go, yield, give away	recession, proceed
cred	believe	credit, credible
dic, dict	speak, say, tell	dictate, dictionary
duc, duct	lead	induce, conductor
fac, fec, fic	do, make	factory, defect, fiction
fer	carry	transfer, ferry
ject	throw, hurl	eject, inject
junct	join	junction, conjunction
miss, mit	send	dismiss, admit
mot, mov	move	motion, movie
par	get ready	prepare, repair
pon, pos, posit	place, put	component, deposit
port	carry	porter, portable
puls	throb, urge	pulsate, compulsory
scrib, script	write	scribble, scripture
spec, spic	look, see	spectacle, conspicuous
stat	stand, put in a place	statue, stature
ten	stretch, hold	tendon, tenant
tract	pull, move	tractor, retract
ven, vent	come	convene, event
vers, vert	turn	versatile, invert
vid, vis	see	video, vista
voc, vok	call	vocation, invoke
vol	wish	volunteer, malevolent
volv	roll	revolve, involve

Determining Word Meaning Through Prefixes and Suffixes Draw lines to separate each of the following words into three parts—prefix, base word, and suffix. Determine the meaning of the prefix and suffix. Then, by adding the meanings of the prefix and suffix to the base word, write the meaning of each complete word.

1. entrapment _____

2. disconsolation _____

3. postoperative _____

4. transcontinental _____

5. interplanetary _____

6. dehumanize _____

7. reaffirmation _____

8. hypersensitivity _____

9. unalterable _____

10. indelicacy _____

Number correct _____ (total 10)

Determining Word Meaning Through Prefixes, Suffixes, and Roots Each of the following words consists of a Greek or Latin root and a prefix or suffix. Use your knowledge of roots, prefixes, and suffixes to put together the meanings of the word parts, and write a definition for each word. You may check your definitions with a dictionary.

1. benefactor _____

2. convocation _____

3. intractable _____

4. hyperacidity _____

5. extrovert _____

6. transmittal _____

7. repulsive _____

8. circumspect _____

9. interpose _____

10. abduction _____

Number correct _____ (total 10)

Number correct in Unit _____ (total 40)

UNIT 1

Part A *Target Words and Their Meanings*

The twenty words below will be the focus of this first unit. You will find them in the reading selection and in the exercises in this unit. By working with these words, you will master their meanings. For a guide to the pronunciations of these words and others found in this book, refer to the **Pronunciation Key** on page 223.

1. acclimate (akʹ lə māt′, klīʹ mət) v.	11. fervent (furʹ vənt) adj.
2. ancestral (an sesʹ trəl) adj.	12. foretell (fôr telʹ) v.
3. aspire (ə spīrʹ) v.	13. impending (im pendʹ iŋ) adj.
4. crescendo (krə shenʹ dō) n., adj., adv.	14. incredible (in kredʹ ə b'l) adj.
5. dependent (di penʹ dənt) adj., n.	15. ingenious (in jēnʹ yəs) adj.
6. despite (di spītʹ) prep.	16. meager (mēʹ ger) adj.
7. evolve (i välvʹ) v.	17. precipitate (pre sipʹ ə tāt') v.
8. exquisite (eksʹ kwi zit, ik skwizʹ it) adj.	18. suffrage (sufʹ rij) n.
9. extreme (ik strēmʹ) adj., n.	19. thrive (thrīv) v.
10. exuberant (ig zoōʹ bər ənt) adj.	20. unsung (un suŋʹ) adj.

Inferring Meaning from Context

For each sentence write the letter of the word or phrase that is closest to the meaning of the word or words in italics. Use context clues to help you determine the correct answer. (For information about how context helps you understand vocabulary, see pages 1-5.)

_____ 1. After living for years in Maine, Richard could not *acclimate to* the hot weather in Arizona.

a. get upset about   b. get interested in   c. get ready for   d. get accustomed to

_____ 2. Gloria discussed her family's *ancestral* background with her grandfather, who revealed that they had relatives in both Mexico and Colombia.

a. athletic   b. educational   c. family   d. financial

_____ 3. Renee *aspired* to become a doctor; her hopes were raised when the medical school accepted her.

a. failed   b. hoped   c. did not want   d. had studied

_____ 4. The *crescendo* of applause assured me that my speech had been a success.

a. brief ripple   b. lack   c. growing wave   d. expectation

_____ 5. Our plans for a picnic are *dependent on* the weather.

a. relying upon   b. the cause of   c. spoiled by   d. similar to

_____ 6. *Despite* our warnings, Joe bought the old, rusty car. One week later the car broke down.

a. Because of   b. In regard to   c. Against   d. During

_____ 7. By training diligently for several years, Jenny *evolved into* a fine gymnast.

a. met   b. developed into   c. refused to become   d. failed to become

_____ 8. People were impressed with the Masons' *exquisite* clothing and manners.

a. strangely colored   b. sloppy   c. beautiful   d. shabby

_____ 9. Helen Keller's *extreme* handicaps—lack of sight and hearing—did not keep her from becoming a world-famous author and lecturer.

a. severe   b. mild   c. underestimated   d. imaginary

_____ 10. Leroy was *exuberant* when he learned that he had won first place in the music contest.

a. elated   b. exhausted   c. talented   d. unemotional

_____ 11. Maurice made a *fervent* plea for contributions to help the drought victims.

a. careless   b. selfish   c. comical   d. intensely earnest

_____ 12. Dark clouds, shifting winds, and rapidly falling barometric pressure are weather signs that *foretell* a rainstorm.

a. come after   b. prevent   c. predict   d. forestall

_____ 13. Often in old movies, gloomy background music hinted at *impending* danger.

a. imaginary   b. previous   c. necessary   d. approaching

_____ 14. It seemed *incredible* that a violent storm could occur when just a few hours earlier the weather had been so mild.

a. logical   b. unbelievable   c. typical   d. lucky

_____ 15. Janet's *ingenious* solution to the problem convinced everyone of her intelligence and creativity.

a. silly   b. difficult   c. clever   d. unworkable

_____ 16. Mr. Howe's earnings were so *meager* that he was barely able to buy food and clothes for his family.

a. generous   b. regular   c. skimpy   d. deserved

_____ 17. The car company announced a breakthrough in the development of a new, high-performance engine. This announcement *precipitated* a rush to buy the company's stocks.

a. followed   b. slowed   c. joined   d. caused

_____ 18. U.S. citizens demonstrate their right to *suffrage* whenever they go to the polls to elect their officials.

a. a speedy trial   b. free speech   c. vote   d. suffering

_____ 19. Unlike plants that require direct sunlight, Impatiens *thrive* in partial shade.
   a. die fast   b. grow vigorously   c. wither away   d. break apart

_____ 20. Larry was the *unsung* hero in his town's fight to save the old village hall; he worked tirelessly behind the scenes and received no recognition.
   a. unpraised   b. musical   c. uninvited   d. glorified

Number correct _____ (total 20)

Part B   *Target Words in Reading and Literature*

You should now have a general idea of the meaning of each target word. Refine your understanding by examining the shades of meaning the words have in the following excerpt.

Women on the Move

Howard D. Peet

The issue of women's equality is not a new one. In America alone, concern over the rights and recognition of women has been apparent for close to 150 years. In this passage the author focuses on some significant early battles for women's rights.

The **ancestral** heritage of the American woman before the twentieth century was one of **unsung** accomplishments and legal constrictions. In fact, the **extreme** legal limitations of a wife in early nineteenth century America seem **incredible** now. Her status in this period was the same as a black slave. She could not lawfully retain title to property after marriage, nor could she vote. 5 What was worse, it was not unlawful for a husband to beat his wife. As the mid-nineteenth century approached, the women of America were far from being **acclimated** to such a **dependent** role. By 1840 women were attempting to improve their status, and the leaders of a budding **suffrage** movement were **aspiring** to equality under the law. 10

Even American homemakers with the most **exquisite** of homes or the happiest of families could not escape hearing the call for women's rights. One outstanding suffrage leader, Elizabeth Cady Stanton, was a mother of seven. Among other things, Stanton had insisted on leaving the word *obey* out of her marriage vows. In addition, she read a "Declaration of Sentiments" at the 15 Women's Rights Convention in Seneca Falls, New York, in 1848. This **ingenious** document, modeled carefully on the Declaration of Independence, declared that "We hold these truths to be self evident: That all men and women are created equal."

Nevertheless, the Seneca Falls convention did not **precipitate** similar meet- 20 ings. The reason, of course, was the country's preoccupation with the **impending** Civil War. However, from that **meager** beginning a **fervent** core of leaders concerned with women's rights emerged.

15

In May 1869, Susan B. Anthony joined Elizabeth Cady Stanton to found the National Woman's Suffrage Association. **Despite** the fact that many members of the association had been active in the abolitionist cause, they loudly opposed the Fifteenth Amendment, which declared that the right to vote could not be denied because of race or color. These women could not be **exuberant** about a law that failed to mention discrimination based on sex.

Since neither the Constitution nor any of the amendments actually denied women the right to vote, Susan Anthony along with fifteen other women decided to actively test the situation. They successfully registered and voted in the 1872 election. Three weeks later the voters were arrested, tried, and fined for voting illegally. Their actions, however, led to a growing call for a suffrage amendment. From that point on, events began to **foretell** the passage of the Nineteenth Amendment in August 1920, which finally extended voting rights to all women.

The issue of women's rights slowly **evolved** to include other concerns beyond the right to vote. The movement began to **thrive** in the 1960's and the 1970s. Interest in the Equal Rights Amendment reached a **crescendo** with the International Women's Year Conference in Houston, Texas, in November 1977. This conference, financed by the federal government, was charged with the task of analyzing the needs of women in an effort to make Elizabeth Cady Stanton's remark—"all men and women are created equal"—a truth in American law.

Refining Your Understanding

For each of the following questions, consider how the target word is used in the passage. Write the letter of the word or phrase that best completes each sentence.

_____ 1. If women were "far from being *acclimated* to such a . . . role" (line 8), they probably   a. were content about the unequal treatment
b. aspired to sexual equality   c. felt they were thriving under the conditions of the time.

_____ 2. An example of the "*dependent* role" of women before the 1900's (line 8) was   a. the word *obey* in marriage vows   b. the "Declaration of Sentiments"   c. the founding of the National Woman's Suffrage Association.

_____ 3. In line 28, which meaning of *exuberant* is conveyed?
a. angry   b. enthusiastic   c. disappointed.

_____ 4. The use of the word *evolved* (line 37) suggests that concern for women's rights grew   a. suddenly   b. gradually   c. not at all.

_____ 5. "The movement began to *thrive* in the 1960's and the 1970's" (line 38). From this fact, one can conclude that   a. women then were suffering greater abuse than they had previously   b. by the 1960's and 1970's women's salaries and working conditions needed no further improvement   c. more women were becoming informed about women's issues.

Number correct _____ (total 5)

Part C   Ways to Make New Words Your Own

By now you are familiar with the target words and their meanings. This section presents a variety of reinforcement activities that will help you make the words part of your permanent vocabulary.

Using Language and Thinking Skills

Understanding Multiple Meanings   Each box in this exercise contains a boldfaced word and its various definitions. Read the definitions, and then read the sentences using the word. Write the letter of the definition that applies to each sentence.

---

thrive
a. to prosper; to succeed (v.)
b. to grow vigorously; to bloom (v.)

_____ 1. Corn thrives in a moist climate.

_____ 2. A healthy diet makes growing children thrive.

_____ 3. Hotels and restaurants will *thrive* when the convention center opens.

```
extreme
   a. at the end or outermost point; remote (adj.)
   b. a very pronounced or excessive degree (n.)
```

_____ 4. The *extreme* northwest portion of our state is famous for cattle ranching.

_____ 5. Joan's sensitivity to any criticism was carried to an *extreme*.

Number correct _____ (total 5)

Practicing for Standardized Tests

Antonyms Write the letter of the word that is most nearly *opposite* in meaning to the capitalized word.

_____ 1. ASPIRE: (A) climb   (B) aim   (C) despair   (D) dignify   (E) delight

_____ 2. CRESCENDO: (A) diminishing   (B) hindrance   (C) increase
           (D) invitation   (E) intention

_____ 3. DEPENDENT: (A) needful   (B) incredible   (C) virtuous
           (D) dignified   (E) self-reliant

_____ 4. EXQUISITE: (A) scornful   (B) shabby   (C) magnified   (D) perpetual
           (E) elegant

_____ 5. FORETELL: (A) evolve   (B) predict   (C) show   (D) conceal   (E) advocate

_____ 6. INCREDIBLE: (A) believable   (B) peculiar   (C) ironic   (D) exuberant
           (E) edible

_____ 7. INGENIOUS: (A) clever   (B) unique   (C) fervent   (D) moral
           (E) uninventive

_____ 8. MEAGER: (A) shy   (B) dependent   (C) ample   (D) sparse   (E) exquisite

_____ 9. THRIVE: (A) wither   (B) grow   (C) evolve   (D) acclimate   (E) save

_____ 10. UNSUNG: (A) demoralized   (B) overtaken   (C) minimized
           (D) praised   (E) menaced

Number correct _____ (total 10)

Word's Worth: crescendo

Crescendo comes from an Italian word meaning "to increase or grow." *Crescendo* is related to the word *crescent*, which describes a shape of the moon as it grows toward fullness. The word *crescendo* is commonly used in music to indicate an increase in loudness in a piece of music. The musical sign for *crescendo* is < , which is reminiscent of the crescent shape.

Spelling and Wordplay

Crossword Puzzle Read each clue to determine what word will fit in the corresponding squares. There are several target words in the puzzle.

ACROSS

1. Inherited
6. Personal pronoun, third person, singular, masculine case
8. An auto
9. Comes after five
10. Gradual increase in volume
14. Abbr. Province of Quebec
15. Not off
16. Contraction of *do not*
19. City in Colombia, S. America
22. Slang for *Mother*
24. Predicts
26. See 23 Down
27. Princess Diana of Wales
29. To be about to happen
31. Gradually develop
34. Mountain pass
36. A coughing sound
38. Scanty
39. In spite of
41. Abbr. teaspoon
42. To be ambitious

DOWN

1. To get accustomed to
2. Abbr. National Association of Realtors
3. Statement of belief
4. Abbr. Strategic Air Command
5. Past tense of *run*
6. Joint at each thigh
7. Beautifully made
11. Greatest degree
12. Opposite of 16 Across
13. One time
17. Not on
18. Opposite of *yes*
20. Nickname of Alphonse
21. Abbr. Doctor of Laws
23. Morning
25. High-school student
28. Large woods
29. A climbing plant
30. To pull
32. Lights
34. To choke for air
35. A fruit
36. To total
37. Male pronoun
38. ___ ___ ___ CULPA; Latin for "I am to blame"
40. Abbr. Ice Point

Part D Related Words

A number of words are closely related to the target words you have studied. Use your knowledge of the target words and of word parts to determine the meanings of these words. (For information about word parts analysis, see pages 6-12.) If you are unsure of any definitions, use your dictionary. Learning these related words expands your vocabulary and helps you learn the target words more thoroughly.

1. ancestor (an′ ses′ tər,-sə s-) n.
2. ancestry (an′ ses′ trē, -sə s-) n.
3. aspiration (as′ pə rā′ shən) n.
4. credibility (kred′ ə bil′ ə tē) n.
5. credible (kred′ ə b'l) adj.
6. credulous (krej′ oo ləs) adj.
7. creed (krēd) n.
8. extremity (ik strem′ ə tē) n.
9. forecast (fôr′ kast′) n., v.
10. forerunner (fôr′ run′ ər) n.
11. foresight (fôr′ sīt′) n.
12. genius (jēn′ yəs, jē′ nē əs) n.
13. incredibility (in kred′ ə bil′ ə tē) n.
14. independent (in′ di pen′ dənt) adj., n.
15. precipitation (pri sip′ ə tā′ shən) n.
16. spite (spīt) n., v.
17. suffragette (suf′ rə jet′) n.

Understanding Related Words

Sentence Completion In the blank write the word from the list that best completes the sentence.

_____ 1. The Kellys trace the _?_ of their family back to seventeenth-century Ireland.

_____ 2. At an early age, Abe Lincoln's _?_ was to become a lawyer.

_____ 3. Huntington, West Virginia, is in the western _?_ of the state.

_____ 4. Wouldn't a _?_ like Susan B. Anthony be exuberant to know that today millions of women exercise their right to vote!

_____ 5. Threats of a strike resulted in the _?_ of negotiation talks and the drafting of a new contract.

_____ 6. Displaying amazing _?_ , Angela took her money out of the stock market one week before the stock prices crashed.

_____ 7. George I, who ruled England in the eighteenth century, is one of Queen Elizabeth II's many royal _?_ (s).

_____ 8. Einstein, the scientist whose theories explained such concepts as mass and energy, was a true _?_ .

_____ 9. In 1963 Kenya declared itself _?_ of Great Britain and formed a new country.

_____ 10. Several inconsistencies that became apparent during cross-examination made the jury doubt the _?_ of the witness.

Number correct _____ (total 10)

20

Analyzing Word Parts

The Prefix *fore-* The target word *foretell* contains the prefix *fore-*, which means "before." Some other words containing this prefix are: *forerunner*, *forecast*, *foresight*, *forestall*, and *foreshadow*. Using your knowledge of *fore*, write the letter of the answer that is closest to the meaning of the italicized word.

_____ 1. The weather *forecast* for this week includes rain and cooler temperatures.
a. precipitation   b. outlook   c. certainty   d. record

_____ 2. Harry   T. Kendall showed considerable *foresight* when he opened a mine in Montana that later yielded great amounts of gold.
a. wealth   b. stubbornness   c. ability to predict   d. willingness to change

_____ 3. Our family's *forefathers* came to North America in 1886 from Germany.
a. grandchildren   b. friends   c. ancestors   d. neighbors

_____ 4. The abacus could be considered a *forerunner* of the modern calculator.
a. follower   b. predecessor   c. competitor   d. copy

_____ 5. The executives *forestalled* bankruptcy by re-organizing the company.
a. explained   b. caused   c. prevented   d. sought

Number correct _____ (total 5)

The Latin Root *cred* and the Prefix *in-* The target word *incredible* comes from the Latin *credere*, "to believe." The prefix *in-* means "not." When *in-* is placed in front of a word, it often forms a new word that means the opposite of the original word. For example, *in* + *capable* means "not capable." Using your knowledge of *in-* and *cred*, write the letter of the word that is closest to the meaning of the word in italics.

_____ 1. We were *incredulous* about the story of the young boy setting a world record.
a. doubtful   b. angered   c. sorry   d. pleased

_____ 2. Little Bobby is very *credulous;* Johnny convinced him that the eclipse would keep the earth in darkness for the next ten days.
a. knowledgeable   b. small   c. trusting   d. disbelieving

_____ 3. After telling those lies, Lynn's *credibility* was shattered.
a. reliability   b. disbelief   c. health   d. credit rating

_____ 4. The *incredibility* of their venture—crossing the Antarctic continent on foot—generated worldwide interest.
a. unknown aspect   b. astounding nature   c. cost   d. problem

_____ 5. According to that philosopher's *creed,* the greatest act a person can perform is to save the life of another.
a. behavior   b. experience   c. set of beliefs   d. large family

Number correct _____ (total 5)

Number correct in Unit _____ (total 60)

Turn to **The Final Silent** *e* on pages 200-202 of the **Spelling Handbook.** Read the rules and complete the exercises provided.

The Last Word

Writing

One of the principal jobs of an editor is to rewrite material using clear, concise language. Try your hand at editing. Rewrite each sentence below, making use of one of the words from the list below.

Original: The robins flew for hundreds of miles to the south for the winter.
Revision: The robins *migrated* south for the winter.

acclimated   exuberant   meager   unsung   aspired   foretold   thrive

1. Cats get along very well on a diet of good food and lots of affection.

   _____

2. By the third week of classes, Nicole had become very used to the schedule.

   _____

3. Sarah made it her goal to become a lawyer.

   _____

4. The hockey team members were in very high spirits after their victory.

   _____

5. The corner restaurant is infamous for serving small, inadequate food portions.

   _____

6. Jose is the hero who did all the work without recognition.

   _____

7. Rita told others that she had the feeling there would be an earthquake in April.

   _____

Group Discussion

"Every great action is extreme when it is undertaken. Only when it has been accomplished does it seem possible to those creatures of more common stuff."—Stendhal
1. With a group of your classmates, identify the meaning of *extreme* as it is used in this quotation.
2. Describe situations that illustrate Stendhal's quotation. Discuss whether you agree with Stendhal's statement or not.

UNIT 2

Part A Target Words and Their Meanings

1. assuage (ə swāj′) v.
2. brandish (bran′ dish) v.
3. cynical (sin′ i k'l) adj.
4. demoralize (di môr′ ə līz′) v.
5. despair (di sper′) n., v.
6. dignify (dig′ nə fī′) v.
7. engulf (in gulf′) v.
8. ennoble (i nō′ b'l) v.
9. grotesque (grō tesk′) adj.
10. impede (im pēd′) v.
11. inert (in urt′) adj.
12. magnificent (mag nif′ ə s'nt) adj.
13. menace (men′ is) n., v.
14. minimize (min′ ə mīz′) v.
15. misconception (mis′ kən sep′ shən) n.
16. overtake (ō′ vər tāk′) v.
17. profound (prə found′) adj.
18. sheepishly (shēp′ ish lē) adv.
19. splendor (splen′ dər) n.
20. staid (stād) adj.

Inferring Meaning from Context

For each sentence write the letter of the word or phrase that is closest to the meaning of the word or words in italics. Use context clues to help you determine the correct answer. (For information about how context helps you understand vocabulary, see pages 1–5.)

_____ 1. Soaking in a warm bath will help to *assuage* the aches and pains you may have after a strenuous workout.

    a. cause b. relieve c. intensify d. acclimate

_____ 2. The painting depicted a Civil War hero *brandishing* his sword in the air as he charged the enemy.

    a. waving   b. throwing c. sharpening d. demonstrating

_____ 3. Colleen became *cynical* when the promise made to her was broken.

    a. appreciative b. hopeful c. distrustful d. indifferent

_____ 4. We started to get *demoralized* when our opponent scored forty-eight points to our ten in the first half of the basketball game.

    a. disheartened b. lucky c. injured d. spirited

_____ 5. The long jumper was filled with *despair* after failing in her final attempt to make the Olympic team.

    a. a sense of relief   b. joy c. depression d. energy

_____ 6. The president *dignified* Ms. Chan by referring to her as a leader.

    a. ridiculed b. honored c. boasted to d. angered

_____ 7. The firefighters were *engulfed* by flames as they attempted to save the people trapped in the burning building.
a. assuaged   b. surrounded   c. corrupted   d. enchanted

_____ 8. At the speaker's table sat the important guests, *ennobled* scientists from around the world.
a. insulted   b. unknown   c. honored   d. demoralized

_____ 9. People at the Halloween party were frightened by Tony's *grotesque* mask.
a. bizarre   b. exquisite   c. filthy   d. ridiculous

_____ 10. The heavy traffic *impeded* our progress.
a. encouraged   b. sustained   c. delayed   d. caused

_____ 11. For hundreds of years, the volcano remained *inert*, causing little threat to nearby villages.
a. inactive   b. incredible   c. invisible   d. interesting

_____ 12. The *magnificent* new building added to the beauty of the city's skyline.
a. grotesque   b. ordinary   c. impressive   d. disguised

_____ 13. The whirlpool was *a menace* to ships traveling through that channel.
a. a memory   b. a threat   c. a pleasure   d. an accident

_____ 14. To *minimize* the chance of severe injury, seat belts are required.
a. prolong   b. illustrate   c. increase   d. reduce

_____ 15. The scenes in the preview of the movie were responsible for our *misconception*. We thought our favorite actor had the lead role; in reality, he had only a small, walk-on part.
a. inspiration   b. ingenious idea   c. misunderstanding   d. mischief

_____ 16. The storm *overtook* us before we could get the boat back to the harbor.
a. conquered   b. assisted   c. avoided   d. caught up with

_____ 17. The philosophers engaged in a *profound* discussion on the meaning of life.
a. productive   b. unimportant   c. unknown   d. deep

_____ 18. After forgetting her lines in the school play, Annette exited *sheepishly* from the stage.
a. proudly   b. loudly   c. self-consciously   d. forcefully

_____ 19. Visitors to the Louvre, the famous art museum in Paris, experience the *splendor* of the art as well as the beauty of the museum itself.
a. inferiority   b. majesty   c. boredom   d. reaction

_____ 20. The guards at Buckingham Palace have been trained to maintain a *staid* expression no matter how hard visitors try to get them to laugh.
a. friendly   b. silly   c. serious   d. changeable

Number correct _____ (total 20)

You should now have a general idea of the meaning of each target word. Refine your understanding by examining the shades of meaning the words have in the following excerpt.

The Day the Dam Broke

James Thurber

James Thurber was an American humorist known for his clever portrayals of human nature. In this reading selection Thurber combines humor with his personal experience to relate an occurrence from his youth.

My memories of what my family and I went through during the 1913 flood in Ohio I would gladly forget. We were both **ennobled** and **demoralized** by the experience. Grandfather especially rose to **magnificent** heights which can never lose their **splendor** for me, even though his reactions to the flood were based upon a **profound misconception;** namely, that Nathan Bedford Forrest's[1] 5 cavalry was the **menace** we were called upon to face. The only possible means of escape for us was to flee the house, a step which grandfather sternly forbade, **brandishing** his old army sabre[2] in his hand. Meanwhile hundreds of people were streaming by our house in a wild panic, screaming "Go east! Go east!" We had to stun grandfather with the ironing board. **Impeded** as we were by the 10 **inert** form of the old gentleman—he was taller than six feet and weighed almost a hundred and seventy pounds—we were passed, in the first half-mile, by practically everybody else in the city. Had grandfather not come to, at the corner of Parsons Avenue and Town Street, we would unquestionably have been **overtaken** and **engulfed** by roaring waters—that is, if there had been any 15

---

[1] Nathan Bedford Forrest: A Confederate general in the Civil War.
[2] sabre: a heavy sword with a slightly curved blade

roaring waters. Later, when the panic had died down and people had gone rather **sheepishly** back to their homes and their offices, **minimizing** the distances they had run and offering various reasons for running, city engineers pointed out that, even if the dam had broken, the water level would not have risen more than two additional inches in the West Side. The East Side (where 20 we lived and where all the running occurred) had never been in any danger at all. Only a rise of some ninety-five feet could have caused the flood waters to flow over High Street—the thoroughfare that divided the east side of town from the west—and engulf the East Side.

The fact that we were all as safe as kittens under a cookstove did not, 25 however, **assuage** in the least the fine **despair** and the **grotesque** desperation which seized upon the residents of the East Side when the cry spread like a grass fire that the dam had given way. Some of the most **dignified, staid, cynical,** and clear-thinking people in town abandoned their homes and offices and ran east. There are few alarms in the world more terrifying than "The dam 30 has broken!" There are few persons capable of stopping to reason when that clarion cry[3] strikes upon their ears, even persons who live in towns no nearer than five hundred miles to a dam.

---

[3] clarion cry: reference to an announcement made by a clarion, a trumpet of the Middle Ages producing clear, sharp, or shrill tones

Refining Your Understanding

For each of the following questions, consider how the target word is used in the passage. Write the letter of the word or phrase that best completes each sentence.

_____ 1. Grandfather's *profound misconception* (line 5) was that a. he believed that the town was in great danger from a flood b. he felt that the family was in no danger c. he thought that the Confederate cavalry was about to attack.

_____ 2. The narrator's grandfather became an *"inert* form" (line 11) because a. the blow from the ironing board had knocked him out b. he was old and arthritic c. he was wildly brandishing his sword.

_____ 3. After the incident, the people came home *sheepishly* (line 17) because a. they had panicked when they were in no danger b. they had taken the flood news too lightly c. their homes had been looted while they were gone.

_____ 4. When the people returned to their homes and jobs, they *minimized* the distances they had run (line 17) because a. they were tired and wanted a shortcut b. they were proud of their accomplishments c. they felt foolish.

_____ 5. The people's *"despair* and . . . *grotesque* desperation" (line 26) had resulted from their a. realizing that they had been in no danger b. fear of a flood c. embarrassment.

Number correct _____ (total 5)

26

Part C   Ways to Make New Words Your Own

Using Language and Thinking Skills

Finding the Unrelated Word. Write the letter of the word that is not related in meaning to the other words in the set.

_____ 1. a. devalue b. ennoble c. underrate d. detract

_____ 2. a. shallow b. deep c. thoughtful d. profound

_____ 3. a. demoralize b. encourage c. discourage d. dispirit

_____ 4. a. aggravate b. assuage c. ease d. lighten

_____ 5. a. harm b. menace c. benefit d. threaten

_____ 6. a. accuracy b. misunderstanding c. misconception d. error

_____ 7. a. flourish b. brandish c. show off d. repress

_____ 8. a. grotesque b. bizarre c. familiar d. unusual

_____ 9. a. forcefully b. sheepishly c. boldly d. confidently

_____ 10. a. minimize b. reduce c. downplay d. glamorize

Number correct _____ (total 10)

Practicing for Standardized Tests

Synonyms Write the letter of the word whose meaning is closest to that of the capitalized word.

_____ 1. DIGNIFY: (A) detract (B) aspire (C) fear (D) hear (E) honor

_____ 2. ENGULF: (A) avoid (B) cleanse (C) overwhelm (D) threaten (E) impend

_____ 3. IMPEDE: (A) input (B) yield (C) hinder (D) help (E) progress

_____ 4. INERT: (A) incredible (B) exquisite (C) ominous (D) motionless (E) meager

_____ 5. MAGNIFICENT: (A) great (B) ingenious (C) insignificant (D) malicious (E) exuberant

_____ 6. MENACE: (A) obstacle (B) benefit (C) grimace (D) threat (E) remark

_____ 7. PROFOUND: (A) foolish (B) deep (C) unfortunate (D) unsung (E) ancestral

_____ 8. MINIMIZE: (A) lessen (B) increase (C) impend (D) evolve (E) explain

_____ 9. SPLENDOR: (A) size (B) drabness (C) beauty (D) genius (E) comfort

_____ 10. DESPAIR: (A) fear (B) extremity (C) incredibility (D) faith (E) hopelessness

Number correct _____ (total 10)

Spelling and Wordplay

Word Maze Find and circle the target words in this maze.

A	B	G	R	O	T	E	S	Q	U	E	C	R	D	E
E	S	H	J	M	P	N	T	R	T	W	Z	I	A	C
N	D	S	F	G	Y	N	E	P	C	G	A	A	R	A
O	N	V	U	D	E	O	R	M	S	T	D	P	S	N
I	F	M	H	A	J	B	N	P	S	I	N	S	H	E
T	R	U	A	W	G	L	L	T	V	O	U	E	E	M
P	F	L	U	G	N	E	Y	A	E	V	O	D	E	I
E	H	S	I	D	N	A	R	B	P	E	F	I	P	N
C	L	N	Q	D	Z	I	E	H	A	R	O	G	I	I
N	T	V	O	C	E	S	F	L	N	T	R	N	S	M
O	N	R	U	T	R	E	N	I	I	A	P	I	H	I
C	G	J	L	A	C	I	N	Y	C	K	B	F	L	Z
S	D	X	N	R	U	Z	T	V	O	E	L	Y	Y	E
I	M	P	E	D	E	E	F	H	S	J	N	P	A	Q
M	D	E	M	O	R	A	L	I	Z	E	W	T	U	R

assuage
brandish
cynical
demoralize
despair
dignify
engulf
ennoble
grotesque
impede
inert
magnificent
menace
minimize
misconception
overtake
profound
sheepishly
splendor
staid

Part D   Related Words

A number of words are closely related to the target words you have studied. Use your knowledge of the target words and of word parts to determine the meanings of these words (For information about word parts analysis, see pages 6-12.) If you are unsure of any definitions, use your dictionary. Learning these related words expands your vocabulary and helps you learn the target words more thoroughly.

1. assuagement (ə swāj′ mənt) n.
2. concept (kän′ sept) n.
3. cynic (sin′ ik) n.
4. desperation (des′ pə rā′ shn) n.
5. dignity (dig′ nə tē) n.
6. grotesqueness (grō tesk′ nes) n.
7. impediment (im ped′ ə mənt) n.
8. inertia (in ʉr′ shə) n.
9. magnificence (mag nif′ ə s′ns) n.
10. magnify (mag′ nə fī′) v.
11. minimum (min′ ə məm) adj., n.
12. nobility (nō bil′ ə tē) n.
13. profundity (prə fun′ də tē) n.
14. splendid (splen′ did) adj.

Understanding Related Words

Finding Examples   Match each noun in the list with its appropriate example below. In the corresponding blank write the noun's letter.

a. assuagement   e. grotesqueness   i. minimum
b. concept   f. impediment   j. nobility
c. cynic   g. inertia
d. dignity   h. magnificence

_____ 1. a broken foot that halts a runner's training for the Olympics

_____ 2. the calming influence of a friend who tells you not to worry

_____ 3. Thomas Edison's original idea for what became the phonograph

_____ 4. King Olaf V of Norway

_____ 5. an ambassador behaving in a stately manner

_____ 6. the lowest wage one can receive for a job

_____ 7. a person who refuses to believe that others appreciate kindness

_____ 8. the terrifying appearance of monsters in a horror movie

_____ 9. the beauty and elegance of Queen Elizabeth's crown

_____ 10. the feeling of a person whose energy has been drained by hot weather

Number correct _____ (total 10)

Analyzing Word Parts

Close Relatives   The target word *magnificent* is an adjective. Its two related words, *magnificence* and *magnify*, are not. Look up their parts of speech on page 28. Write the word that best completes each sentence below.

1. From the top of the Empire State Building, the view of New York City

   was _____ .

2. The _____ of the new spacecraft thrilled the tourists.

3. Kevin's emotional description of his unfortunate dilemma seemed to

   _____ the seriousness of the situation.

4. A _____ rainbow appeared in the sky after the storm.

5. Astronomers' telescopes _____ planets and other heavenly bodies.

Number correct _____ (total 5)

Number correct in Unit _____ (total 60)

Turn to **The Letter g** on page 209 of the **Spelling Handbook.** Read the rule and complete the exercises provided.

The Last Word

Writing

Write an imaginative story that includes three of the items listed below. Choose one item from each of the three columns.

Characters	Incidents	Conditions
• a *cynical* person	• *engulfed* in fire	• in a *splendid* way
• a *dignified* individual	• *impeded* by a heavy load	• under a *misconception*
• a person of *nobility*	• *minimizing* a setback	• with *despair* in her/his voice
• a *menace* to society	• *sheepishly* regretting something	• on a *meager* salary
• a person who cannot overcome *inertia*	• *brandishing* a trophy	• with a *grotesque* appearance
• a *profound* thinker	• *overtaking* a villain	• in an *independent* fashion
• an *ancestor*	• *assuaging* a friend's fears	• *despite* many problems
• a *staid* professor		

Speaking

What is *dignity*? Think of a person you regard as dignified—a friend, a relative, or a public figure. List the qualities that make him or her seem dignified. In a brief speech, describe an incident that shows how and why this person is dignified.

Group Discussion

Share with a small group an experience that had a *profound* effect on you. Explain why the experience affected you so deeply. Determine through discussion if other students have had similar experiences.

Word's Worth: grotesque

Grotesque comes from the Italian word *grottesca*, meaning "a grotto, cave, or crypt." The term was used to describe the odd paintings and designs in underground rooms dating back to ancient Rome—strange artwork that people today still find grotesque.

UNIT 3

Part A   Target Words and Their Meanings

1. advocate (ad′ və kit, -kāt′) n.
   (ad′ və kāt′) v.
2. anticipate (an tis′ ə pāt′) v.
3. circumscribe (sʉr′ kəm skrīb′) v.
4. circumstance (sʉr kəm stans′, -stəns) n.
5. collective (kə lek′ tiv) adj.
6. consensus (kən sen′ səs) n.
7. depreciate (di prē′ shē āt′) v.
8. dispute (dis pyo͞ot′) n., v.
9. enable (in ā′ b'l) v.
10. encompass (in kum′ pəs) v.
11. irony (ī′ rən ē, ī′ ər nē) n.
12. militant (mil′ i tənt) adj., n.
13. morality (mə ral′ ə tē, mô-) n.
14. perpetuate (pər pech′ o͞o wāt′) v.
15. prominent (präm′ ə nənt) adj.
16. satire (sa′ tīr)n.
17. stereotype (ster′ ē ə tīp′, stir′-) n., v.
18. unity (yo͞o′ nə tē) n.
19. urgency (ʉr′ jən sē) n.
20. virtue (vʉr′ cho͞o) n.

Inferring Meaning from Context

For each sentence write the letter of the word or phrase that is closest to the meaning of the word or words in italics. Use context clues to help you determine the correct answers. (For information about how context helps you understand vocabulary, see pages 1–5.)

_____ 1. The action Sam *advocated* was overruled by the committee.
   a. opposed   b. enjoyed   c. inquired about   d. was in favor of

_____ 2. Although we did not *anticipate* having company last week, we were happy to see our friends when they showed up at our house.
   a. dislike   b. announce   c. foresee   d. neglect

_____ 3. The forecaster *circumscribed* three states on the weather map to indicate the region that was expecting snow.
   a. erased   b. circled   c. questioned   d. avoided

_____ 4. Marilyn believed that if Jon had been brought up under more favorable *circumstances*, he would not have been in trouble with the law.
   a. conditions   b. governments   c. handicaps   d. travels

_____ 5. It was a *collective* decision; everyone on the city council finally agreed.
   a. financial   b. disputed   c. cynical   d. group

_____ 6. The club members settled their differences and achieved *a consensus*.
   a. a confrontation   b. an advantage   c. a stalemate   d. an agreement

_____ 7. The house had *depreciated* in value; it hadn't been cared for in years.
a. fluctuated b. increased c. decreased d. remained unchanged

_____ 8. The border *dispute* between those two countries was finally settled.
a. conversation b. distraction c. cooperation d. argument

_____ 9. Len's swimming ability *enabled* him to save the drowning girl.
a. told b. made it impossible for c. utilized d. made it possible for

_____ 10. Trespassers were discouraged by the barbed wire fence that *encompassed* the entire pool area.
a. excluded b. surrounded c. minimized d. covered

_____ 11. It was *an irony* that Eileen did well on the test even though she didn't study.
a. a fortunate thing b. an expected occurrence c. a likely excuse d. an unexpected outcome

_____ 12. The protesters gradually became more *militant*, some even advocating the destruction of property; that's when I left the group.
a. learned b. athletic c. ordinary d. aggressive

_____ 13. Jeffrey's sense of *morality* led him to report the accident he had caused.
a. life style b. what is right and wrong c. competition d. ignorance

_____ 14. In order to *perpetuate* his name after his death, Mr. Clydesdale gave a considerable amount of money for a park to be established in his name.
a. immortalize b. dishonor c. minimize d. change

_____ 15. After twenty years of distinguished accomplishments, Ms. Dubrinski had become *a prominent* figure in the field of mathematics education.
a. an incompetent b. a temporary c. a forgetful d. an outstanding

_____ 16. Many readers initially thought that the newspaper story was just lighthearted fun; upon rereading it, however, they realized it was a cruel *satire* of the new mayor and his policies.
a. glamorized description b. ridiculing account c. inspirational account d. meager picture

_____ 17. Dickens's character Ebenezer Scrooge is *a stereotype* of the lonely miser.
a. an end b. a defense c. a true story d. a popular image

_____ 18. The signing of the contract and the handshakes afterward signaled the achievement of *unity* between the opposing sides.
a. harmony b. devotion c. ambition d. humor

_____ 19. The siren emphasized the *urgency of* the crisis; we dived for cover.
a. accomplishment of b. inertia of c. need for action during
d. impending celebration of

_____ 20. Wrongdoing is not always punished, nor is *virtue* always rewarded.
a. evil b. ancestry c. inertia d. goodness

Number correct _____ (total 20)

Part B Target Words in Reading and Literature

By now you should have a general idea of the meaning of each target word. You can begin to refine your understanding by examining the shades of meaning the words have in the following excerpt.

Indian Humor

Vine Deloria, Jr.

Few people are aware of the importance of humor in the Native American culture. In this excerpt from Custer Died for Your Sins, *Native American Vine Deloria, Jr., reveals the extent of this humor. Written in the early 1970's, Deloria's book seeks to destroy the many myths and misconceptions that most Americans have about Native Americans.*

One of the best ways to understand a people is to know what makes them laugh. Laughter **encompasses** the limits of the soul. In humor, life is redefined and accepted. **Irony** and **satire** provide much keener insights into a group's **collective** psyche and values than do years of research.

It has always been a great disappointment to Indian people that the humorous   5 side of Indian life has not been mentioned by professed experts on Indian affairs. Rather, the image of the granite-faced grunting Indian has been **perpetuated** by American mythology.

People have little sympathy with stolid[1] groups. Dick Gregory did much more than is believed when he introduced humor into the civil rights struggle. He   10 **enabled** nonblacks to enter into the thought world of the black community and experience the hurt it suffered. When all people shared the humorous but ironic situation of the blacks, the **urgency** and **morality** of civil rights was communicated.

---

[1] stolid: having or showing little or no emotion or sensitivity

"WELL, THERE GOES THE NEIGHBORHOOD"

© ROBERT FREEMAN

The Indian people are exactly opposite of the popular **stereotype.** Indians have found a humorous side to nearly every problem, and the experiences of life have generally been so well defined through jokes and stories that they have become a thing in themselves.

For centuries before the white invasion, teasing was a method of control of social situations by Indian people. Rather than embarrass members of the tribe publicly, people used to tease individuals they considered out of step with the **consensus** of tribal opinion. In this way egos were preserved, and **disputes** within the tribe of a personal nature were held to a minimum.

Gradually people learned to **anticipate** teasing and began to tease themselves as a means of showing humility and at the same time **advocating** a course of action they deeply believed in. People would **depreciate** their feats to show they were not trying to run roughshod over tribal desires. This method of behavior served to highlight their true **virtues** and gain them a place of influence in tribal policy-making circles.

Humor has come to occupy such a **prominent** place in national Indian affairs that any kind of movement is impossible without it. Tribes are being brought together by sharing humor of the past. Columbus jokes gain great sympathy among all tribes, yet there are no tribes extant[2] who had anything to do with Columbus. But the fact of white invasion from which all tribes have suffered has created a common bond in relation to Columbus jokes that gives a solid feeling of **unity** and purpose to the tribes.

The more desperate the problem, the more humor is directed to describe it. Satirical remarks often **circumscribe** problems so that possible solutions are drawn from the **circumstances** that would not make sense if presented in other than a humorous form.

Often people are awakened and brought to a **militant** edge through funny remarks. I often counseled people to run for the Bureau of Indian Affairs in case of an earthquake because nothing could shake the BIA. And I would watch as younger Indians set their jaws, determined that they, if nobody else, would shake it. We also had a saying that in case of fire call the BIA, and they would handle it because they put a wet blanket on everything. This also got a warm reception from people.

Columbus jokes are the best for penetration into the heart of the matter, however. It is said that when Columbus landed, one Indian turned to another and said, "Well, there goes the neighborhood." Another version has two Indians watching Columbus land and one saying to the other, "Maybe if we leave them alone they will go away." A favorite cartoon in Indian country a few years back showed a flying saucer landing while an Indian watched. The caption was "Oh, no, not again."

---

[2] extant: in existence

Refining Your Understanding

For each of the following items, consider how the target word is used in the passage. Write the letter of the word or phrase that best completes the sentence.

_____ 1. "A group's *collective* psyche and values" (line 4) suggests that   a. the people in that group share common attitudes   b. individualism in that group does not exist   c. the group thrives by collecting objects.

_____ 2. If "Indian people are exactly opposite of the popular *stereotype*" (line 15), they must be   a. just like most people think they are   b. beyond description   c. not at all like most people think they are.

_____ 3. An example of what people might do when they "*depreciate* their feats" (line 26) would be to   a. brag about their accomplishments   b. ridicule their accomplishments   c. forget their accomplishments.

_____ 4. When the author says "satirical remarks often *circumscribe* problems" (line 38) he means that, through humor, the problems have been   a. defined and limited   b. avoided   c. intensified.

_____ 5. When the author states that "people are awakened and brought to a *militant* edge through funny remarks" (lines 41–42), he is suggesting that humor can   a. incite people to violence   b. persuade poor people to find a career in the military   c. inspire people to be more assertive.

Number correct _____ (total 5)

Part C   Ways to Make New Words Your Own

By now you are familiar with the target words and their meanings. This section presents a variety of activities that will help you make these words part of your permanent vocabulary.

Using Language and Thinking Skills

True-False   Determine whether each statement is true or false. Write **T** for True and **F** for False.

_____ 1. A *satire* would never use ridicule or sarcasm to poke fun at someone.

_____ 2. When people can't agree on how to do a task, it is called a *collective* effort.

_____ 3. The feats of many folk heroes and heroines have been *perpetuated* in legends, songs, and poems.

_____ 4. If you *advocate* the recycling of glass, cans, and paper, you would encourage others to do the same.

_____ 5. A lack of sleep will *enable* you to perform well in your daily activities.

_____ 6. The *urgency* of a situation often causes a person to act quickly.

_____ 7. A huge, muscular person fits the *stereotype* of a football player.

_____ 8. When there is *unity* on a volleyball team, there are many arguments.

_____ 9. If property *depreciates*, the owner will probably lose money.

_____ 10. A person with *virtue* thinks nothing of stealing things.

Number correct _____ (total 10)

Practicing for Standardized Tests

Synonyms Write the letter of the word whose meaning is closest to that of the capitalized word.

_____ 1. ANTICIPATE: (A) brandish   (B) honor   (C) expect   (D) remember
(E) aspire

_____ 2. CIRCUMSTANCE: (A) suffrage   (B) difficulty   (C) miracle
(D) distance   (E) situation

_____ 3. CONSENSUS: (A) disagreement   (B) misconception   (C) crescendo
(D) population   (E) agreement

_____ 4. DISPUTE: (A) agreement   (B) argument   (C) extremity   (D) menace
(E) reason

_____ 5. ENCOMPASS: (A) surround   (B) measure   (C) guide   (D) overtake
(E) ignore

_____ 6. MILITANT: (A) peaceful   (B) aggressive   (C) certain
(D) exuberant   (E) cynical

_____ 7. PERPETUATE: (A) end   (B) persuade   (C) continue   (D) foretell
(E) acclimate

_____ 8. PROMINENT: (A) remote   (B) little-known   (C) ingenious
(D) well-known   (E) prompt

_____ 9. CIRCUMSCRIBE: (A) copy   (B) encircle   (C) free   (D) prevent   (E) dignify

_____ 10. VIRTUE: (A) splendor   (B) evil   (C) manners   (D) goodness
(E) adventure

Number correct _____ (total 10)

Word's Worth: satire

Satire comes from the Latin word *satura*, which was a long poem that ridiculed people's foolishness. People were supposed to see themselves in the satire. However, the English satirist Jonathan Swift once said, "Satire is a sort of glass, wherein beholders do generally discover everybody's face but their own."

Spelling and Wordplay

Crossword Puzzle Read each clue to determine what word will fit in the corresponding squares. There are several target words in the puzzle.

ACROSS
2. A condition
9. Slender
11. Three-toed sloth
12. Abbr. North America
13. Hearing organ
15. Opposite of usual meaning
17. Collective opinion
20. __ __ and behold
21. Single item
22. Objective case of *he*
23. Unit of electrical resistance
24. Not awake
26. Mockeries
29. Ma's partner
30. Abbr. Doctor of Dental Surgery
32. To cause to be continued or remembered
36. Nickname for sister
37. That thing
38. Low singing voice
40. Stick for baseball
42. Nickname for Alex
43. Egyptian cobras
44. Bumble __ __ __
46. The need for quick action
49. Feeling blue
50. Abbr. Regular Army
51. Contraction of *it is*
52. Preposition meaning "position or place"
53. To expect

DOWN
1. Conventional opinion
2. Traced a line around
3. Not out
4. The principal one
5. Knights' titles
6. Belonging to Ann
7. Negative vote
8. To encircle or include
10. A laugh word
14. Abbr. Eastern Standard Time
16. Six per inning
18. Not off
19. Abbr. Northern Ireland
20. Falsehood
22. Opposite of *tails*
24. Abbr. Arsenic
25. Abbr. Long Playing
27. A foot digit
28. To make possible
31. To question the truth of
33. Abbr. Parent Teachers Association
34. Abbr. Tantalum
35. Abbr. Eastern Seaboard
39. To speak
41. To revolve or rotate
42. Abbr. Agriculture
44. Abbr. Boy Scouts of America
45. To devour
47. Large rodent
48. Covering for the head
51. See 37 Across

Part D   Related Words

A number of words are closely related to the target words you have studied. Use your knowledge of the target words and of word parts to determine the meanings of these words. (For information about word parts analysis, see pages 6–12.) If you are unsure of any definitions, use your dictionary. Learning these related words not only expands your vocabulary. It helps you learn the target words more thoroughly.

1. anticipation (an tis′ ə pā′ shən) n.
2. circumstantial (sʉr′ kəm stan′ shəl) adj.
3. collection (kə lek′ shən) n.
4. consent (kən sent′) n., v.
5. depreciation (di prē′ shē ā′ shən) n.
6. disputable (dis pyo͞ot′ ə b'l, dis′ pyo͞ot-) adj.
7. ironical (ī rän′ i k'l) adj.
8. military (mil′ ə ter′ ē) adj., n.
9. moral (môr′ əl, mär′-) adj. n.
10. perpetual (pər pech′ o͞o wəl) adj.
11. prominence (präm′ ə nəns) n.
12. satirize (sat′ ə rīz′) v.
13. unify (yo͞o′ nə fī′) v.
14. unison (yo͞o′ nə sən, zən) n.
15. unit (yo͞o′ nit) n.
16. urgent (ʉr′ jənt) adj.
17. virtuous (vʉr′ cho͞o wəs) adj.

Understanding Related Words

Sentence Completion   Write the related word from the list above that best completes each sentence.

1. Before running for political office, Senator West gained _____ as a writer.

2. Ms. Garcia used her column in today's newspaper to _____ those who publicly praise charities but never contribute.

3. _____ evidence in a legal case refers to evidence that helps prove certain circumstances existed when a particular incident occurred.

4. Locked in _____ darkness for thousands of years, the ancient Egyptian tomb was now about to be opened.

5. In our excitement over and _____ of Marissa's visit, we forgot to note the flight number and time of her arrival.

6. Aesop's fables all contain a _____ that teaches a lesson.

7. Fighter planes, tanks, and aircraft carriers represent various types of

    _____ power.

8. Before Mr. McGuire would _____ to the purchase, he insisted that the engine of the car be examined by a mechanic.

9. The protests of the fans suggested that the decision was _____

10. In the speech that awarded her the Nobel Peace Prize, Mother Teresa was praised

for her _____ work among the sick and needy.

Number correct _____ (total 10)

Turn to **Words Ending in *ize* or *ise*** on pages 203-204 of the **Spelling Handbook.** Read the rule and complete the exercise provided.

Matching Ideas   In the blank write the word from the list that matches the idea expressed in each of the following sentences.

collection   ironical   consent   depreciation   urgent

_____ 1. He received a telegram that needed an immediate reply.

_____ 2. Betty removed the foreign stamp from the envelope and pasted it in her stamp book.

_____ 3. The doctor died of the very disease he had tried to cure.

_____ 4. Mr. and Mrs. Henry feared they would have to sell their house for less than they paid.

_____ 5. After pleading with her parents for weeks, Amy finally got their approval to go on the camping trip.

Number correct _____ (total 5)

Analyzing Word Parts

The Latin Root *uni*   The target word *unity* and its related words, *unify, unison,* and *unit,* come from the Latin word *unus,* meaning "one." There are also many other words, such as *unicorn* and *uniform,* that contain this root.   Keeping in mind the meaning of *unus,* match each of the listed words with its correct definition. Write the word in the appropriate blank.

unicorn   uniform   unify   unison   unit

_____ 1. sameness of musical pitch; agreement; harmony (n.)

_____ 2. to combine into one; to become or make united (v.)

_____ 3. a mythical horselike animal with a single horn (n.)

_____ 4. any fixed quantity, amount; a single, distinct part (n.)

_____ 5. not varying (adj.); the official or special clothes worn by members of a particular group (n.)

Number correct _____ (total 5)

Number correct in Unit _____ (total 65)

The Last Word

Writing

Satire is a form of humor and wit used to expose the vice or folly of others. Write a paragraph that satirizes a current custom, fad, or behavior. Write from the point of view of an alien creature who visits earth, observes our habits, and attempts to describe them to a fellow alien upon returning home. For example, what would a visitor from another planet say about the habit of cigarette smoking or the sport of boxing? Read your paragraph aloud in class.

Speaking

Native Americans are not the only group of people that have been stereotyped. Teenagers have been *stereotyped* too. In a short speech, describe the common stereotypes of teenagers as evidenced in fictional characters, advertisements, or adults' conversations. Then point out specific objections you have to the stereotypes and explain why these stereotypes might have evolved.

Group Discussion

Disputes are an unfortunate but natural part of our lives. Whether these disputes are with family and friends or between nations, it is important for world peace and for our own peace of mind that we deal with them effectively. With group members, discuss some basic principles you feel will help in dealing with disputes. Think about some disputes you have been involved in or that you are concerned about. Identify several principles that you think could help in settling disputes.

U N I T 4: Review of Units 1–3

Part A   Review Word List

Unit 1 Target Words

1. acclimate	11. fervent
2. ancestral	12. foretell
3. aspire	13. impending
4. crescendo	14. incredible
5. dependent	15. ingenious
6. despite	16. meager
7. evolve	17. precipitate
8. exquisite	18. suffrage
9. extreme	19. thrive
10. exuberant	20. unsung

Unit 1 Related Words

1. ancestor	10. forerunner
2. ancestry	11. foresight
3. aspiration	12. genius
4. credibility	13. incredibility
5. credible	14. independent
6. credulous	15. precipitation
7. creed	16. spite
8. extremity	17. suffragette
9. forecast	

Unit 2 Target Words

1. assuage	11. inert
2. brandish	12. magnificent
3. cynical	13. menace
4. demoralize	14. minimize
5. despair	15. misconception
6. dignify	16. overtake
7. engulf	17. profound
8. ennoble	18. sheepishly
9. grotesque	19. splendor
10. impede	20. staid

Unit 2 Related Words

1. assuagement	8. inertia
2. concept	9. magnificence
3. cynic	10. magnify
4. desperation	11. minimum
5. dignity	12. nobility
6. grotesqueness	13. profundity
7. impediment	14. splendid

Unit 3 Target Words

1. advocate	11. irony
2. anticipate	12. militant
3. circumscribe	13. morality
4. circumstance	14. perpetuate
5. collective	15. prominent
6. consensus	16. satire
7. depreciate	17. stereotype
8. dispute	18. unity
9. enable	19. urgency
10. encompass	20. virtue

Unit 3 Related Words

1. anticipation	10. perpetual
2. circumstantial	11. prominence
3. collection	12. satirize
4. consent	13. unify
5. depreciation	14. unison
6. disputable	15. unit
7. ironical	16. urgent
8. military	17. virtuous
9. moral	

Inferring Meaning from Context

For each sentence write the letter of the word or phrase that is closest in meaning to the italicized word or words.

_____ 1. Deep-sea divers must return to the water's surface slowly so that their bodies can *acclimate* to the change in pressure.
   a. minimize   b. aspire   c. adjust   d. inflate

_____ 2. The athlete *advocated* a healthful diet of vegetables and whole grains.
   a. was against   b. was in favor of   c. was cynical about
   d. experimented with

_____ 3. The tiny seedling *evolved* into a lush, fruit-bearing bush.
   a. depreciated   b. aspired   c. developed   d. mutated

_____ 4. News that the young girl had been rescued made us feel *exuberant*.
   a. exhausted   b. independent   c. meager   d. joyous

_____ 5. The gnarled tree cast a *grotesque* shadow on the crumbling stone wall.
   a. cynical   b. credible   c. weird   d. magnificent

_____ 6. Despite various experiments to change its composition, the chemical substance remained *inert*.
   a. urgent   b. explosive   c. inactive   d. menacing

_____ 7. The mountain climbers carried little equipment and only a *meager* supply of food.
   a. skimpy   b. profound   c. fervent   d. excellent

_____ 8. To *minimize* the boy's fears, his older brother accompanied him to the dentist.
   a. increase   b. lessen   c. identify   d. advocate

_____ 9. My grandfather wondered who would *perpetuate* our family's traditions.
   a. terminate   b. unite   c. carry on   d. precipitate

_____ 10. Superintendent Garcia's *profound* comments on the value of education convinced many students of the need to finish high school.
   a. comical   b. militant   c. impending   d. wise

_____ 11. Colleen, *a prominent* leader in various school organizations, was elected sophomore class president.
   a. an outstanding   b. a cynical   c. an ironical   d. a conservative

_____ 12. The *splendor* of the fourteenth-century French cathedral captivated natives and tourists alike.
   a. spirit   b. magnificence   c. grotesqueness   d. poverty

_____ 13. Tony's business will *thrive* if he keeps a careful eye on expenses.
   a. depreciate   b. threaten   c. grow   d. despair

_____ 14. Although the halls were filled with smoke, the hotel guests seemed unaware of the *urgency* of the situation.

a. violence   b. seriousness   c. inertia   d. exuberance

_____ 15. A candidate's *virtue* is not always easy to determine, even though he or she speaks of high ideals.

a. moral excellence   b. misconception   c. desperation   d. political fervor

Number correct _____ (total 15)

Using Review Words in Context

Use context clues to determine which word from the list below fits logically in each blank. Write the word in the blank. Each word may be used once.

anticipate	despaired	exuberance	misconception
assuage	despite	fervent	profound
circumstance	dispute	impedes	prominence
consensus	enable	ingenious	sheepishly
demoralized	extremely	minimize	thrive

The Shyness of Sonia

For Sonia, school brought feelings of joyful _____ as well as a deep and _____ fear. Sonia liked school and did well in her classes. The previous year she had gained _____ as a math whiz, winning an award in the citywide competition for her _____ solution to a difficult algebra problem. In other subjects Sonia proved herself an eager learner. There was a _____ among her teachers that Sonia would go on to do well in college. _____ her scholastic accomplishments, however, Sonia was _____ withdrawn. She tried hard to _____ her contact with others. If Sonia was in a _____ in which a fellow student began conversing with her, she looked down at the floor _____ and said as little as possible. Poor Sonia was under the _____ that other students resented her for doing so well in school.

Sonia's shyness was apparent to all who met her. One day Ms. Groves, Sonia's counselor, decided to call Sonia into her office. Ms. Groves had a sympathetic attitude and always listened to what students had to say.

Sonia began to tell Ms. Groves how she felt. "I know what my problem is, but I don't know how to change," she _____ . She explained her feeling that other students resented her and how it almost made her want to do poorly in school in order to gain some friends. "I'll never be able to handle college—not with all the people—no matter how good my grades are!" Ms. Groves listened patiently and tried to _____ Sonia's fears. "Don't become so _____ ," she said. "I _____ that you'll have great success at college. Has anyone ever told you they resented you?"

Of course, the answer was no. "Fear is the only thing that _____ you," Ms. Groves continued. "A little self-confidence will _____ you to realize that people don't resent you in the least."

Sonia could not _____ what Ms. Groves had said. She looked at Ms. Groves and smiled. Sonia realized she would have to make a _____ effort to change. After all, a little self-confidence would help her to grow and _____ both in and outside of school.

Number correct _____ (total 20)

Part B   Review Word Reinforcement

Using Language and Thinking Skills

True-False   Determine whether each statement is true or false. Write **T** for True and **F** for False.

_____   1. If you research your *ancestral* background, you might learn the occupations of your forefathers.

_____   2. *Crescendo* means that musicians should play with a light, delicate touch.

_____   3. A *cynical* person believes everything people say.

_____   4. You cannot *dispute* the fact that Jefferson City is the capital of Missouri.

_____   5. In ancient myths and fairy tales, many characters claimed that they could *foretell* the future.

_____   6. The Egyptians' construction of the pyramids was an *incredible* feat.

_____   7. Volcanic Mt. St. Helens has never been a *menace* to the surrounding area.

_____   8. The *militant* speeches of Patrick Henry helped bring about the American Revolution.

_____   9. Border disputes between countries have sometimes *precipitated* a war.

_____ 10. Honesty is a *virtue* to be sought and admired.

Number correct _____ (total 10)

Practicing for Standardized Tests

Synonyms   Write the letter of the word whose meaning is closest to that of the capitalized word.

_____   1. ANTICIPATE: (A) await   (B) surprise   (C) advocate   (D) assuage   (E) remember

_____ 2. CIRCUMSTANCE: (A) vacuum (B) menace (C) condition
(D) circumnavigation (E) dignity

_____ 3. DISPUTE: (A) agree (B) reason (C) aspire (D) argue
(E) minimize

_____ 4. EVOLVE: (A) depreciate (B) develop (C) engulf (D) overtake
(E) conserve

_____ 5. EXTREME: (A) meager (B) unsung (C) narrow (D) exotic
(E) excessive

Number correct _____ (total 5)

Antonyms Write the letter of the word whose meaning is most nearly _opposite_ that of the capitalized word.

_____ 1. ASSUAGE: (A) provoke (B) calm (C) impede (D) unite
(E) acclimate

_____ 2. DEMORALIZE: (A) corrupt (B) discourage (C) foretell (D) lie
(E) encourage

_____ 3. EXQUISITE: (A) exuberant (B) hideous (C) profound
(D) superior (E) expensive

_____ 4. FERVENT: (A) healthy (B) fiery (C) indifferent (D) satirical
(E) elated

_____ 5. INCREDIBLE: (A) inflexible (B) unsung (C) ironical
(D) believable (E) grotesque

Number correct _____ (total 5)

Spelling and Wordplay

Word Scramble The words in the box below have been scrambled and then listed in the exercise that follows. Unscramble each word in the column on the left and write it on the line following. Then match each unscrambled target word with its definition on the right. Write the letter of the matching definition in the blank.

assuage	depreciate	meager
consensus	despair	misconception
circumscribe	enable	overtake
crescendo	exquisite	unsung
dependent	ingenious	suffrage

45

_____ 1. nsseusocn _____   a. scanty

_____ 2. petdaicere _____   b. agreement

_____ 3. qetexuiis _____   c. encircle

_____ 4. comisctnpeoin _____   d. high quality

_____ 5. guasesa _____   e. lessen in value

_____ 6. leenba _____   f. gradually getting louder

_____ 7. veratoke _____   g. not sung

_____ 8. siniougen _____   h. misunderstanding

_____ 9. neeneptdd _____   i. right to vote

_____ 10. raisepd _____   j. pacify

_____ 11. snugnu _____   k. loss of hope

_____ 12. fesfurga _____   l. allow or make possible

_____ 13. odensrecc _____   m. relying on someone

_____ 14. rriibumsccce _____   n. catch up with

_____ 15. rageme _____   o. clever

Number correct _____ (total 15)

Part C   Related Word Reinforcement

Sentence Completion   Write the related word from the list that best completes each sentence.

circumstantial	cynic	disputable	prominence	suffragette
credibility	desperation	perpetual	satirize	virtuous

_____ 1. The ?(s) fought for over seventy years to secure women the right to vote.

_____ 2. The police officer challenged the ? of the story when they learned the witness reported seeing UFO's frequently.

_____ 3. Bill Cosby's book *Fatherhood* ?(s) parents and teen-agers.

_____ 4. In ?, one resident jumped from the burning building.

_____ 5. Only people of ? are listed in *Who's Who in America*.

_____ 6. There were no eyewitnesses to the crime; the defendant was convicted on ? evidence.

_____ 7. Only a ? could doubt the motives behind such a large contribution to charity.

_____ 8. Location of the property line was ?, so a survey was made.

46

_____ 9. The monks in the abbey led ⟶?⟵ and disciplined lives.

_____ 10. The trust established funds for the ⟶?⟵ care of the
building and surrounding grounds.

Number correct _____ (total 10)

Reviewing Word Structures

The Prefixes _de-, fore-, in-,_ **and** _uni-_ Use the prefixes and base words below to
form ten words. Then correctly use each word you formed in a sentence.

Prefixes:	de-	fore-	in-	uni-	
Base Words:	cycle	face	cellular	port	head
	efficient	see	direct	lateral	tour

1. _____ Sentence: _____

_____

2. _____ Sentence: _____

_____

3. _____ Sentence: _____

_____

4. _____ Sentence: _____

_____

5. _____ Sentence: _____

_____

6. _____ Sentence: _____

_____

7. _____ Sentence: _____

_____

8. _____ Sentence: _____

_____

9. _____ Sentence: _____

_____

10. _____ Sentence: _____

_____

Number correct _____ (total 10)

Number correct in Unit _____ (total 90)

Vocab Lab 1

FOCUS ON: **Drama**

By now the words you learned in previous units should be part of your active vocabulary. You can expand your vocabulary even further by becoming familiar with the following words used in the dramatic arts.

antagonist (an tag′ ə nist) n. a character or force that works against the main character in a piece of literature, thus creating a conflict. • The play's *antagonist* plotted to stop the marriage of the two main characters.

aside (ə sīd′) n. a character's words spoken to the audience and supposedly not heard by the other characters on stage. • In an *aside* to the audience, the villain revealed his treacherous plans.

characterization (kar′ ik tər i zā′ shən) n. the technique writers use to create and describe characters. • The playwright's effective *characterization* of the old man allowed the audience to understand his loneliness and despair.

climax (klī′ maks) n. the turning point in the plot when interest and intensity reach their peak. • The play reached its *climax* when the detective identified the murderer as one of the dinner guests.

comedy (käm′ ə dē) n. a play with a happy ending or a nontragic theme. • In a *comedy* the characters generally live happily ever after.

comic relief (käm′ ik ri lēf′) n. humorous scenes that relieve the tension created by the development of conflicts. • After the emotional intensity of the second act, the appearance of the clown provided *comic relief*.

conflict (kän′ flikt) n. the struggle between opposing characters or forces in a play. • The play's *conflict* concerned the main character's struggle between family ties and her need to leave home and become independent.

dialogue (dī′ ə lôg′, -läg′) n. a conversation between two or more characters. • The Shakespearean comedy was filled with witty *dialogue*.

farce (färs) n. an exaggerated comedy based on highly unlikely situations. • Although the main character's stupidity was too ridiculous to be believed, the *farce* provoked hearty laughter from those who viewed it.

protagonist (prō tag′ ə nist) n. the central character in a play. • The *protagonist* saves the child in the last act of the play.

setting (set′ iŋ) n. the time and place of the action of a play. • The *setting* of Shakespeare's play *Julius Caesar* is ancient Rome.

soliloquy (sə lil′ ə kwē) n. a speech in which a character speaks as if to himself. A playwright uses this device to reveal the character's inner thoughts to the audience. • The line "To be, or not to be" is from Hamlet's famous *soliloquy*.

theme (thēm) n. the main idea in a work of literature. • The *theme* of the play is that power corrupts.

tragedy (traj′ ə dē) n. a serious play with a sad or unfortunate ending brought about by fate, a moral weakness in a character, or social conditions. ● The play is a *tragedy* dealing with the struggles encountered by people during war.

tragic hero (traj′ ik hir′ ō, hē′rō) n. the central character in a tragedy. ● *Tragic heroes* often make errors in judgment that lead to their downfall.

Matching Match each drama term from the list with the appropriate example below. Write the term in the blank.

_____ 1. Two characters interrupt a serious scene with a silly ditty, sung off-key.

_____ 2. The curtain rises on turn-of-the-century America.

_____ 3. In this play, people give up sleeping in order to watch television twenty-four hours a day.

_____ 4. At the end, the star-crossed lovers die in each other's arms.

_____ 5. Sherlock Holmes is the hero in the Conan Doyle mystery stories.

_____ 6. The high point in the drama came when the defendant spoke in his own behalf to the jury.

_____ 7. After some hilarious twists and turns, the play ends happily, and the audience leaves the theater chuckling.

_____ 8. A character turns to the audience and reveals that she is really John's long-lost sister.

_____ 9. The main idea of the story is that people are basically good.

_____ 10. The conversations of two characters disclose their love for each other.

_____ 11. Realizing that his greediness caused his mother's death, the hero commits suicide.

_____ 12. A character cuts the brake cables on the heroine's car.

_____ 13. While thinking aloud, a character unveils his secret plan to flee to another country.

_____ 14. A character is always dressed in black, walks with a limp, and speaks with a heavy Russian accent.

_____ 15. A character struggles between warning the town about an advancing army and saving her own life.

Number correct _____ (total 15)

FOCUS ON: *Analogies*

In the first four units of this book, you completed activities that help build vocabulary skills, such as synonym, antonym, and sentence completion exercises. An analogy exercise is another way to enrich your understanding of words. An **analogy** shows a relationship between words. A typical analogy problem looks like this:

> Choose the lettered pair of words that best expresses a relationship similar to that of the original pair.

> ___ HAPPY : SAD ::   (A) dim : dark   (B) terrible : terrifying   (C) good : bad (D) able : capable   (E) plain : unadorned

The analogy can be expressed this way: *"Happy* is to *sad* as ? is to ? ."

To answer an analogy problem, first determine the relationship between the original pair of words. State this relationship in a sentence:

"Happy is the opposite of *sad."*

Then decide which of the other word pairs expresses a similar relationship. You can test your choice by substituting the pair of words for the original pair in the sentence. It becomes apparent that (C) is the best answer to this problem when you use the test:

"Good is the opposite of *bad."*

Here are the most common types of relationships used in analogies:

Type of Analogy	Example
cause to effect	virus : cold :: carelessness : errors
part to whole	finger : hand :: spoke : wheel
object to purpose	car : transportation :: lamp : illumination
action to object	dribble : basketball :: fly : kite
item to category	salamander : amphibian :: corn : vegetable
age	kitten : cat :: cygnet : swan
type to characteristic	owl : nocturnal :: lion : carnivorous
word to synonym	nice : pleasant :: gratitude : thankfulness
synonym variants	pliant : flexibility :: unruly : disobedience
word to antonym	nice : unpleasant :: lazy : industrious
antonym variants	spotless : filth :: faultless : accuracy
object to its material	shoe : leather :: necklace : gold
product to source	apple : tree :: milk : cow
worker and creation	composer : symphony :: author : novel
worker and tool	carpenter : hammer :: surgeon : scalpel
worker and workplace	mechanic : garage :: judge : courtroom
time sequence	sunrise : sunset :: winter : spring
spatial sequence	mountaintop : valley :: engine : caboose
word and derived form	act : action :: image : imagine
degree of intensity	pleased : ecstatic :: drizzle : downpour
manner	shout : speak :: swagger : walk

Analogies Solve the following analogy problems, which use words from previous units. Write the letter of the word or word pair that best completes the analogy.

_____ 1. DESPAIR : HOPELESSNESS :: (A) dejection : elation (B) serenity : agitation (C) exuberance : enthusiasm (D) fear : courage (E) laziness : ambition

_____ 2. HONESTY : VIRTUE :: (A) failure : success (B) objective : goal (C) hope : desperation (D) search : discovery (E) winter : season

_____ 3. CYNICAL : PESSIMIST :: (A) satirical : tragedy (B) well-known : celebrity (C) staid : comedian (D) illiterate : poet (E) sad : optimist

_____ 4. OBSTRUCTION : IMPEDIMENT :: (A) escape : get away (B) acclimation : climate (C) dispute : evidence (D) foresight : hindsight (E) virtue : vice

_____ 5. PERPETUAL : MOMENTARY :: (A) sheepish : aggressive (B) uncertain : disputable (C) confident : haughty (D) thoughtful : meditative (E) incredible : unbelievable

_____ 6. CRIMINAL : MENACE :: (A) excitement : boredom (B) overeating : indigestion (C) greed : generosity (D) letter : communication (E) misconception : comprehension

_____ 7. SPLENDID : BRILLIANT :: (A) clumsy : agile (B) growing : dying (C) magnificent : wonderful (D) odd : common (E) chilly : freezing

_____ 8. URGENT : UNIMPORTANT :: (A) intense : tense (B) sad : despairing (C) fervent : unfeeling (D) chubby : obese (E) profound : meaningful

_____ 9. SOLDIER : MILITARY :: (A) chef : food (B) advocate : spokesperson (C) author : book (D) physician : nurse (E) senator : legislature

_____ 10. PRECIPITATE : HASTEN :: (A) reap : sow (B) advocate : recommend (C) magnify : minimize (D) perpetuate : wreck (E) impede : assist

_____ 11. DIGNIFY : ENNOBLE :: (A) thrive : flourish (B) circumscribe : erase (C) initiate : continue (D) foretell : recall (E) compose : destroy

_____ 12. SUFFRAGE : SUFFRAGIST :: (A) vote : election (B) right : duty (C) environment : environmentalist (D) quiet : loudness (E) issue : idea

_____ 13. KING : NOBILITY :: (A) criminal : crime (B) dawn : dusk (C) gem : diamond (D) knight : crusade (E) peasant : working class

_____ 14. INVENTOR : INGENIOUS :: (A) author : illiterate (B) philosopher : meditative (C) physician : surgical (D) priest : irreverent (E) child : old

_____ 15. DISAGREEMENT : CONSENSUS :: (A) believability : credibility (B) practice : competence (C) exercise : energy (D) hope : despair (E) work : employment

Number correct _____ (total 15)

Number correct in Vocab Lab _____ (total 30)

51

UNIT 5

Target Words and Their Meanings

1. appall (ə pôl´) v.
2. apparently (ə per´ ənt lē) adv.
3. characteristic (kar´ ik tə ris´ tik) adj., n.
4. deadpan (ded pan´) adj.
5. decade (dek´ ād) n.
6. deny (di nī´) v.
7. excel (ik sel´) v.
8. extend (ik stend´) v.
9. fluster (flus´ tər) v.
10. forethought (fôr´ thôt´) n.
11. ordeal (ôr dēl´) n.
12. routinely (ro͞o tēn´ lē) adv.
13. stake (stāk) n., v.
14. stolid (stäl´ id) adj.
15. stun (stun) v.
16. subject (sub´ jikt) n. (səb jekt´) v.
17. suitor (so͞ot´ ər) n.
18. tedious (tē´ dē əs) adj.
19. vibrant (vī´ brənt) adj.
20. whim (hwim, wim) n.

Inferring Meaning from Context

For each sentence write the letter of the word or phrase that is closest to the meaning of the word or words in italics. Use context clues to help you determine the correct answer. (For more information on context clues, see pages 1-5.)

_____ 1. *Appalled* by the polluted water, the Peace Corps workers dug a new well.
   a. dignified   b. horrified   c. unaffected   d. bored

_____ 2. No one is sure, but *apparently* the longest Ferris wheel ride went on for twenty-nine hours!
   a. profoundly   b. unquestionably   c. it seems   d. ingeniously

_____ 3. Geese hover over the water before landing; similarly, it is *characteristic* for pheasants to glide a few feet above the ground before landing.
   a. unheard of   b. typical   c. awkward   d. harmful

_____ 4. Some comedians maintain *a deadpan* expression so that the audience will be caught off guard by the punch line of a joke.
   a. a funny   b. an emotionless   c. an exuberant   d. an angry

_____ 5. During the *decade* from 1860 to 1870, Americans fought the Civil War.
   a. evolution   b. century   c. best of times   d. ten-year period

_____ 6. The police officer arrested Tim for speeding, but Tim *denied* the charges.
   a. refused to accept   b. advocated   c. dignified   d. dreamed up

_____ 7. One basketball player who *excelled* at shooting made 840 free throws for Los Angeles in a single season!
   a. was inferior   b. was average   c. was fair   d. was very good

_____ 8. The state of Iowa *extends* from the Mississippi River on the east to the Missouri River on the west.

a. floods   b. can be seen   c. increases   d. reaches

_____ 9. Although Senator Jones was an experienced public speaker, the heckling by a boisterous member of the audience *flustered* him.

a. amused   b. upset   c. assuaged   d. disgusted

_____ 10. Had Napoleon given the matter more *forethought*, he might not have led his troops on the disastrous march to Moscow.

a. financing   b. planning   c. publicity   d. consent

_____ 11. The five-mile run was a real *ordeal* for the new members of the track team.

a. irony   b. mystery   c. hardship   d. circumstance

_____ 12. Several decades ago, eye surgery was seldom attempted, but today doctors do it *routinely*.

a. awkwardly   b. sheepishly   c. rarely   d. regularly

_____ 13. It was important that Rick, last year's tennis champion, win the match; at *stake* was the trophy that his school hoped to keep.

a. risk   b. first   c. harm   d. odds

_____ 14. Vine Deloria tells us that Native Americans, contrary to popular stereotypes, are not *stolid* people but have a great sense of humor.

a. panicky   b. happy   c. unemotional   d. silly

_____ 15. Flying into the picture window *stunned* the yellow warbler, but less than ten minutes later the bird jolted upright and then flew away.

a. seized   b. encompassed   c. dazed   d. reflected

_____ 16. All recruits in the armed forces *are subjected to* a thorough physical exam.

a. are required to have   b. learn about   c. try to avoid   d. are dignified by

_____ 17. The Capulets would not accept Romeo as Juliet's *suitor* and did everything they could to discourage the romance.

a. tailor   b. forefather   c. boyfriend   d. casual acquaintance

_____ 18. Being out at sea on a calm day, far from shore and waiting for the wind to blow, must be *tedious* for sailors.

a. energizing   b. grotesque   c. tiresome   d. exuberant

_____ 19. Mr. Snyder is a humorless man with a deadpan expression; his wife, on the other hand, has a *vibrant* personality.

a. dull   b. sheepish   c. militant   d. lively

_____ 20. Jack went to Las Vegas on a *whim*, without making any travel plans until the morning he left.

a. sudden notion   b. secret lead   c. threat   d. aspiration

Number correct _____ (total 20)

You should now have a general idea of the meaning of each target word. Refine your understanding by examining the shades of meaning the words have in the following excerpt.

An American Childhood

Annie Dillard

The author, Annie Dillard, is known for her keenly perceptive descriptions of nature. In An American Childhood, *she applies her talent to describing her childhood years in Pittsburgh. The following excerpt describes Dillard's mother, a thoroughly unique, always surprising woman.*

On a long, sloping beach by the ocean, she [Mother] lay stretched out sunning with Father and friends, until the conversation gradually grew **tedious,** when without **forethought** she gave a little push with her heel and rolled away. People were **stunned.** She rolled **deadpan** and **apparently** effortlessly, arms and legs **extended** and tidy, down the beach to the distant water's edge, where she lay at   5 ease just as she had been, but half in the surf, and well out of earshot.

She dearly loved to **fluster** people by throwing out a game's rules at **whim**—when she was getting bored, losing in a dull sort of way, and when everybody else was taking it too seriously. If you turned your back, she moved the checkers around on the board. When you got them all straightened out, she   10

denied she'd touched them; the next time you turned your back, she lined them up on the rug or hid them under your chair. In a rummy game called Michigan, she **routinely** played out of turn, or called out a card she didn't hold, or counted backward, simply to amuse herself by causing an uproar and watching the rest of us do double takes and have fits. (Much later, when serious **suitors** came to call, Mother **subjected** them to this fast card game as a trial by **ordeal;** she used it as an intelligence test and a measure of spirit. If the poor man could stay around without breaking down or running out, he got to marry one of us, if he still wanted to.)

She **excelled** at bridge, playing fast and boldly, but when the **stakes** were low and the hands dull, she bid slams[1] for the devilment of it, or raised her opponents' suit to bug them, or showed her hand, or tossed her cards in a handful behind her back in a **characteristic** swift motion accompanied by a **vibrantly** innocent look. It drove our **stolid** father crazy. The hand was over before it began, and the guests were **appalled.** How do you score it, who deals now, what do you do with a crazy person who is having so much fun? Or they were down seven, and the guests were appalled. "Pam!" He groaned. What ails such people? What on earth possesses them? He rubbed his face.

She was an unstoppable force; she never let go. When we moved across town, she persuaded the U.S. Post Office to let her keep her old address— forever—because she'd had stationery printed. I don't know how she did it. Every new post office worker, over **decades,** needed to learn that although the Doaks' mail is addressed to here, it is delivered to there.

_____
[1] slams: winning all the tricks in a hand of bridge

Refining Your Understanding

For each of the following items, consider how the target word is used in the passage. Write the letter of the word or phrase that best completes the sentence.

_____ 1. The people who were *stunned* (line 4)   a. probably sat motionless for a few seconds   b. shouted for joy   c. had been expecting Mother's action.

_____ 2. The fact that Mother loved to *fluster* people (line 7) shows that she a. was considerate of others' feelings   b. was competitive   c. enjoyed stirring things up.

_____ 3. From the word *routinely* (line 13) we infer that Mother's strange card-playing behavior happened   a. often   b. seldom   c. monthly.

_____ 4. In a card game, if the *stakes* (line 20), are low, there must be a. high bets   b. little to lose or gain   c. no betting taking place.

_____ 5. If the author's father was *stolid* (line 24), he and his wife's personalities were   a. much the same   b. opposite   c. impossible to compare.

Number correct _____ (total 5)

Part C   Ways to Make New Words Your Own

This section presents a variety of reinforcement activities that will help you make these words part of your permanent vocabulary.

Using Language and Thinking Skills

Understanding Multiple Meanings   Read the definitions of the boldfaced target word, and then read the sentences that use the word. Write the letter of the definition that applies to each sentence.

> **stake**
> a. a piece of wood that is pointed and can be driven into the ground (n.)
> b. money or other valuables risked in a game of chance (n.)
> c. a share or interest in an enterprise (n.)
> d. to show the boundaries of property, usually with stakes (v.)

_____ 1. Having invested over a million dollars, Mr. Kowalski had a large *stake* in the Ruby Gulch Mine.

_____ 2. We all helped Mr. Carpenter pound the tent *stakes* into the ground.

_____ 3. Jeff had a large *stake* in the game; college recruiters had come to watch him play.

_____ 4. First the contractor *staked* out the area the patio was to cover, then he built concrete forms, and finally he poured the cement.

_____ 5. Everyone has a *stake* in world economy; if it doesn't thrive, neither do we.

> **deny**
> a. to say that something is not true (v.)
> b. to refuse to believe (v.)
> c. to refuse access to (v.)

_____ 6. Border officials *denied* the drug offenders entrance to the country.

_____ 7. The forest ranger accused Charlie of starting a fire, but he *denied* it.

_____ 8. Roxy continued to *deny* that her abrupt manner kept her from making friends.

_____ 9. Colleges and universities *deny* admission to people with poor grades.

_____ 10. After seeing the film *Miracle on Thirty-fourth Street*, can you *deny* the existence of Santa Claus?

Number correct _____ (total 10)

Practicing for Standardized Tests

Analogies Each item below consists of a related pair of words followed by five other pairs of words. Write the letter of the pair of words that best expresses a relationship similar to that of the original pair.

_____ 1. PASSIONATE : STOLID ::   (A) conservative : thrifty   (B) owl-like : nocturnal   (C) exquisite : grotesque   (D) cool : cold   (E) Canadian : neighboring

_____ 2. EXCEL : NOBEL PRIZE ::   (A) rain : flood   (B) explore : territory   (C) surpass : award   (D) fail : rejection   (E) fly : airplane

_____ 3. TEDIOUS : MONOTONY ::   (A) tired : exhaustion   (B) quiet : din   (C) victorious : victor   (D) exuberant : loser   (E) incredulous : credibility

_____ 4. FORETHOUGHT : AFTERTHOUGHT ::   (A) blacksmith : horseshoe   (B) idea : thought   (C) clouds : rain   (D) panic : stampede   (E) prediction : remembrance

_____ 5. DECADE : TEN ::   (A) anticipation : expectation   (B) measurement : meter   (C) radish : vegetable   (D) precipitation : rain   (E) century : hundred

_____ 6. DIFFICULT : ORDEAL ::   (A) erroneous : truth   (B) disputable : opinion   (C) beneficial : menace   (D) cynical : believer   (E) orange : color

_____ 7. FLUSTER : UPSET ::   (A) consent : disapprove   (B) walk : strut   (C) crawl : swirl   (D) argue : dispute   (E) enable : impede

_____ 8. ROUTINELY : NORMALLY ::   (A) luckily : fortunately   (B) frequently : infrequently   (C) early : tardy   (D) unskillfully : deftly   (E) cautiously : carelessly

_____ 9. EXTEND : REACH ::   (A) unify : separate   (B) forecast : recall   (C) ennoble : dignify   (D) trot : gallop   (E) speak : mumble

_____ 10. APPARENTLY : PROBABLY ::   (A) seldom : often   (B) sternly : sympathetically   (C) urgently : seriously   (D) partially : wholly   (E) never : frequently

Number correct _____ (total 10)

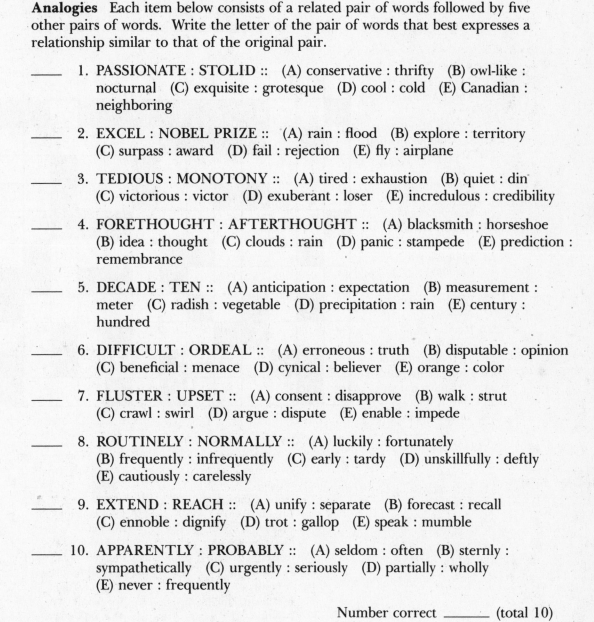

Word's Worth: ordeal

Ordal, in Old English, meant "judgment" and was often used in the phrase "trial by ordeal." In the trial, or ordeal, a defendant might be asked to prove his or her innocence by carrying a red-hot iron without being burned or by plunging his or her hand into boiling oil without flinching. Today, _ordeal_ has changed in meaning from a severe test of character to a very trying experience.

Spelling and Wordplay

Crossword Puzzle Read each clue to determine what word will fit in the corresponding squares. There are several target words in the puzzle.

ACROSS

1. Distinguishing trait
6. Abbr. Associated Press
8. Periods of ten years
13. Showing no emotion
17. Abbr. Receiving Office
18. Prefix meaning "without or from"
19. Hearing organ
20. Abbr. Postscript
21. An advertisement
22. Abbr. North Carolina
23. Tiresome
27. Word expressing agreement
30. Member of a convent
31. To try to persuade
33. Abbr. Lieutenant
34. To stretch out
35. Bets or wagers
38. To settle debts
39. ___ ___ ___ de Janeiro
40. Prefix meaning "three"
41. Exclamation of triumph
43. Type of grass or grain
44. Passing notion
45. A play on words

DOWN

2. A laugh word
3. Evidently
4. Ocean
5. Abbr. Columbia Broadcasting System
7. Sweetened fruit drink
9. Period of time
10. A family of food fish in the North Atlantic
11. To refuse to believe
12. To exceed or outdo
14. To consume
15. Abbr. Army Post Office
16. Abbr. Northwestern State University
24. Payable
25. Hotels
26. Men courting women
28. Unexcitable
29. Pungent spice used as food flavoring
32. Organ of sight
35. Spanish for *yes*
36. To hold or save
37. To astound or bewilder
39. Male sheep
41. Sigh of relief
42. Slang for *hello*

Part D Related Words

A number of words are related to the target words you have studied. Use your knowledge of the target words and of word parts to determine the meanings of these words. (For information about word parts analysis, see pages 6-12.) Use your dictionary as needed.

1. apparent (ə per′ ənt) adj.
2. character (kar′ ik tər) n.
3. denial (di nī′ əl) n.
4. excellent (ek′ s'l ənt) adj.
5. extension (ik sten′ shən) n.
6. routine (rōō tēn′) n.
7. stunning (stun′ iŋ) adj.
8. subjective (səb jek′ tiv) adj.
9. tedium (tē′ dē əm) n.
10. vibrate (vī′ brāt) v.
11. vibrato (vi brät′ ō, vē-) n.
12. whimsical (hwim′ zi k'l, wim′- zik'l) adj.

Understanding Related Words

Sentence Completion Write the related word from the list above that best fits each sentence.

_____ 1. If a car's steering wheel starts to _?_ , one thing the driver should check is the wheel alignment.

_____ 2. _?_ of credit means that one cannot borrow money.

_____ 3. The helicopter was on a _?_ mission, but the crew will never forget what happened.

_____ 4. The trembling _?_ of the flute melody haunted us long after the notes had died away.

_____ 5. To alleviate the _?_ of the repetitive task, Jan took a break.

_____ 6. The fire chief said that the fire's cause was not _?_ , but he thought that the fire probably began in the kitchen.

_____ 7. Wearing a _?_ red dress, the actress waved to the crowd.

_____ 8. One characteristic employers look for in hiring employees is strength of _?_ .

_____ 9. "There's no one answer to the question," Dr. Johnson reassured the students. "I just want your _?_ opinion."

_____ 10. If Anne hadn't been so _?_ in choosing an apartment, she wouldn't have to move so soon again.

Number correct _____ (total 10)

Turn to **The Prefix _ex-_** on page 197 of the **Spelling Handbook.** Read the rule and complete the exercise provided.

Analyzing Word Parts

The Prefix *ex-* *Ex-* is a widely used English prefix. It has two common meanings: "from" and "out" or "out of." When you encounter an unfamiliar word with the prefix *ex-*, try applying one of these meanings along with considering sentence context to determine the meaning of the word.

In addition to the related words *excellent* and *extension*, many other words are formed using this prefix. In the exercise below, fill in the blank with the word from the list that fits the context of each sentence. Use your dictionary as needed.

exaggerate   exhale   extension   excellent   exile

1. Some fishermen _____ the size of the fish that got away.

2. A robot should not be looked on as a replacement for humans but as an

   _____ of them.

3. After being forced out of the Philippines, former President Ferdinand Marcos

   lived in _____ in the United States.

4. By listening to you _____ , a doctor can detect heart problems.

5. Martin got an _____ score on the test even though he had not studied.

Number correct _____ (total 5)

Number correct in Unit _____ (total 60)

The Last Word

Writing

If you've been waiting with bated breath to get to "The Last Word," you can finally breathe a sigh of relief. In fact, if you read the last sentence again, you'll even have a good idea of what this feature is about. Phrases such as "waiting with bated breath" and "breathe a sigh of relief" are clichés—overused expressions that once were clever but have become so predictable that they are no longer vivid. "Calm, cool, and collected," "lady of the house," "last but not least," and "running the gauntlet" are a few more of the thousands of clichés in American English. To make your writing original and interesting, you should avoid clichés. You have a unique way of looking at the world, so why not use language in a way that will make you "stand out from the crowd?"

Each of the next ten sentences contains a cliché printed in italics. From the word list below, find a word that has roughly the same meaning as the italicized cliché. Then revise the sentence, using the word or a form of that word.

| apparent | excel | fluster | routine | vibrant |
| denial | excellent | ordeal | stun | whim |

1. Toby *swore up and down* that he had nothing to do with the Halloween prank.

   _____

2. When the car behind him honked repeatedly, Chris *blew his cool*.

   _____

3. The Bakers didn't know they were going anywhere until Friday morning, when *on the spur of the moment* they decided to fly to Mexico.

   _____

4. Taking attendance and grading papers is *all in a day's work* for a teacher.

   _____

5. Benjy cooked a gourmet dinner that was *fit for a king*.

   _____

6. Spiro *saw stars* when he was hit in the head with a golf ball.

   _____

7. The mechanic looked under the hood and said the problem with the engine was *as plain as the nose on his face*.

   _____

8. The aerobics instructor was *such a ball of fire* that no one in the class could keep up with him.

   _____

9. Gloria's team *went over the top* in candy sales for the school band.

   _____

10. The burglar dreaded the *moment of truth* he was about to face—an avalanche of questions from detectives and police officers.

    _____

Number correct _____ (total 10)

Speaking

The excerpt from *An American Childhood* serves as a character sketch of Annie Dillard's mother. Ms. Dillard uses a series of incidents to illustrate a particular character trait of her mother. Try to write a similar character sketch of your own by following these steps:

- Choose someone you know well, perhaps a family member, a close friend, or a neighbor.
- Identify one dominant character trait in that person.
- Describe several incidents that illustrate that character trait and help the reader "see" the person you have chosen to describe.

As your teacher directs, share your character sketch with the class.

UNIT 6

Part A   Target Words and Their Meanings

1. acclaim (ə klām′) n., v.
2. accommodate (ə käm′ ə dāt′) v.
3. admirably (ad′ mər ə b′lē) adv.
4. apprehend (ap′ rə hend′) v.
5. attribute (a′ trə byoōt′) n.
    (ə trib′ yoōt) v.
6. competence (käm′ pə təns) n.
7. depth (depth) n.
8. efficiency (ə fish′ ən sē, i-) n.
9. enthusiastic (in thoō′ zē as′ tik, -thyoō′-) adj.
10. finesse (fi nes′) n.
11. gratitude (grat′ ə toōd′, -tyoōd) n.
12. mortal (môr′ t′l) adj., n.
13. provision (prə vizh′ shn) n.
14. reproach (ri prōch′) n., v.
15. scrupulously (skroō′ pyə ləs lē) adv.
16. sophisticated (sə fis′ tə kāt′ id) adj.
17. sufficient (sə fish′ ′nt) adj.
18. tact (takt) n.
19. unmercifully (un mur′ si fə lē) adv.
20. virtually (vur′ choo wəl ē, -choo lē) adv.

Inferring Meaning from Context

For each sentence write the letter of the word or phrase that is closest to the meaning of the word or words in italics. Use context clues to help you.

_____ 1. Dr. Salk received great *acclaim* for his discovery of the polio vaccine.
a. assuagement   b. criticism   c. inertia   d. praise

_____ 2. Although I had made reservations for only four people, the maitre d' at the restaurant was able to *accommodate* our additional two people.
a. deny   b. adjust for   c. admit to   d. depend on

_____ 3. Mr. Ott performs his job *admirably*; his hard work and his desire to help others make him one of our most valued employees.
a. commendably   b. curiously   c. militantly   d. tediously

_____ 4. Fortunately, the police *apprehended* the bank robbers outside of town.
a. caught   b. passed   c. lost   d. frightened

_____ 5. One of Jenny's *attributes* is her willingness to be a loyal friend.
a. qualities   b. faults   c. problems   d. triumphs

_____ 6. One must demonstrate *competence* in driving to receive a driver's license.
a. willingness   b. enthusiasm   c. ability   d. competitiveness

_____ 7. Although only twenty-five feet wide, the building site has *a depth* of over two hundred feet.
a. an engulfment   b. a neighboring lot   c. a density
d. a distance from front to back

_____ 8. The milk-bottling machine operates with remarkable *efficiency*, producing a bottle of milk every three seconds.

a. effectiveness   b. ability to consume great amounts
c. lack of productivity   d. safety

_____ 9. Terri was not merely interested in being in the variety show; she was *enthusiastic* about it.

a. cynical   b. grave   c. eagerly excited   d. reluctant

_____ 10. Using his *finesse* for settling disputes, Judge Mayfield arranged an agreeable compromise between the two angry lawyers.

a. exuberance   b. trickery   c. fame   d. skillfulness

_____ 11. The village presented a plaque to the paramedics out of *gratitude* for their efforts and service to the community.

a. thankfulness   b. funds collected   c. sympathy   d. concern

_____ 12. Unlike *mortals*, the gods and goddesses of Greek myths could take part in dangerous adventures without fear of death.

a. human beings   b. animals   c. historians   d. physicians

_____ 13. We camped in the woods but made trips into town to replace our *provisions*.

a. procedures   b. supplies   c. conditions   d. finesse

_____ 14. Fred was often *reproached* for failing to do his math assignments.

a. scolded   b. relieved   c. praised   d. reminded

_____ 15. Mary runs the treasurer's office *scrupulously*; no one could ever accuse her of misusing funds.

a. ignorantly   b. in an easygoing manner   c. menacingly   d. honestly

_____ 16. The last time I saw Mark, he was awkward and shy, but today, as he talked about his European travels, he seemed very *sophisticated*.

a. worldly   b. desperate   c. well dressed   d. clumsy

_____ 17. We don't need any more logs because our supply of firewood is *sufficient*.

a. low   b. enough   c. unknown to us   d. depreciating

_____ 18. Although Anita had a good solution to the conflict, she lacked the *tact* needed to express her views without angering either side.

a. consent   b. diplomacy   c. impediment   d. irony

_____ 19. Tom's friends teased him so *unmercifully* about his dream of becoming a talk-show host that he stopped talking about it.

a. slightly   b. sympathetically   c. amusingly   d. cruelly

_____ 20. That type of whale has been hunted so relentlessly that today it is *virtually* nonexistent.

a. for all practical purposes   b. far from being   c. prevented from being   d. strangely

Number correct _____ (total 20)

Part B   *Target Words in Reading and Literature*

You should now have a general idea of the meaning of each target word. Refine your understanding by examining the shades of meaning the words have in the following excerpt.

What Makes a Good Police Officer?

Clarence M. Kelley

According to Clarence M. Kelley, former Director of the FBI, people expect much from police officers but give them little support. This selection is an excerpt from a speech given in Birmingham, Alabama.

We expect not only the very best in our officers, but a range and **depth** of **attributes** that no **mortal** could possibly possess. All too frequently we expect of officers what we do not require of ourselves.

They must, in our eyes, be above **reproach** at all times, **scrupulously** honest, and **virtually** without a fault. They must make no mistakes, and if they do, we criticize them **unmercifully**. 5

We expect them to handle all situations with **finesse**, **tact**, and **competence**, but seldom do we realize that as a community we have not provided them with the professional training needed to cope with today's **sophisticated**, changing society.We expect them to risk their lives to **apprehend** a hijacker, bank robber, 10 and murderer, yet we often fail to pay them livable salaries, and we make few, if any, **provisions** for their families in case of death during the line of duty.

We expect them to be **enthusiastic** and never to complain or gripe (as all of us do), yet we refuse to take the time to acquaint ourselves with their working conditions at headquarters, the precinct station, or wherever they may be. 15

We expect them to perform at top **efficiency**, for long hours, often being called out in the middle of the night or on weekends, and forget that they, too, are human, that they get tired and hungry, and, like us, may have children with whom they like to play.

We expect them to **accommodate** our desires immediately when we call them, forgetting that we have not given them **sufficient** personnel and equipment to provide the kind of service we expect and deserve. 20

Yet these men and women in blue, despite these handicaps, perform **admirably**—and I think the citizens across the great state of Alabama—and the nation—owe them a tremendous debt of **gratitude**. 25

I have worked with police officers all my life. I have been an officer myself. I know their gripes. I know their joys. I think I know the men and women themselves—as human beings. And I can tell you, honestly and truthfully, you will never meet a finer group of Americans. They work not for the salary alone; if they did, they would not be there. They work not for public **acclaim**; if so, they 30 wouldn't be there. They work not to be heroes; if so, they would long ago have resigned.

They walk your streets, safeguard your homes, keep your traffic going . . . why? Because they believe in the dignity of the law, in the triumph of right over might, and, above all, because they want to do their share in helping protect 35 their communities.

Refining Your Understanding

For each of the following items, consider how the target word is used in the passage. Write the letter of the word or phrase that best completes the sentence.

_____ 1. "We expect . . . in our officers . . . a range and *depth* of *attributes* that no mortal could . . . possess" (lines 1–2). By this the author suggests that police officers are expected to   a. have few good qualities   b. have the same qualities as everyone else   c. be perfect.

_____ 2. A good definition for "above *reproach*" (line 4) would be   a. keenly intelligent   b. wise and mature   c. scrupulously honest.

_____ 3. "*Provisions* for their families in case of death during the line of duty" (line 12) might include   a. life insurance   b. higher salary c. promotions.

_____ 4. By "*accommodate* our desires" (line 20) the author means that we expect the police to   a. furnish shelter for us   b. assist us   c. adapt to our changing community.

_____ 5. From the statement "they work not for public *acclaim*" (lines 30–31) we can infer that police officers   a. like being mentioned in the newspapers b. like to be considered heroes   c. find satisfaction in serving people.

Number correct _____ (total 5)

Part C *Ways to Make New Words Your Own*

By now you are familiar with the target words and their meanings. This section presents a variety of reinforcement activities that will help you make the words part of your vocabulary.

Using Language and Thinking Skills

Finding Examples Write the letter of the situation that best demonstrates each word's meaning.

Example:

<u>a</u> **careful**

    a. using a seat belt every time you are in a car
    b. paying no heed to a flashing yellow light
    c. taking the expressway because it saves time

_____ 1. **acclaim**

    a. getting a standing ovation for an excellent performance
    b. receiving a *C* on a test
    c. going on a trip to a favorite place

_____ 2. **depth**

    a. a person who forgets to change a light bulb
    b. a character in a play who laughs, even in serious situations
    c. intense despair that seems to have no end

_____ 3. **tact**

    a. explaining in a nice way why you do not want to see a particular movie
    b. testing a varnished surface to see if it is dry
    c. yelling at an employee for being late

_____ 4. **efficiency**

    a. using a calculator to add a long column of figures
    b. taking all the time you want on each item during a timed test
    c. lounging on a beach in the hot sun

_____ 5. **admirably**

    a. to question the value of another's efforts to do volunteer work
    b. to answer a question truthfully even if it is difficult or embarrassing
    c. to laugh at another's inability to understand a math problem

Number correct _____ (total 5)

Identifying Word Function Three target words, *acclaim*, *attribute*, and *reproach*, can be used as both nouns and verbs. Fill in the appropriate target word in each of the sentences that follow, and identify how the word is being used—noun or verb. In some cases you will have to add an appropriate word ending.

Example: The teacher's greatest *attribute* was her patience. (**noun**)
            I *attribute* the success of the book to the fact that its movie counterpart was released at the same time. (**verb**)

1. Gauguin's paintings were not given _____ until he died.

2. Several students were _____ for talking during the assembly.

3. The _____ of a good actor or actress include the ability to understand the personality of the character being portrayed.

4. Scientists _____ the recent drought to the greenhouse effect.

5. An investigation revealed that the mayor's actions were above _____ .

6. Critics _____ Meryl Streep's performance.

7. Huck Finn ignored the _____ of Aunt Polly and did as he pleased.

8. The combined _____ of many students made a great team.

9. Jonas Salk was greatly _____ for developing the polio vaccine.

10. The supervisor _____ anyone who comes in late.

Number correct _____ (total 10)

Practicing for Standardized Tests

Antonyms Write the letter of the word whose meaning is most nearly *opposite* that of the capitalized word.

_____ 1. ADMIRABLY: (A) poorly (B) splendidly (C) urgently (D) collectively (E) incredibly

_____ 2. APPREHEND: (A) arrest (B) aspire (C) understand (D) approach (E) release

_____ 3. ENTHUSIASTIC: (A) half-hearted (B) unsung (C) clever (D) stern (E) exuberant

_____ 4. FINESSE: (A) splendor (B) skill (C) clumsiness (D) end (E) course

_____ 5. GRATITUDE: (A) praise (B) thanklessness (C) aspiration (D) inertia (E) hatred

_____ 6. REPROACH: (A) depart (B) compliment (C) decline (D) obey (E) scold

_____ 7. SCRUPULOUSLY: (A) profitably (B) honestly (C) humorously (D) carelessly (E) quickly

_____ 8. SOPHISTICATED: (A) wise (B) dignified (C) naive (D) exquisite (E) disputed

_____ 9. SUFFICIENT: (A) adequate (B) deficient (C) usual (D) pleasurable (E) magnificent

_____ 10. UNMERCIFULLY: (A) credibly (B) cynically (C) enough (D) kindly (E) cruelly

Number correct _____ (total 10)

Spelling and Wordplay

Word Maze Find and then circle the target words in this maze.

```
S  C  R  U  P  U  L  O  U  S  L  Y  E  V        acclaim
U  O  E  T  C  H  G  J  W  Y  L  D  N  I        accommodate
F  P  P  R  A  M  R  E  Z  L  X  C  T  R        admirably
F  R  R  H  P  C  A  F  U  B  A  O  H  T        apprehend
I  O  O  A  I  Q  T  F  M  A  T  M  U  U        attribute
C  V  A  P  M  S  I  I  I  R  T  P  S  A        competence
I  I  C  P  O  C  T  C  A  I  R  E  I  L        depth
E  S  H  R  R  D  U  I  L  M  I  T  A  L        efficiency
N  I  S  E  T  E  D  E  C  D  B  E  S  Y        enthusiastic
T  O  M  H  A  P  E  N  C  A  U  N  T  E        finesse
Q  N  J  E  L  T  V  C  A  H  T  C  I  K        gratitude
U  K  X  N  R  H  Z  Y  L  W  E  E  C  G        mortal
P  W  S  D  O  F  I  N  E  S  S  E  D  F        provision
B  L  G  E  T  A  D  O  M  M  O  C  C  A        reproach
```

acclaim
accommodate
admirably
apprehend
attribute
competence
depth
efficiency
enthusiastic
finesse
gratitude
mortal
provision
reproach
scrupulously
sophisticated
sufficient
tact
unmercifully
virtually

Part D   Related Words

A number of words are closely related to the target words you have studied. Use your knowledge of the target words and of word parts to determine the meanings of these words. (For information about word parts analysis, see pages 6-12.) If you are unsure of any definitions, use your dictionary. Learning these related words expands your vocabulary and helps you learn the target words more thoroughly.

1. acclamation (ak′ lə mā′ shən) n.
2. accommodation (ə käm′ ə dā′ shən) n.
3. admire (əd mīr′, ad-) v.
4. apprehension (ap′ rə hen′ shən) n.
5. attributable (ə trib′ yoot ə b'l) adj.
6. competent (käm′ pə tənt) adj.
7. comprehension (käm′ prə hen′ shən) n.
8. efficient (ə fish′ ənt) adj.
9. enthusiasm (in thoo′ zē az'm, -thyoo′-) n.
10. exclamation (eks′ klə mā′ shən) n.
11. grateful (grāt′ fəl) adj.
12. immortality (i′ môr tal′ ə tē) n.
13. inefficient (in′ ə fish′ ənt) adj.
14. irreproachable (ir′ i prō′ chə b'l) adj.
15. mercy (mur′ sē) n.
16. mortality (môr tal′ ə tē) n.
17. scruple (skroo′ p'l) n.
18. sophistication (sə fis′ tə kā′ shən) n.
19. tactful (takt′ fəl) adj.
20. virtue (vur′ choo) n.

Understanding Related Words

Sentence Completion Complete each sentence below with the appropriate related word or words from the preceding list.

1. Judging from the small amount of work completed, there was good reason to accuse Jesse of being _____ .

2. "Bravo!" and "Encore!" were two of the _____ made by the audience after the concert. In addition, the soloist received _____ from three newspaper critics the following day.

3. Although Terry's _____ of the history chapter was thorough, her nervous _____ about the test kept her from doing well.

4. I had to _____ and respect the salesperson's honesty when she pointed out how much more _____ this car was compared to the more expensive model.

5. The senator's record is _____ : he has never been touched by even a hint of scandal.

Number correct _____ (total 5)

Matching Ideas Write the related word from the list below that best matches the idea conveyed in each sentence.

| accommodation | sophistication | virtue | tactful | mercy |
| enthusiasm | scruple | mortality | competent | grateful |

_____ 1. A trip across the country gave Anne a more worldly outlook; afterward, she seemed more mature.

_____ 2. The young girl hesitated and then put the candy bar back. She had been taught not to steal and couldn't take it even if no one would find out.

_____ 3. The aged philosopher, talking about the brevity of life, remarked, "None of us is going to get out of this alive."

_____ 4. Andrew spoke with fervor about the proposed legislation and all the benefits the new law would give young people who lack the means to pay for a college education.

_____ 5. Passengers wondered whether a pilot who looked so young had the skills, knowledge, and good judgment necessary to pilot a jumbo jet.

_____ 6. Judge Sanchez decided not to send the young shoplifter to prison this time but gave him one more chance to change.

_____ 7. The youth assured Judge Sanchez that he would never forget the great favor she did for him.

_____ 8. We reserved two rooms with an adjoining bath.

_____ 9. Victoria was praised for her honesty and patience.

_____ 10. Gloria pointed out that although Greta's favorite dress was beautiful, it would not be appropriate for a formal dance.

Number correct _____ (total 10)

Analyzing Word Parts

Negative Prefixes Several prefixes in English have a negating effect on a word. That is, when added to a base word, these prefixes cause the newly formed word to mean the opposite of the base word. For example, adding *in-* to *credible* changes the word's meaning from "believable" to "unbelievable." Five common negative prefixes are *in-*, *un-*, *im-*, *il-*, and *ir-*. All five mean "not."

Add a negative prefix to each of the following words. If you do not know the correct prefix to add, use a dictionary. Then write the meaning of the new word.

1. capable: _____

2. replaceable: _____

3. literate: _____

4. legal: _____

5. usual: _____

6. personal: _____

7. comprehensible: _____

8. resistible: _____

9. moral: _____

10. bearable: _____

Number correct _____ (total 10)

Number correct in Unit _____ (total 75)

Word's Worth: scrupulous

How is a *scrupulous* person like the fairy-tale princess who could sense a tiny pea under her mattress? In ancient Rome a *scrupulus* was a tiny stone used to represent the smallest unit of weight. Gradually the word came also to mean "anxiety," "uneasiness," and "doubt." So if the two meanings were combined, a *scrupulous* person would be one with great sensitivity. He or she would be the kind of person to become anxious about a matter as small as a pebble in his or her shoe. An unscrupulous person, on the other hand, would probably not even notice the annoyance, much less care about it. Later, the French shaped the meaning further to match our use today, "oversensitivity to small matters of conscience."

Turn to **The Prefix ad-** on pages 194-195 of the **Spelling Handbook**. Read the rule and complete the exercises provided.

The Last Word

Writing

Imagine that you are in the process of completing an application for the job or college of your dreams. You are asked to write a short essay in which you convey your unique strengths, areas of *competence*, and *enthusiasm*. As you write, keep in mind that you want to convince your readers that they should choose you for the job or the college because of your special *attributes* and interests. Be as creative in your writing as possible.

Speaking

Choose a situation in which an *efficient* use of time is appropriate and beneficial. Possible situations include how to study, how to practice playing a musical instrument, how to complete chores, or how to shop. Prepare a speech in which you give specific suggestions as to how a person in this situation might save time.

Group Discussion

Whom do you *admire* in the fields of politics, science, literature, and music? As a class, choose at least three people (they may be contemporary figures or those from the past) who have received great *acclaim* in politics, science, literature, or music. Then discuss the attributes you most admire in these people.

UNIT 7

Part A   Target Words and Their Meanings

1. adage (ad′ ij) n.
2. aerial (er′ ē əl) adj., n.
3. agility (ə jil′ ə tē) n.
4. conceal (kən sēl′) v.
5. cycle (sī′ k'l) n., v.
6. excess (ek′ ses′) adj. (ik ses′, ek ′ ses′) n.
7. expanse (ik spans′) n.
8. expediency (ik spē′ dē ən sē) n.
9. forage (fôr′ ij, fär′-) n., v.
10. inconspicuous (in′ kən spik′ yōō wəs) adj.
11. keynote (kē′ nōt′) n., v., adj.
12. liable (lī′ ə b'l, lī′ b'l) adj.
13. maintenance (mān′ t'n əns) n.,
14. majestic (mə jes′ tik) adj.
15. predator (pred′ ə tər) n.
16. prescribe (pri skrīb′) v.
17. recognition (rek′ əg nish′ ən) n.
18. seclude (si klōōd′) v.
19. secretive (sē krə tiv) adj.
20. stealth (stelth) n.

Inferring Meaning from Context

For each sentence write the letter of the word or phrase that is closest to the meaning of the word or words in italics. Use context clues to help you determine the correct answer. (For information about how context helps you understand vocabulary, see pages 1-5.)

_____ 1. Benjamin Franklin is credited with the old *adage* "a penny saved is a penny earned."

a. law b. saying c. reproach d. resource

_____ 2. To get an overview of the campus, we looked at *aerial* photographs.

a. close-up b. color c. daring d. from the air

_____ 3. Ron thought that tap-dancing was simple. After stumbling through his first lesson, however, he realized that tap-dancing requires a great deal of *agility*.

a. cooperation b. intelligence c. nimbleness d. tact

_____ 4. Weeds and bushes *concealed* the sign so that we could not see it.

a. hid b. damaged c. controlled d. magnified

_____ 5. The tadpole is one of the first stages in the life *cycle* of the frog.

a. migration b. accommodation c. series of events d. purpose

_____ 6. The Schmidts cooked more than they needed for the party; they gave the *excess* food to their next-door neighbors.

a. wasted b. surplus c. overcooked d. anticipated

_____ 7. The early pioneers found vast *expanses* of prairie suitable for farming.
a. urban areas   b. wooded areas   c. enclosures   d. open areas

_____ 8. The senator's decision was based on political *expediency*. If he voted for the bill, he would receive support from an important block of voters.
a. expeditions   b. self-serving advantage   c. impracticality   d. balance of power

_____ 9. During the harsh winter months, rabbits *forage for* food—they will eat twigs, bark, and the fruit left on trees.
a. fight for   b. search for   c. destroy   d. save

_____ 10. The stop sign was so *inconspicuous* that the bus driver failed to see it.
a. easy to see   b. extraordinary   c. unnoticeable   d. appealing

_____ 11. The *keynote* speaker delivered a speech on the central issue of our convention: the importance of local recycling efforts.
a. second   b. main   c. eloquent   d. well-dressed

_____ 12. The judge concluded that Mr. Wagner was *liable* for the damages caused in the car accident and therefore had to pay for all repairs.
a. responsible   b. prepared   c. sorry   d. not responsible

_____ 13. *Maintenance* of the railroad has declined so much in recent months that track 13 is showing signs of neglect.
a. Upkeep   b. Public support   c. Use   d. Expansion

_____ 14. I am always impressed by the *majestic* mountain peaks of Colorado.
a. diminutive   b. sophisticated   c. ordinary   d. grand

_____ 15. Because the cat is a *predator* of the mouse, our cat keeps the mouse population under control in our home.
a. hunter   b. friend   c. relative   d. protector

_____ 16. Dr. Monacelli *prescribed* a new type of medication to treat Susan's severe hay fever; after taking the medicine for two days, Susan's head cleared.
a. predicted   b. ordered   c. described   d. postponed

_____ 17. Formal *recognition* was given to Ms. Muhlenberg for her many contributions.
a. acknowledgment   b. ownership   c. sympathy   d. authority

_____ 18. The doctor recommended that Gina be *secluded* in her room so that her sisters and brothers would not contract the chicken pox.
a. encompassed   b. acclimated   c. isolated   d. apprehended

_____ 19. George's quiet, *secretive* manner made people suspicious of his actions.
a. open   b. close-mouthed   c. exuberant   d. inspiring

_____ 20. The fox crept with such *stealth* that the hens were caught off guard.
a. slyness   b. noise   c. independence   d. selfishness

Number correct _____ (total 20)

You should now have a general idea of the meaning of each target word. Refine your understanding by examining the shades of meaning the words have in the following excerpt.

An Owl's Place

Mike Sawyers

The owl is one of the most common predators, but one that most people have never seen. In the following selection the author describes the life of this familiar yet mysterious bird.

Predacious,[1] fierce, **secretive, majestic,** and even wise are adjectives that describe the owl. Seen only occasionally, the owl quietly goes about its business of living in its **prescribed** natural way. Covered by the veil of night, the owl skims the top from **excess** populations of insects, reptiles, small mammals, and birds.

The owl seemingly requires no personal **recognition** for its part in the natural scheme of things. Its whole life **cycle** is **keynoted** by darkness, **stealth**, and secrecy. A missing figure in the daytime, the owl is everywhere at night, quietly ruling the darkened woodland.

"Hoot" plays the role of the heavy in the **predator** versus prey drama. It is well equipped for its part and fulfills its mission with efficiency. The necessity of birds of prey in the **maintenance** of a balanced system of life was a once-disputed fact now taken for granted.

Eagles and hawks are usually the topic in predatory bird discussions, while the owl often goes unmentioned. Because they hunt mostly at night, observations of owl kills are few. Out of sight, out of mind is an **adage** the owl uses to its advantage. But it is there, swiftly going about its business. Since it is so **inconspicuous**, the names great horned or screeched are not on the tips of most tongues as are redtail, golden, or bald.

5

10

15

---

[1] predacious: characteristic of a predator

A predator, the owl works only as hard for its meals as is necessary. Small animals and birds that are plentiful and close to its roost are the ones that most often grace the owl's dinner table. `20`

Great horned owls are the most common of North American owls. Abundant in Wyoming, they work the nightshift out of **expediency**. That is when likely candidates for a meal will be up and about. `25`

The darkness that envelops half of the world each night offers protection to prey and predator alike. The mouse and rabbit waiting until sunset to **forage** for food run the risk of predacious attack from a snake hidden in the darkness. The great horned owl can now swoop down from its perch with no fear of casting a shadow or being silhouetted against a daytime sky. Snake and rabbit alike are **liable** to end up in the owl's sharp talons. `30`

A large muscular bird, the horned owl can weigh up to five pounds and spread its wings to five feet. It prefers a medium-size meal, and its **aerial agility** and pointed talons give it the weapons to capture these quick prey animals.

Skunks, marmots, chipmunks, muskrats, small birds, and insects all fall prey to this night flyer. If game birds are available, the owl includes them in its menu. `35`

The great horned owl is a homebody, spending the entire year in the same patch of woods or area of the forest. Each season, as some of the hawks and crows depart, the horned owl will look over their nests and take up residence in the best-looking one. A pair of horned owls will mate for life. Once the male picks the right nest, the female will join him and they will spend the winter there. `40`

The hunting range of the horned owl is accordingly small. A square mile will usually encompass this big owl's aerial safari[2] route.

In late winter the female owl will lay her eggs in the nest and stay with them until they hatch a little more than a month later. The nest will usually be **concealed** within the top of a broken tree or in some other high **secluded** place. Young owls will be helpless for a while and need the protection from returning hawks and crows. In Wyoming the great horned owl will nest in sagebrush **expanses** if no suitable wood lots are available. `45`

_____

[2] safari: a journey or hunting expedition, especially in eastern Africa

Refining Your Understanding

For each of the following items, consider how the target word is used in the passage. Write the letter of the word or phrase that best completes each sentence.

_____ 1. If owls live in a "*prescribed* natural way" (line 3), they apparently
a. choose where and how they will live   b. live according to the laws of nature   c. make the rules for other creatures in a region.

_____ 2. The owl "skims the top from *excess* populations" (line 4) of various creatures, meaning that the owl   a. helps hold animal populations in check   b. eats only part of its prey   c. takes endangered species as prey.

_____ 3. If snakes and rabbits are "*liable* to end up in the owl's sharp talons" (line 31), they are   a. unusual prey for the owl   b. likely prey for the owl   c. treacherous prey for the owl.

_____ 4. *Aerial agility* (line 33) is also a necessary trait for a   a. piano player   b. seamstress   c. high-wire artist.

_____ 5. The fact that the owl's nest is described as *concealed* and *secluded* (line 46) suggests that an owl   a. advertises where its nest is   b. prefers its nest to be hidden   c. constructs its nest with wood and sticky material.

Number correct _____ (total 5)

Part C   Ways to Make New Words Your Own

This section presents a variety of reinforcement activities that will help you make these words part of your permanent vocabulary.

Using Language and Thinking Skills

Finding Examples Write the letter of the situation that best demonstrates the meaning of each word. For example:

__c__ **careful**

a. rarely using a seatbelt when you are in a car
b. paying no heed to a flashing yellow light
c. trying hard not to knock over a valuable vase

_____ 1. **adage**

a. A stitch in time saves nine.
b. A weather forecaster is seldom correct.
c. Squids and snails are mollusks.

_____ 2. **aerial**

a. a dispenser for insecticide
b. a squirrel leaping from branch to branch
c. something mysterious or weird

_____ 3. **cycle**

a. the phases of the moon
b. a farm implement
c. a first-run movie

_____ 4. **expanse**

a. a doctor's waiting room
b. a financial cost or fee
c. a wheat field stretching as far as you can see

_____ 5. **forage**

a. a forester fighting fires
b. a cow grazing in a pasture
c. a salesperson negotiating a deal

_____ 6. **inconspicuous**
   a. a deer blending in with its surroundings
   b. a boy wearing an orange shirt
   c. a stoplight

_____ 7. **maintenance**
   a. forgetting to change the oil in a car
   b. painting a house every five years
   c. purchasing a new bicycle

_____ 8. **predator**
   a. a hunter tracking a deer
   b. a rabbit eating carrots in a carrot patch
   c. a gardener chasing a rabbit from her garden

_____ 9. **seclude**
   a. denying some people the right to join a club
   b. selecting members of a team
   c. choosing to live alone in the backwoods

_____ 10. **stealth**
   a. a one-hundred-piece brass band marching down Main Street
   b. a burglar checking a store for unlocked windows
   c. a steelworker demanding higher wages

Number correct _____ (total 10)

Practicing for Standardized Tests

Synonyms Write the letter of the word whose meaning is closest to that of the capitalized word.

_____ 1. KEYNOTE: (A) opening (B) theme (C) genius (D) melody (E) trivia

_____ 2. CONCEAL: (A) deny (B) develop (C) hide (D) display (E) mistreat

_____ 3. EXPANSE: (A) range (B) expense (C) exit (D) suitor (E) concept

_____ 4. EXPEDIENCY: (A) laziness (B) enthusiasm (C) convenience
   (D) finesse (E) tact

_____ 5. FORAGE: (A) seize (B) praise (C) dispute (D) grow (E) search

_____ 6. LIABLE: (A) exempt (B) free (C) tedious (D) responsible (E) false

_____ 7. MAINTENANCE: (A) circumstance (B) upkeep (C) goodness
   (D) stealth (E) depth

_____ 8. PREDATOR: (A) wedge (B) device (C) hero (D) ancestor (E) hunter

_____ 9. RECOGNITION: (A) tact (B) forethought (C) identification
   (D) memory (E) concealment

_____ 10. SECLUDE: (A) impede (B) isolate (C) uncover (D) exhibit (E) acclaim

Number correct _____ (total 10)

Analogies Write the letter of the word pair that best expresses a relationship similar to that expressed in the original pair.

_____ 1. DEFICIENCY : EXCESS : : (A) breeze : air (B) shortfall : overabundance (C) mortal : William Shakespeare (D) infant : childhood (E) vegetable : potato

_____ 2. STRAIGHTFORWARD : SECRETIVE : : (A) apprehensive : nervous (B) northern : western (C) brave : courageous (D) timid : shy (E) inexact : accurate

_____ 3. MONKEY : AGILITY : : (A) dog : hound (B) stealth : fox (C) smirk : smile (D) turtle : sluggishness (E) robbery : apprehension

_____ 4. ADAGE : SAYING : : (A) brain : intelligence (B) silo : storage (C) mortal : immortal (D) chaos : disorder (E) ordeal : relief

_____ 5. HIDDEN : INCONSPICUOUS : : (A) honest : unscrupulous (B) obvious : conspicuous (C) downtrodden : ennobled (D) solar : lunar (E) healthy : sick

_____ 6. SECRECY : STEALTH : : (A) impediment : help (B) inertia : activity (C) unity : country (D) stone : statue (E) anger : fury

_____ 7. DOCTOR : PRESCRIBE : : (A) medicine : cure (B) airport : travel (C) pool : swim (D) architect : design (E) hospital : recover

_____ 8. AIRPLANE : AERIAL : : (A) ship : oceanic (B) train : fast (C) whim : fanciful (D) pilot : reliable (E) consensus : agreeable

_____ 9. MAJESTIC : MODEST : : (A) profound : deep (B) menacing : dangerous (C) wintry : snowy (D) impressive : ordinary (E) meager : abundant

_____ 10. CONCEAL : IDENTITY : : (A) laugh : joke (B) elect : election (C) win : pride (D) seek : search (E) grow : plant

Number correct _____ (total 10)

Word's Worth: liable

Liable comes from the Latin word _ligare_, meaning "to bind." It is related to such English words as _alloy, ally, league, leech, obligate,_ and _religion,_ all of which have to do with binding. Bonds can be pleasant or unpleasant. Most people, for example, seek out _allies_ but shun _leeches. Leagues_ bind and organize sports teams, but only the most loyal fans feel _obligated_ to support a losing team. When you are liable, you are legally bound to make good on any damage you cause, which is why people purchase _liability_ insurance.

Spelling and Wordplay

Crossword Puzzle Read each clue to determine what word will fit in the corresponding squares. There are several target words in the puzzle.

ACROSS

1. Suitability for a given purpose
8. Abbr. Radium
10. Having color
11. Hunter
13. Abbr. California
14. Past tense of *see*
16. Ground-level cloud
17. __ __ and behold
18. To hunt for food
19. Poetical word for *forefathers*
21. A __ __ __ can
22. Not out
23. Roman numeral 9
24. Abbr. Ancient
25. Nickname for Lillian
27. Abbr. Before Christ
28. Totaled
29. 7th tone on the musical scale
30. To crawl
32. By way of
33. A recurring period
36. Abbr. Obstetrics
37. To touch with the lips
39. Prefix meaning "again"
40. Abbr. South America
41. Printer's abbr. New Line
42. __ __ or don't
43. Toward
45. Abbr. Registered Nurse
48. To pull behind
49. Sun god of ancient Egyptians
51. Nickname for Edward
53. Attracting little attention

DOWN

1. Large open area
2. To advocate a treatment
3. Speaks slowly
4. Abbr. Economics
5. Neither . . .
   __ __ __
6. Abbr. Chlorine
7. Exclamation of pain
8. Acknowledgment
9. A proverb
12. Abbr. District Attorney
15. Hides
16. To be unsuccessful
18. To discover
20. Surplus
21. __ __ __ pole; young frog
26. Likely
31. Sudden hostile attack
33. Large black birds
34. Biblical word for *you*
35. Part of cornstalk that bears the corn
38. In the way shown
43. 2,000 pounds
44. Prefix meaning "three"
46. Prefix meaning "new"
47. Slang for *hello*
48. See 43 Across
50. Abbr. Alternating Current
52. Abbr. Dutch

Part D   Related Words

A number of words are closely related to the target words you have studied. Use your knowledge of the target words and of word parts to determine the meaning of these words. (For information about word parts analysis, see pages 6-12.) Learning these related words expands your vocabulary and helps you learn the target words more thoroughly.

1. aerialist (er′ ē əl ist) n.	8. maintain (mān tān′) v.
2. cognizant (käg′ nə zənt) adj.	9. majesty (maj′ is tē) n.
3. concealment (kən sēl′ mənt) n.	10. predacious (pri dā′ shəs) adj.
4. cyclical (sik′ lik k'l) adj.	11. prescription (pri skrip′ shən) n.
5. excessive (ik ses′ iv) adj.	12. seclusion (si klōō′ zhən) n.
6. expeditious (ek′ spə dish′ əs) adj.	13. stealthy (stel′ thē) adj.
7. liability (lī′ ə bil′ ə tē) n.	14. subscription (səb skrip′ shən) n.

Understanding Related Words

Sentence Completion   Complete each sentence with the correct related word from the list above.

_____ 1. Arnie was not _?_ of the time and continued to read the mystery novel until dawn.

_____ 2. Foxes, lions, and tigers are examples of _?_ animals.

_____ 3. The _?_ cat leapt onto the kitchen table and quickly lapped the milk from the saucer.

_____ 4. The Millers were overcome by the _?_ of the Taj Mahal.

_____ 5. The audience watched in amazement as the _?_ performed dives, handstands, somersaults, and pirouettes on the tightrope.

_____ 6. Because the movie star was often hounded by fans and photographers, he valued the total _?_ of his home in the country.

_____ 7. The landlord demanded that the tenants pay damages for the _?_ wear and tear they had inflicted on the apartment.

_____ 8. The salesperson's shy, reserved behavior was considered a (an) _?_.

_____ 9. Wanda resuscitated the child and then called an ambulance; her _?_ action saved the child's life.

_____ 10. The _?_ of weapons by civilians is prohibited by law.

Number correct _____ (total 10)

Analyzing Word Parts

The Latin Root *ced* The target word *excess* comes from the Latin word *cedere*, meaning "to go" or "to yield." Other words with the *cedere* root include *concede*, *exceed*, *precede*, *recede*, and *succeed*. Look up the meanings of each of these words in your dictionary. Then use each word in one of the following sentences.

_____ 1. During the ebb tide, the water began to ⸮ , and soon the beach was wide enough for sunbathing.

_____ 2. To avoid getting another traffic ticket, Mr. Elms tried not to ⸮ the speed limit.

_____ 3. Greta was able to ⸮ at the task because she worked hard and never lost confidence in herself.

_____ 4. When the members of the scholastic team could not recall the name of the eighth President of the United States, they were forced to ⸮ defeat to their opponents.

_____ 5. Richard was asked to ⸮ the dignitaries into the banquet hall and direct them to their seats.

Number correct _____ (total 5)

Turn to **Words with the "Seed" Sound** on pages 207-208 of the **Spelling Handbook**. Read the rule and complete the exercises provided.

The Latin Root *ten* The target word *maintenance* and the related word *maintain* come from the Latin word *tenere*, meaning "to hold." The following words also come from this Latin word: *contain*, *detain*, *pertain*, and *retain*. Keeping in mind the meaning of *tenere*, fill each blank below with the correct word.

_____ 1. We decided to ⸮ the first draft of our ad in case we needed it.

_____ 2. The train was coming, so I could not ⸮ him any longer.

_____ 3. My mother is always reminding me that buying a car is one thing; continuing to ⸮ it is an altogether different matter.

_____ 4. The lawyer's question did not ⸮ to the case that would be heard later in the day.

_____ 5. The cartons that we collected for our school's semi-annual food drive ⸮ all kinds of canned and boxed foods.

Number correct _____ (total 5)

Number correct in Unit _____ (total 75)

The Last Word

In this unit you have learned the target word *adage*. Adages are often important statements of advice that have been passed down through the ages. Many of today's adages can be traced to ancient Greek and Roman literature, the Bible, and sages such as Benjamin Franklin and Mark Twain.

Group Discussion

Read and discuss three of the following adages. What do they mean, and are they true in today's world? Can you think of situations in which the adage isn't true? Be sure to consider differences in interpretation among class members.

1. Look before you leap.
2. Practice makes perfect.
3. Knowledge is power.
4. It never rains but it pours.
5. All things come to those who wait.
6. Rome was not built in a day.
7. An empty wagon rattles the loudest.
8. The nearer the dawn, the darker the night.
9. To understand is to forgive.
10. Good and quickly seldom meet.

Writing

Choose one of the adages above, and write a journal entry or a longer composition, using the adage as your thesis, or controlling idea. Give explanations and examples to prove or disprove the truth expressed by the adage. Write your composition so that a reader unfamiliar with the adage will understand it after reading your explanation.

Speaking/Writing/Discussion

Adages are interesting and useful, but some have become clichés through overuse. Creating fresh, original expressions will make your point more effectively than using worn-out adages such as "You can't teach an old dog new tricks." Create new sayings of your own that communicate the same idea as the following adages. Use imagination and humor.

1. Birds of a feather flock together.
2. When the cat's away, the mice will play.
3. A stitch in time saves nine.
4. Every cloud has a silver lining.

U N I T 8: Review of Units 5–7

Part A Review Word List

Unit 5 Target Words

1. appall
2. apparently
3. characteristic
4. deadpan
5. decade
6. deny
7. excel
8. extend
9. fluster
10. forethought
11. ordeal
12. routinely
13. stake
14. stolid
15. stun
16. subject
17. suitor
18. tedious
19. vibrant
20. whim

Unit 5 Related Words

1. apparent
2. character
3. denial
4. excellent
5. extension
6. routine
7. stunning
8. subjective
9. tedium
10. vibrate
11. vibrato
12. whimsical

Unit 6 Target Words

1. acclaim
2. accommodate
3. admirably
4. apprehend
5. attribute
6. competence
7. depth
8. efficiency
9. enthusiastic
10. finesse
11. gratitude
12. mortal
13. provision
14. reproach
15. scrupulously
16. sophisticated
17. sufficient
18. tact
19. unmercifully
20. virtually

Unit 6 Related Words

1. acclamation
2. accommodation
3. admire
4. apprehension
5. attributable
6. competent
7. comprehension
8. efficient
9. enthusiasm
10. exclamation
11. grateful
12. immortality
13. inefficient
14. irreproachable
15. mercy
16. mortality
17. scruple
18. sophistication
19. tactful
20. virtue

Unit 7 Target Words

1. adage
2. aerial
3. agility
4. conceal
5. cycle
6. excess
7. expanse
8. expediency
9. forage
10. inconspicuous
11. keynote
12. liable
13. maintenance
14. majestic
15. predator
16. prescribe
17. recognition
18. seclude
19. secretive
20. stealth

Unit 7 Related Words

1. aerialist
2. cognizant
3. concealment
4. cyclical
5. excessive
6. expeditious
7. liability
8. maintain
9. majesty
10. predacious
11. prescription
12. seclusion
13. stealthy
14. subscription

Inferring Meaning from Context

Write the letter of the word or phrase that is closest to the meaning of the word or words in italics.

_____ 1. Before the game, we bragged about an easy victory. After we lost by 64 to 14, the *adage* "Pride goeth before a fall" came to mind.
a. liability   b. attribute   c. saying   d. provision

_____ 2. The head cheerleader displayed her *agility* by performing six cartwheels.
a. clumsiness   b. ability to move easily   c. ability to be clever
d. sophistication

_____ 3. Mara's most amazing *characteristic* is her ability to quickly figure logarithms in her head.
a. trait   b. ordeal   c. accommodation   d. tact

_____ 4. Living within walking distance of work was *expeditious* for Alex because he didn't have a car.
a. convenient   b. tedious   c. routine   d. inefficient

_____ 5. The foreman of the jury presented his arguments with such *finesse* that the dissenting jurors changed their votes.
a. accommodation   b. virtue   c. skillfulness   d. reproach

_____ 6. Carla's dark coat made her *inconspicuous* as she hurried down the path.
a. unnoticeable   b. irresponsible   c. irreproachable   d. unmerciful

_____ 7. Miss Andersen's final examination was such *an ordeal* that we were all exhausted when it was over.
a. an excursion   b. an attribute   c. a trial   d. a whim

_____ 8. Eagles are *predators* that feed on rodents such as mice and gophers.
a. ancestors   b. social animals   c. hunters   d. foragers

_____ 9. Since the Lawsons retired, they *routinely* walk to the park every day.
a. expediently   b. enthusiastically   c. apparently   d. habitually

_____ 10. The cabin was old but freshly painted and *scrupulously* clean.
a. carelessly   b. painstakingly   c. majestically   d. irresponsibly

_____ 11. Kim's *sophisticated* black prom dress made her look older than seventeen.
a. mortal   b. maintained   c. inconspicuous   d. worldly

_____ 12. Kris had *a sufficient* number of books to write an informative report.
a. an arbitrary   b. an expeditious   c. an adequate   d. a scrupulous

_____ 13. Billy's rudeness displayed a total lack of *tact*.
a. stealth   b. coordination   c. enthusiasm   d. finesse

_____ 14. Washing the dishes was *a tedious* job shared by all the campers in turn.
a. an excessive   b. a reproachful   c. a tiresome   d. an efficient

_____ 15. On *a whim,* without thinking, we jumped into the pool with our clothes on.
   a. a sudden fancy   b. a dare   c. a secretive plan   d. a mortal provision

Number correct _____ (total 15)

Using Review Words in Context

Using context clues, determine which word from the list fits best in each blank in the story below. Each word from the list will be used only once.

acclaim	decades	extend	mortal	stunning
admired	denied	inconspicuous	scrupulously	virtually
character	depth	liability	seclusion	whim

Private I Versus Public Eye

"I want to be alone."

You might expect that such a desire for _____ would be expressed by a hermit retreating to the wilderness to live off the land. However, one of the most popular motion picture stars of all time, Greta Garbo, not only said just that but _____ made it happen.

Garbo's career spanned the 1920's and 1930's, _____ that saw the demise of silent pictures and the birth of the modern cinema. Although the fans who _____ her knew Garbo only by the two-dimensional image they saw on the movie screen, she had a complexity and _____ that made her more fascinating than any _____ she portrayed.

Garbo was born Greta Lovisa Gustafsson in Stockholm, Sweden, in 1905. She began working at menial jobs in her early teens, but she did not long remain _____ . Swedish motion picture director, Mauritz Stiller, gave her a stage name as well as her first important part, the title role in *The Story of Gosta Berling*. In 1925, when Stiller was hired by Metro-Goldwyn-Mayer in Hollywood, he insisted that they _____ a contract to Garbo as well. Garbo accompanied Stiller to the United States, where she starred in twenty-four films, and became one of the few actresses to successfully make the transition from silent to talking pictures. She often played tragic heroines and won _____ not only for her _____ beauty and extraordinary talent, but also for the low, sultry voice that gave her an air of mystery and inaccessibility.

In fact, Garbo was, and remains, an enigma. She chose a career in the public eye, yet was indifferent to her audience's opinion and _____ a need for their approval. Her greatest asset as an actress, her ability to make people respond to and care about her, became a _____ . She _____ guarded her private life, resisting Hollywood's attempts to

85

make her into a goddess. Perhaps to prove that she was only _____ , or maybe just on a _____ , she withdrew into isolation at the height of her fame.

"I want to be alone," Garbo insisted. However, can a private person who has become public property ever really be alone?

Number correct _____ (total 15)

Part B   Review Word Reinforcement

Using Language and Thinking Skills

Words on a Continuum   In each of the five sets below, a **1** is placed beside a target word; find that word's antonym and place a **4** beside it. Then number the two remaining words. Put **2** beside the word that is closer in meaning to word **1**. Put **3** next to the word that is closer in meaning to word **4**.

Example:

<u>3</u> modest

<u>2</u> fine

<u>4</u> lowly

<u>1</u> magnificent

1.

<u>1</u> agile

____ active

____ clumsy

____ sluggish

2.

____ qualified

____ ineligible

<u>1</u> competent

____ careless

3.

____ unnoticed

<u>1</u> conspicuous

____ indistinct

____ noticeable

4.

<u>1</u> excellent

____ poor

____ average

____ good

5.

<u>1</u> tactful

____ polite

____ careless

____ rude

Number correct _____ (total 15)

Practicing for Standardized Tests

Analogies   Write the letter of the word pair that best expresses a relationship similar to that expressed in the original pair.

____ 1. PERSON : MORTAL ::   (A) atheist : pious   (B) god : immortal
(C) actor : inhuman   (D) characteristic : stolid   (E) railroad : efficient

____ 2. CHAMPION : EXCEL ::   (A) hermit : seclude   (B) farmer : forage
(C) spotlight : conceal   (D) explanation : confuse   (E) engineer : destroy

____ 3. GRATITUDE : THANKFULNESS ::   (A) finesse : clumsiness
(B) impulsiveness : thoughtfulness   (C) ingratitude : ungratefulness
(D) praise : winner   (E) tedium : unexpectedness

_____ 4. REPROACH : ACCUSER ::   (A) discover : discovery   (B) acclaim : actor (C) question : interrogator   (D) spoil : success   (E) snow : winter

_____ 5. SOPHISTICATED : WORLDLY ::   (A) concealed : obvious (B) inconspicuous : unnoticed   (C) stolid : whimsical   (D) vibrant : deadpan (E) tedious : exciting

_____ 6. AGILE : CLUMSY ::   (A) expansive : broad   (B) mortal : human (C) secretive : open   (D) grateful : appreciative   (E) southern : eastern

_____ 7. EAGLE : AERIAL ::   (A) snail : slow   (B) giraffe : terrestrial   (C) fish : egg-laying   (D) butterfly : colorful   (E) horse : domesticated

_____ 8. DETECTIVE : INVESTIGATE ::   (A) police : arrest   (B) aerialist : swim (C) speaker : listen   (D) suitor : argue   (E) soldier : disobey

_____ 9. FORAGE : ANIMAL ::   (A) stun : expectation   (B) teach : subject (C) cook : hunger   (D) stalk : predator   (E) exaggerate : understatement

_____ 10. PREDATOR : PREY ::   (A) chef : kitchen   (B) fox : hound   (C) hunter : game   (D) boxer : ring   (E) suitor : flowers

Number correct _____ (total 10)

Antonyms Write the letter of the word whose meaning is most nearly _opposite_ that of the capitalized word.

_____ 1. ACCOMMODATE: (A) extend   (B) appall   (C) inconvenience (D) adjust   (E) admire

_____ 2. ADMIRABLY: (A) shamefully   (B) majestically   (C) mercifully (D) whimsically   (E) scrupulously

_____ 3. DEADPAN: (A) routine   (B) reproachful   (C) expressionless (D) expressive   (E) efficient

_____ 4. DENY: (A) refuse   (B) attribute   (C) appall   (D) seclude   (E) admit

_____ 5. ENTHUSIASTIC: (A) liable   (B) reluctant   (C) vibrant (D) sophisticated   (E) tactful

_____ 6. EXCEL: (A) surpass   (B) stun   (C) fail   (D) prescribe   (E) subject

_____ 7. MORTAL: (A) godly   (B) tedious   (C) characteristic   (D) agile (E) competent

_____ 8. SECLUDE: (A) fluster   (B) forage   (C) separate   (D) reveal   (E) hide

_____ 9. STOLID: (A) secretive   (B) enthusiastic   (C) admirable   (D) impassive (E) sophisticated

_____ 10. UNMERCIFULLY: (A) kindly   (B) whimsically   (C) virtually (D) unkindly   (E) charmingly

Number correct _____ (total 10)

Synonyms Write the letter of the word whose meaning is closest to that of the capitalized word.

_____ 1. ATTRIBUTE: (A) quality (B) whim (C) provision (D) failing (E) stake

_____ 2. CHARACTERISTIC: (A) proviso (B) adage (C) cycle (D) feature (E) suitor

_____ 3. EXPANSE: (A) forethought (B) routine (C) expense (D) cubicle (E) range

_____ 4. GRATITUDE: (A) thanklessness (B) appreciation (C) mercy (D) accommodation (E) majesty

_____ 5. LIABLE: (A) likely (B) tedious (C) doubtful (D) grateful (E) efficient

_____ 6. MAINTENANCE: (A) efficiency (B) neglect (C) upkeep (D) tact (E) finesse

_____ 7. ORDEAL: (A) provision (B) virtue (C) attribute (D) routine (E) trial

_____ 8. REPROACH: (A) acclaim (B) scold (C) exceed (D) appall (E) excel

_____ 9. ROUTINELY: (A) successfully (B) competently (C) virtually (D) habitually (E) scrupulously

_____ 10. STEALTH: (A) stolidness (B) forethought (C) sneakiness (D) vibrancy (E) majesty

Number correct _____ (total 10)

Spelling and Wordplay

Proofreading Find the ten misspelled words, and write them correctly in the blanks.

Weather Sentinel

Weather forecasting is a sofisicated subjekt that has flustured people for dekades. However, an article in a recent issue of the _Gardener's Honest Almanac_ describes an old homemade forecasting device and prerscribes it for use by all serious gardeners.

The device is easy to build and when placed in the garden is efficiant and requires very little maintenence. Construction is simple. All you do is nail a short length of chain on top of a fence post.

Then the weather vertually forecasts itself. If the chain becomes wet, the weather is rainy. If the device is covered with snow, then there are snow conditions. If the chain is hanging straight down, the weather is calm. If the chain is out from the post at an angle, there is a wind. And finally, if the chain is extanded straight out, it is storming.

So, set up your own weather sentinel in an inconspicuos corner of the garden. You will soon be forecasting the weather at least as well as the experts.

1. _____   6. _____

2. _____   7. _____

3. _____   8. _____

4. _____   9. _____

5. _____   10. _____

Number correct _____ (total 10)

Part C   *Related Word Reinforcement*

Using Related Words

Understanding Multiple Meanings   Each word in this exercise contains a boldfaced word with its definitions. Read the definitions and then the sentences that follow. Write the letter of the definition that applies to each sentence.

---

depth
a. distance from the surface to the bottom or from the front to the back (n.)
b. most inner part (n.)
c. quality of deepness (n.)

_____ 1. The scholar's analysis of the problem showed unusual *depth* of thought.

_____ 2. The hunters were lost in the *depth* of the forest.

_____ 3. Jorge's mother said he could not dive off the rocks because the *depth* of the water was not great enough and he might hit his head on the bottom.

---

subject
a. likely to have (adj.)
b. a person under the authority of someone or some rule (n.)
c. a course of study (n.)
d. the main theme of a discussion, speech, composition, or work of art (n.)

_____ 4. Of the four academic *subjects* I'm taking this year, I like English best.

_____ 5. The *subject* of the editorial in today's newspaper is acid rain.

_____ 6. Mary's mother is *subject to* fainting spells.

_____ 7. Before the American Revolution, the colonists were *subjects* of the King of England.

> **cycle**
> a. a recurring time period with a definite number of years (n.)
> b. a bicycle, tricycle, or motorcycle (n.)
> c. a historical age (a very long period of time) (n.)

_____ 8. Locusts appear in *cycles*, some returning every seven years, and some every seventeen years.

_____ 9. The *cycle* of the ice age is also known as the glacial epoch.

_____ 10. Chris works after school at The Village *Cycle* Shop.

Number correct _____ (total 10)

Reviewing Word Structures

Three Latin Roots   The Latin roots *ced* ("to go" or "to yield"), *ten* ("to hold"), and *scrib* ("to write") are contained in several related words in Units 5, 6, and 7. In each sentence below, write the correct related word based on one of these roots.   Refer to the Related Word list on page 83.

1. Old cars are costly to _____ because their parts start to break down regularly.

2. Dr. Martinez gave me a _____ for some medicine for my cough.

3. If you are unable to file your income tax by the deadline, you can request

   an _____ from the IRS.

4. Our driving instructor told us to slow down when he felt our speed

   was _____.

5. I didn't get my favorite magazine last month because my

   _____ ran out, and I failed to renew it.

Number correct _____ (total 5)

Number correct in Unit _____ (total 100)

Vocab Lab 2

FOCUS ON: *The Constitution*

For a change of pace, take a look at the following words pertaining to the United States Constitution and its provisions.

amendment (ə mend′ mənt) n. a change that deletes from, modifies, or adds to a document. • The *amendment* limits the President to two consecutive terms.

bicameral (bī kam′ ər əl) adj. consisting of two separate chambers or legislative bodies. • The Congress, which consists of the Senate and the House of Representatives, is *bicameral.*

confederation (kən fed′ ə ra′ shən) n. a group of nations or states united in a league or alliance for joint action. • The *confederation* of nations signed the treaty.

constituent (kən stich′ oo wənt) n. a citizen or resident who elects another to represent him or her in legislative or public office. • The representative listened attentively to her *constituents*' requests.

delegated powers (del′ ə gā ted pou′ ərz) n. specific, assigned powers. • The federal government has *delegated powers* that are listed in the Constitution.

double jeopardy (dub′′l jep′ ər dē) n. putting a person on trial twice for the same offense. • Since *double jeopardy* is prohibited by the U.S. Constitution, the defendant could not be tried again for the murder.

impeachment (im pēch′ mənt) n. the formal act of accusing a public official of misconduct. • The official's *impeachment* was a result of his flagrant stealing of state funds.

inalienable rights (in āl′ yən ə b'l rīts) n. rights that cannot be surrendered, denied, or transferred. • Our *inalienable rights* are guaranteed by the Constitution.

jurisdiction (joor is dik′ shən) n. the legal power to exercise authority; the range of authority. • The crime was committed in a neighboring state and therefore was not within the judge's *jurisdiction.*

mandate (man′ dāt) n. an authorization to act; an order or plea given by citizens to their elected representative. • The people's *mandate* forced the representative to approve the bill.

pro tempore (prō tem′ pə rē) (often shortened to **pro tem**) adj. chosen to occupy a position for the time being, or during the absence of the regularly elected official. • When the Senate president is absent, the president *pro tempore* takes charge of the proceedings.

ratification (rat′ ə fi kā′ shən) n. confirmation; the act of making something valid or legal. • The *ratification* of the treaty brought peace to the two countries.

residual powers (ri zij′ oo wəl pou′ ərz) n. the powers that remain after other powers have been accounted for. • Those powers not granted to the federal government are called *residual powers* and belong to the states.

servitude (sur′ və tood, -tyood) n. slavery; bondage. • In order to avoid a lifetime of *servitude*, many slaves fled along the escape route known as the Underground Railroad.

statute (stach′ oot, -oot) n. a law passed by a legislative body; an established rule. • The new *statute* prohibits smoking in public places.

Sentence Completion   Choose the correct word from the list to complete each sentence. Each word may be used only once.

_____ 1. The British Parliament is __?__, being composed of the House of Commons and the House of Lords.

_____ 2. Three of our __?__ are life, liberty, and the pursuit of happiness.

_____ 3. United by the treaty, the __?__ of countries agreed on a mutual defense plan.

_____ 4. Involuntary __?__ was abolished by the Constitution.

_____ 5. The __?__ of the new contract by a majority of union members officially ended the strike.

_____ 6. Congresswoman Jackson was appointed to be chairperson __?__ until an election could be held to fill the vacancy.

_____ 7. The __?__ from the people told the representative how to vote on the issue.

_____ 8. Once they crossed the county line, the fugitives were outside the sheriff's __?__

_____ 9. There was one constitutional __?__ to enact Prohibition and another to repeal it.

_____ 10. Each branch of government has __?__ specifically assigned by law.

_____ 11. Several of the senator's __?__(s) sent letters conveying their strong disagreement with her voting record.

_____ 12. The House of Representatives voted for the official's __?__ after hearing evidence of his professional and personal misconduct.

_____ 13. The legislature voted into law several new __?__.

_____ 14. If __?__ were legal, a person might be tried more than once for the same offense.

_____ 15. Although a special committee has been appointed to carry out the investigation, the House of Representatives still holds __?__ to determine what course of action should be taken.

Number correct _____ (total 15)

FOCUS ON: *The Thesaurus*

Imagine you have written this introductory sentence to a science fiction story:

"The pale sun rose like a frosted 40-watt bulb over the city, bathing the deserted streets in pale light."

Your sentence creates a vivid image, but notice that the word *pale* has been used twice. Replacing this repeated adjective with a synonym would not only make your sentence sound better, but it also could emphasize the mood or clarify the setting. Where can you find the word you're looking for? Your dictionary probably won't help much—you already know the definition of *pale*. However, there is a reference book—the thesaurus—made to order for such situations.

What Is a Thesaurus and How Is It Used?

A thesaurus is a dictionary of synonyms and antonyms. The word *thesaurus* comes from the Greek word for "treasure," and that's exactly what a thesaurus is—a treasury of words. It groups related words that have various shades of meaning so you can find the one that expresses your thought exactly. It is a reference source no good writer should be without.

The first thesaurus, the *Thesaurus of English Words and Phrases*, was written in 1852 by an English physician, Peter Roget (rō zhā′). That original thesaurus, and many others, group words into categories based on meaning. Some categories in Roget's thesaurus include "Time," "Space," and "Means of Communicating Ideas." To use this type of thesaurus, you look up a specific word in an alphabetical index at the back of the book, note the number that is printed beside the word, and then look under that number in the main part of the book to find synonyms for the word.

Other thesauruses are used like a dictionary; they are arranged in alphabetical order, with synonyms grouped after each entry.

To discover how a thesaurus can help you improve the introduction to your science fiction story, look at this dictionary-type entry for *pale* from *The Random House Thesaurus:*

> **pale¹** *adj.* **1** *She looks so pale, she must be ill:* colorless, white, pasty, ashen, ash-colored, wan, pallid, sallow, drained of blood, bloodless, anemic, cadaverous, deathly, deathlike, ghostlike, ghastly. **2** *The walls were painted a pale green:* light, light-colored, light-toned, bleached, whitish. —*v.* **3** *She paled when we told her the news:* become pale, blanch, whiten.
> *Ant.* **1** ruddy, rosy-cheeked, rosy, rubicund, high-colored, florid, flushed. **2** dark, deep, vivid. **3** flush, blush.

This entry presents a sentence for each of the major meanings of *pale,* followed by a list of synonyms. (Note that antonyms for each meaning are also listed at the end of the entry.) Depending on the mood you want to establish for your story, you might choose to replace the word *pale* with *anemic, deathly, ghostly,* or *bleached.*

If none of these adjectives seems to capture your meaning precisely, you could choose the closest in meaning and then look up that word in the thesaurus. For example, *ghostly* may approximate the mood you want because it suggests that something out of the ordinary is coming. However, the word has a supernatural connotation that may not fit your story exactly. If you look at the thesaurus entry for *ghostly,* you'll find more synonyms, such as *spectral, wraithlike, phantasmal, unearthly,* and *uncanny.* Soon you'll have found just the word you're looking for:

"The pale sun rose like a frosted 40-watt bulb over the city, bathing the deserted streets in unearthly light."

Using a thesaurus in this way is like digging for buried treasure. You'll discover that the payoff is clearer and more precise language.

Using a Thesaurus Use a thesaurus to find two synonyms for each of the words below. Use each synonym in a sentence that clearly expresses its precise meaning.

PREPARE 1. _____

2. _____

SYMPATHETIC 3. _____

4. _____

INSIGNIFICANT 5. _____

6. _____

OCCASION 7. _____

8. _____

Number correct _____ (total 8)

Choosing Synonyms Each of the following capitalized words is followed by several synonyms. In the blank, write the synonym that best describes each situation. Use your dictionary if necessary.

FALSEHOOD: lie, fib, forgery

_____ 1. Signing your mother's name to a permission slip.

_____ 2. Telling your friend that you thought his piano solo was wonderful when it was only fair.

_____ 3. Telling the principal that you did not see Marci cheat even though you actually did.

RENEW: reestablish, rejuvenate, extend, restore

_____ 4. Meeting a friend you haven't seen since second grade.

_____ 5. Subscribing to *Mechanics* magazine for an additional year.

_____ 6. Having your carpet cleaned and seeing original colors again.

_____ 7. Taking a two-week vacation at the beach.

Number correct _____ (total 7)

Number correct in Vocab Lab _____ (total 30)

Special Unit Taking Standardized Vocabulary Tests

Employment tests, placement tests, and college entrance examinations include vocabulary questions in order to measure your basic skills in language. One way to prepare for these tests is to study the different types of questions you are likely to encounter. These types of questions include **antonyms, analogies,** and **sentence completion.**

The exercises in this book have provided practice with these types of vocabulary questions. This unit offers additional practice and specific strategies for taking standardized tests.

Part A   *Antonyms*

As you know, **antonyms** are words that are opposite in meaning. Standardized test questions covering antonyms are answered by selecting the choice most opposite in meaning to the given word. A typical question looks like this:

___ CAREFUL: (A) easy   (B) acute   (C) careless   (D) unprepared
(E) cautious

To answer an antonym question, use the following strategies:

1. Remember that you must find a word that is *opposite* in meaning. Do not be thrown off by *synonyms*—words that are similar in meaning. In the example above, choice *E, cautious,* is a synonym for the given word, *CAREFUL.*

2. Decide whether the given word is positive or negative, and then eliminate all possible choices that are in the same category. *CAREFUL* has a positive connotation. Therefore, *A, easy,* and *E, cautious,* can be eliminated.

3. Remember that many words have more than one meaning. If no word seems to fit your sense of the opposite meaning, think about other meanings for the given word. *Acute* means both "sharp" and "serious." However, since neither of these meanings is opposite to *CAREFUL,* choice *B* also can be eliminated.

4. If you do not know the meaning of a given word, try to analyze the word's parts—the prefix, suffix, base word, or root—in order to define it. *Careful* and *careless* share the same root. Their suffixes, *-ful* and *-less,* have opposite meanings, however. Therefore, the words themselves have opposite meanings, and choice *C* is the correct answer.

Exercise   Using the strategies listed above, complete the following exercises.

___ 1. EXOTIC: (A) foreign   (B) alien   (C) poisonous   (D) commonplace
(E) tropical

___ 2. PIOUS: (A) devout   (B) self-righteous   (C) unhealthy   (D) irreverent
(E) intelligent

___ 3. COARSE: (A) refined   (B) inexpensive   (C) scratchy   (D) unexplored
(E) crude

___ 4. EXPEND: (A) shrink   (B) extend   (C) conserve   (D) exhaust
(E) destroy

_____ 5. URGE: (A) conceal (B) oppose (C) persuade (D) surge (E) drive

_____ 6. DELETE: (A) define (B) exhaust (C) consume (D) add (E) drain

_____ 7. SORDID: (A) clean (B) unclear (C) disreputable (D) simple (E) low

_____ 8. PRECEDE: (A) progress (B) follow (C) proceed (D) eliminate (E) intercede

_____ 9. COMPULSION: (A) explosion (B) habit (C) pressure (D) incomprehension (E) choice

_____ 10. ACUTE: (A) ugly (B) sharp (C) critical (D) sensitive (E) dull

Number correct _____ (total 10)

Part B Analogies

Analogies, as you will recall, are pairs of words that are related to each other. In many analogy problems on standardized tests, you are given two words that are related to each other in some way. Your job is to find another pair of words that are related to each other in the same way. A typical analogy question looks like this:

_____ RING : JEWELRY :: (A) bell : tower (B) boat : cargo (C) pencil : pen (D) fir : tree (E) drink : milk

To answer an analogy question, use the following strategies:

1. First, recognize the many types of relationships expressed in analogies. Refer to the chart on page 50 for a listing of the most common of these relationships.

2. Second, determine the relationship between the first pair of words given. Then, create a sentence that contains both words and that shows a relationship between them. The relationship of the first pair of words in the example can be expressed in this way:

   A _ring_ is a type of _jewelry_.

3. Third, find the pair of words among the answer choices that can logically replace the first pair in your sentence. In the example, answer _D_ does this.

   A _fir_ is a type of _tree_.

Exercise Write the letter of the word pair that best expresses a relationship similar to that expressed in the original pair.

_____ 1. INTERMITTENTLY : CONTINUOUSLY :: (A) regularly : periodically (B) rarely : steadily (C) infrequently : seldom (D) always : constantly (E) usually : generally

_____ 2. FEARLESS : CONFIDENT :: (A) fearful : apprehensive (B) healthy : frail (C) bold : timid (D) plump : slender (E) steady : shaky

_____ 3. OVERWORK : STRESS :: (A) relaxation : anxiety (B) gardening : plants (C) advertising : sales (D) play : work (E) dreaming : sleep

_____ 4. NAVIGATE : BOAT :: (A) travel : train (B) paint : brush (C) run : exercise (D) steer : car (E) eat : kitchen

_____ 5. FENCE : ENCLOSURE :: (A) flowers : garden (B) box : container (C) menu : food (D) propeller : airplane (E) saddle : horse

_____ 6. NURTURE : CHILD :: (A) feed : pet (B) misbehave : punishment (C) hire : employer (D) befriend : enemy (E) teach : school

_____ 7. EXERT : PRESSURE :: (A) exercise : basketball (B) preserve : conservation (C) discharge : energy (D) sew : thread (E) reflect : mirror

_____ 8. APERTURE : CAMERA :: (A) doorway : entrance (B) film : photograph (C) hole : enclosure (D) window : building (E) whale : mammal

_____ 9. IMMIGRATION : EMIGRATION :: (A) arrival : departure (B) submergence : emergency (C) tourist : sightseer (D) migration : relocation (E) departure : move

_____ 10. IMMODERATE : UNREASONABLE :: (A) immature : aged (B) warm : hot (C) reasonable : irrational (D) excessive : overabundant (E) immodesty : modesty

Number correct _____ (total 10)

Part C   Sentence Completion

Sentence completion problems test your ability to use words and to recognize relationships among parts of a sentence. You are given a sentence in which one or two words are missing. You must then choose the word or words that best complete the sentence. A typical sentence completion problem looks like this:

_____ The argument _?_ but Tyrone felt his anger gradually _?_.
(A) proceeded . . . grow (B) stopped . . . disappear
(C) returned . . . remember (D) erupted . . . established
(E) continued . . . diminish

To answer sentence completion problems, use the following strategies:

1. Read the sentence carefully, noting key words. Pay special attention to words that indicate contrast or similarity. For example, the word _but_ in the sample gives you the clue that the correct word pair will contain words that contrast. Therefore the correct answer is _(E) continued . . . diminish_.

2. Try each of the choices in the sentence. Eliminate those choices that make no sense or those that contradict some other part of the statement.

3. Look for grammatical clues. Does the sentence structure call for a verb, an adjective, a noun? If the answer is a verb, what tense must the verb be?

Exercise Write the letter of the word or words that best complete the sentence.

_____ 1. The dealer gave the painting a quick ? and ? that it was worth $1,000.
(A) inspection . . . pervaded (B) appraisal . . . estimated (C) reputation
. . . ventured (D) picturesque . . . urged (E) utilization . . . proclaimed

_____ 2. As Kevin descended the stairs to the subway, he proved to be a(n) ? in
the path of the ? who were trying to exit.
(A) spectacle . . . organisms (B) mechanism . . . intruders (C) strategist
. . . sophisticated (D) obstacle . . . hordes (E) visionary . . . species

_____ 3. She was known as the class ? because her answers were ? correct.
(A) philosopher . . . unpredictably (B) militant . . . mysteriously
(C) genius . . . unerringly (D) brilliance . . . constantly
(E) symbol . . . abundantly

_____ 4. The campers were ? by the ? sound in the night.
(A) propelled . . . rigid (B) involved . . . hearty (C) overwhelmed . . .
moderate (D) expended . . . mysterious (E) bewildered . . . ominous

_____ 5. The critic wrote with ? about the performance and ? that the play
was not worth the price of admission.
(A) derision . . . proclaimed (B) appraised . . . heralded (C) exertion
. . . envisioned (D) qualification . . . accomplished
(E) indictment . . . ascertained

_____ 6. Because of the ? involved in his work, Guy found his job ?.
(A) glamour . . . technological (B) repetition . . . tedious (C) stress . . .
exotic (D) technique . . . mobile (E) reflection . . . intent

_____ 7. The ? realized that planning was ? to the operation's success.
(A) descendant . . . innovative (B) professional . . . restorative
(C) crowd . . . impossible (D) strategist . . . integral
(E) psychologist . . . sufficient

_____ 8. The ? weight of the grand piano made moving it a(n) ? undertaking.
(A) uncharted . . . enormous (B) output . . . treacherous (C) sheer . . .
cumbersome (D) meager . . . potent (E) deficient . . . exhausting

_____ 9. ? plant growth could not occur in such a(n) ? climate.
(A) Perpetual . . . indefinite (B) Hazardous . . . sordid (C) Inferior . . .
overwhelming (D) Brilliant . . . abundant (E) Luxuriant . . . arid

_____ 10. It would have been difficult for our ancestors to have ? today's ?.
(A) envisioned . . . technology (B) continued . . . uniformity
(C) encountered . . . compulsion (D) approached . . . phenomenon
(E) determined . . . thrust

Number correct _____ (total 10)

Number correct in Unit _____ (total 30)

Part D General Strategies

No matter what type of question you are answering, certain strategies can be applied to any part of a standardized test. Keep the following guidelines in mind:

Basic Strategies for Taking Standardized Tests

1. **Read and listen to directions carefully.** This may seem obvious, but many students do poorly on tests because they misunderstand the directions. Read all the answer choices for a question before deciding on an answer.

2. **Budget your time carefully.** Most standardized tests are timed. It is important that you not spend too much time on any single item.

3. **Complete the test items you know first.** Go back and tackle the more difficult items later.

4. **Mark the answer sheet carefully and correctly.** Most standardized tests make use of computerized answer sheets. Students are required to fill in a circle corresponding to the correct answer in the test booklet, as follows:

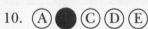

When using such computerized answer sheets, follow these guidelines:

a. Always completely fill in the circle for the correct answer.
b. Periodically check your numbering on the answer sheet, particularly if you skip an item. Make sure the number of the question you are answering matches the number on the answer sheet.
c. Never make notes or stray marks on the answer sheet. These could be misread as wrong answers by the scoring machine. Instead, write on the test booklet itself or on scratch paper, as indicated in the directions.

5. **Be aware of distractors.** Distractors are answer choices that may seem correct at first glance but are actually wrong. For example:

_____ HOT : COLD   (A) cool : frozen   (B) good : bad   (C) first : second   (D) warm : lukewarm   (E) run : ran

Two choices, *(A) cool : frozen* and *(D) warm : lukewarm,* are distractors. Both relate to temperature, as does *HOT : COLD.* You may be tempted to choose one of these as the correct answer. However, neither of these choices presents the same relationship as *HOT : COLD.* The correct answer, *(B) good : bad,* shows the relationship of opposites shown by *HOT : COLD.*

6. **Do not make random guesses.** Guessing is unlikely to improve your score. In fact, in some standardized tests, points are deducted for incorrect answers. On such a test, you should guess only if you are almost certain of an answer. If no points are deducted for a wrong answer, guess if you can eliminate one or more of the choices.

These strategies can help you increase your chances of success on standardized tests. Remember, too, that a good mental attitude, plenty of rest the night before a test, and the ability to relax can be important factors.

UNIT 9

Target Words and Their Meanings

1. absolutely (ab′ sə loot′ lē) adv.
2. adorn (ə dôrn′) v.
3. assemblage (ə sem′ blij) n.
4. avaricious (av′ ə rish′ əs) adj.
5. dauntless (dônt′ lis, dänt′-) adj.
6. disfigure (dis fig′ yər) v.
7. disturb (dis turb′) v.
8. endow (in dou′) v.
9. flourish (flur′ ish) n., v.
10. lucrative (loo′ krə tiv) adj.
11. militia (mə lish′ ə) n.
12. peerless (pir′ lis) adj.
13. principality (prin′ sə pal′ ə tē) n.
14. procession (prə sesh′ ən, prō-) n.
15. prosperous (präs′ pər əs) adj.
16. rife (rīf) adj.
17. simper (sim′ pər) v., n.
18. solitude (säl′ ə tood′, -tyood′) n.
19. stalwart (stôl′ wərt) adj., n.
20. vigorous (vig′ ər əs) adj.

Inferring Meaning from Context

For each sentence write the letter of the word or phrase that is closest to the meaning of the word or words in italics. Use context clues to help you determine the correct answer. (For information about how context helps you understand vocabulary, see pages 1-5.)

_____ 1. Although she was unsure of other formulas, Ann was *absolutely* certain that πr^2 was the formula for the area of a circle.

    a. never b. sometimes c. completely d. sternly

_____ 2. Queen Elizabeth's cape was *adorned* with glittering jewels that sparkled as she passed.

    a. hidden b. decorated c. magnified d. concealed

_____ 3. *An assemblage* of friends and relatives was in the hall, waiting to celebrate Grandmother Mayer's eightieth birthday.

    a. A branch b. An expanse c. A mural d. A group

_____ 4. The man was *avaricious*; he did everything he could to make money and refused to part with a cent of it.

    a. greedy b. fearless c. liable d. agile

_____ 5. According to legend, Prince Valiant was *a dauntless* young man known for his heroic deeds.

    a. an avaricious b. a brave c. a menacing d. an irresponsible

_____ 6. Heavy rains *disfigured* the hillside, creating unsightly gullies.

    a. flattened b. contrived c. marred d. minimized

_____ 7. Noisy car mufflers *disturb* people, particularly when they are sleeping.
a. demoralize   b. reproach   c. agree with   d. annoy

_____ 8. Dorothy was *endowed with* great musical talent; when she was only a year old, she could sing in tune.
a. surrounded by   b. apprehended by   c. impressed with   d. gifted with

_____ 9. Corn *flourishes* in warm, moist climates and does poorly in dry, cold ones.
a. grows vigorously   b. grows slowly   c. depreciates   d. recedes

_____ 10. Jean became wealthy through her *lucrative* accounting business.
a. circumstantial   b. artificial   c. profitable   d. dilapidated

_____ 11. On the eve of the Revolutionary War, ordinary people such as farmers and tradesmen formed a *militia* to fight the British.
a. committee   b. legislature   c. citizen army   d. professional army

_____ 12. According to legend, Helen of Troy was the most beautiful woman in the world; her *peerless* beauty was the envy of the gods and caused a war.
a. unequaled   b. inconspicuous   c. diminutive   d. flawed

_____ 13. The prince ruled his *principality* very well; everyone who lived there respected his decisions.
a. territory   b. ancestry   c. army   d. temper

_____ 14. In columns of eight, the *procession* of soldiers marched down the road.
a. disorderly group   b. orderly, forward-moving group   c. mob   d. expanse

_____ 15. Many Christmas cards include wishes for a happy and *prosperous* New Year.
a. militant   b. meager   c. successful   d. humble

_____ 16. Rumors were *rife* in Centerville after the mayor suddenly announced his resignation; most of the stories centered on the mayor's health problems.
a. minimal   b. abundant   c. humorous   d. expeditious

_____ 17. When their classmates saw Tom and Sue holding hands, the two *simpered* in embarrassment.
a. cried immediately   b. argued loudly   c. smiled self-consciously   d. joked

_____ 18. The few people living on that remote island during the winter when no tourists were present enjoyed their *solitude*.
a. seclusion   b. solicitation   c. assemblage   d. acclaim

_____ 19. Ann is one of the most *stalwart* people I know; she once walked thirty miles through rugged territory when her car broke down.
a. efficient and honest   b. intelligent and profound   c. strong and determined   d. careful and shy

_____ 20. Tom enjoys playing *vigorous* sports such as football, soccer, and rugby.
a. winter   b. energetic   c. independent   d. sedate

Number correct _____ (total 20)

You should now have a general idea of the meaning of each target word. Refine your understanding by examining the shades of meaning the words have in the following excerpt.

California—Character of Population

Mark Twain

In 1848, at Sutter's Mill in California, James Marshall discovered gold. By the next year, the greatest gold rush in U.S. history was under way as thousands traveled to California to seek their fortunes. In this excerpt from Roughing It, *Mark Twain describes the towns and the men of the California gold rush.*

It was in the Sacramento Valley that a deal of the most **lucrative** of the early gold mining was done, and you may still see, in places, its grassy slopes and levels torn and guttered[1] and **disfigured** by the **avaricious** spoilers of fifteen and twenty years ago. You may see such disfigurements far and wide over California—and in some such places, where only meadows and forests are visible—not a living creature, not a house, no stick or stone or remnant of a ruin, and not a sound, not even a whisper to **disturb** the Sabbath stillness—you will find it hard to believe that there stood at one time a fiercely **flourishing** little city of two thousand or three thousand souls, with its newspaper, fire company, brass band, volunteer **militia,** bank, hotels, noisy Fourth of July **processions** and speeches, and rough-bearded men

of all nations and colors, with tables heaped with gold dust sufficient for the revenues of a German **principality**—streets crowded and **rife** with business—town lots worth four hundred dollars a front foot—labor, laughter, music, dancing—everything that delights and **adorns** existence—all the appointments and appurtenances[2] of a thriving and **prosperous** and promising young city—and now nothing is left of it all but a lifeless, homeless **solitude.** The men are gone, the houses have vanished, even the name of the place is forgotten. In no other land in modern times have towns so **absolutely** died and disappeared as in the old mining regions of California.

It was a driving, **vigorous,** restless population in those days. It was a curious population. It was the only population of the kind that the world has ever seen gathered together, and it is not likely that the world will ever see its like again. For, observe, it was an **assemblage** of two hundred thousand young men—not **simpering,** dainty, kid-gloved weaklings, but **stalwart,** muscular, **dauntless** young braves, brimful of push and energy, and royally **endowed** with every attribute that goes to make up a **peerless** and magnificent person—the strangest population, the finest population, the most gallant host that ever trooped down the startled solitudes of an unpeopled land.

---

[1] guttered: with ditches, the result of mining and soil erosion
[2] appurtenances: something added to a more important thing

Refining Your Understanding

For each of the following items, consider how the target word is used in the passage. Write the letter of the word or phrase that best completes each sentence.

_____ 1. An *avaricious* person would not care if the landscape became *disfigured* (line 3) because such a person a. believes the land is sacred b. cares only about getting rich c. doesn't realize the land is being spoiled.

_____ 2. "Streets crowded and *rife* with business" (line 13) probably indicates that a. mining was good for the economy b. many poor people lived on the streets c. an economic slowdown was coming soon.

_____ 3. "Everything that delights and *adorns* existence" (line 15) probably refers to a. the basic necessities of life b. clothing stores c. luxuries and other extras.

_____ 4. Mark Twain uses the phrase *"absolutely* died" (line 19) to emphasize a. how abandoned the mining towns had become b. how violent the miner's life was c. how important law and order was in the mining towns.

_____ 5. From this selection we can infer that what brought the "*assemblage* of two hundred thousand young men" (line 24) together in California was most likely a. solitude b. charity c. avarice.

Number correct _____ (total 5)

Part C *Ways to Make New Words Your Own*

By now you are familiar with the target words and their meanings. This section presents a variety of reinforcement activities that will help you make these words part of your vocabulary.

Using Language and Thinking Skills

Finding the Unrelated Word Write the letter of the word that is not related in meaning to the other words in the set.

_____ 1. a. unique   b. peerless   c. equaled   d. unequaled

_____ 2. a. avaricious   b. greedy   c. miserly   d. generous

_____ 3. a. profitable   b. worthless   c. lucrative   d. productive

_____ 4. a. stalwart   b. afraid   c. fearless   d. strong

_____ 5. a. beautify   b. adorn   c. decorate   d. disfigure

_____ 6. a. wither   b. shrivel   c. flourish   d. decay

_____ 7. a. disturb   b. bother   c. disrupt   d. rejoice

_____ 8. a. simper   b. frown   c. glare   d. scowl

_____ 9. a. rife   b. abundant   c. plentiful   d. meager

_____ 10. a. supply   b. endow   c. deplete   d. bestow

Number correct _____ (total 10)

Practicing for Standardized Tests

Analogies Write the letter of the pair of words that best expresses a relationship similar to that expressed in the original pair.

_____ 1. ABSOLUTELY : DOUBTFULLY ::   (A) doubtlessly : completely (B) positively : questionably   (C) horizontally : diagonally   (D) abruptly : anxiously   (E) perpetually : continually

_____ 2. DISFIGURE : BEAUTIFY ::   (A) precede : proceed   (B) impede : thwart   (C) bark : meow   (D) compose : sing   (E) fail : excel

_____ 3. AGITATE : DISTURB ::   (A) disrupt : unsettle   (B) upset : calm (C) shake : separate   (D) trust : distrust   (E) haughty : meek

_____ 4. ENDOW : GIFT ::   (A) conduct : copper   (B) bestow : award (C) enter : exit   (D) save : payment   (E) defend : trial

_____ 5. VIGOROUS : LIFELESS ::   (A) stalwart : robust   (B) healthy : sturdy (C) cloudy : rainy   (D) spirited : feeble   (E) routine : ordinary

_____ 6. HERMIT : SOLITUDE ::   (A) music : harmony   (B) group : discussion   (C) bird : aviation   (D) prisoner : confinement (E) expedience : convenience

104

_____ 7. FLOURISHING : PROSPEROUS :: (A) lucrative : unprofitable
(B) peerless : dauntless (C) successful : intelligent (D) rich : wealthy
(E) ephemeral : lasting

_____ 8. MISER : AVARICIOUS :: (A) benefactor : kind (B) doctor :
medicinal (C) king : harsh (D) prey : animalistic (E) desert : rainy

_____ 9. RIFE : SURPLUS :: (A) leathery : shoe (B) tedious : excitement
(C) mortal : eternity (D) triumphant : contest (E) meager : shortage

_____ 10. HERO : DAUNTLESS :: (A) coward : peerless (B) history : recent
(C) disc jockey : musical (D) winner : triumphant (E) spy : open

Number correct _____ (total 10)

Spelling and Wordplay

Crossword Puzzle

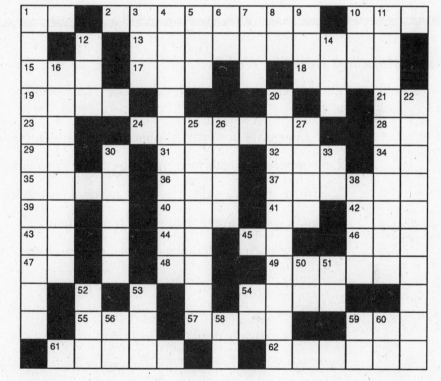

ACROSS
1. 3.14159265
2. Sturdy
10. Flying mammal
13. See 4 Down
15. Abbr. International
Phonetic Alphabet
17. Insane
18. Finishes
19. Bird's home
21. Initials of poet Ezra
Pound
23. Abbr. Civil
Engineer
24. To annoy
28. Man's title
29. Abbr. Ireland
31. Dove's call
32. Petroleum
34. Abbr. Back Order
35. Scheme
36. Sick
37. Creeps
39. Abbr. Account
Executive
40. See 32 Across
41. Nickname for
Edward
42. Sharp knock
43. Abbr. Landing Ship
44. Utah
45. Abbr. Arsenic
46. Era
47. Third person
singular of *be*
48. Abbr. Southern
University
49. Silly smile
54. Widespread
55. Much _ _ _
about nothing

57. Reflected sound
59. Abbr. Oregon State
University
61. To decorate
62. *PM*'s

DOWN
1. A prince's territory
3. _ _ _ O'
Shanter
4. Greedy
5. Young boy
6. Abbr. World
Record
7. To help

8. Abbr. Red Cross
9. To knot
10. Flower shoot
11. Gathering of people
12. Ma's and _ _ _
14. A single item
16. Without equal
20. Parade
22. Wealthy
25. Isolation
26. A bridge tax
27. Flying creature
30. To give money or
property
33. Abbr. Los Angeles

38. An outer covering
50. In case that . . .
51. Myself
52. Unhappy
53. In favor of
54. _ _ factor, a
characteristic of
blood
56. _ _ or don't
58. Abbr. Certificate of
Deposit
59. Exclamation of
surprise
60. Abbr. Saint

105

Part D Related Words

A number of words are closely related to the target words you have studied. Use your knowledge of the target words and of word parts to determine the meanings of these words. Learning these related words expands your vocabulary and helps you learn the target words more thoroughly.

1. absolute (ab′ sə lo͞ot′, ab′ sə lo͞ot′) adj., n.
2. adornment (ə dôrn′ ment) n.
3. avarice (av′ ər is) n.
4. disfigurement (dis fig′ yər mənt) n.
5. endowment (in dou′ mənt) n.
6. invigorate (in vig′ ə rāt′) v.
7. militant (mil′ i tənt) adj., n.
8. military (mil′ ə ter′ ē) adj.
9. peer (pir) n., v.
10. perturb (pər turb′) v.
11. proceed (prə sēd′, prō-) v.
12. solitary (säl′ ə ter′ ē) adj.
13. undaunted (un dôn′ tid, -dän′-) adj.
14. vigor (vig′ ər) n.

Understanding Related Words

True–False Decide whether each statement is true or false. Write **T** for True and **F** for False.

_____ 1. If a person is in *solitary* confinement, he or she has no contact with others.

_____ 2. A person who feels *invigorated* must take frequent naps.

_____ 3. *Avarice* is a personality trait that makes a person well liked.

_____ 4. People usually avoid things that *perturb* them.

_____ 5. If the silence in a room is *absolute*, one can hear a pin drop.

_____ 6. Members of a jury are *peers*.

_____ 7. When you *proceed* to pack your suitcase, you start removing things.

_____ 8. A puppy usually displays a great deal of *vigor*.

_____ 9. A person who becomes discouraged easily is obviously *undaunted*.

_____ 10. A two-thousand-dollar gift to a hospital can be called an *endowment*.

Number correct _____ (total 10)

Turn to **The Addition of Prefixes** on pages 193-194 of the **Spelling Handbook.** Read the rule and complete the exercises provided.

Analyzing Word Parts

The Prefix *pro-* conveys the meaning of forward movement. It often means "before," "in front of," or "forth." A rocket *propels* a satellite, meaning the rocket shoots the satellite forward. When you *propose* a solution to a problem, you are putting forth that idea to be considered. A *prophet* speaks of things to come.

The Prefix *dis-* means "away," as in *discharge* or *dismiss*. It can also mean "apart," as in *disassemble* or *dismantle*. Finally, *dis-* also means "opposite of," as in *dislike* or *disarmament*. In this latter meaning, *dis-* acts much like the negative prefixes *un-* and *im-*.

In the following exercise, the words in the left column contain the prefix *pro-* or *dis-*. In the right column are definitions. Match the appropriate definition to each word, writing the letter in the blank. If you are unsure of a word's meaning, use your dictionary.

_____ 1. prohibit   a. to force something from a position

_____ 2. produce   b. to scatter or distribute widely

_____ 3. prolong   c. to stir up action or to anger

_____ 4. profess   d. to melt or become liquid

_____ 5. provoke   e. to cut apart

_____ 6. discontinue   f. to bring forth or yield

_____ 7. dislodge   g. to stop using

_____ 8. dissect   h. to lengthen in time

_____ 9. disperse   i. to forbid by law

_____ 10. dissolve   j. to openly declare

Number correct _____ (total 10)

Number correct in Unit _____ (total 65)

Word's Worth: lucrative

The origins of the word *lucrative* and its related word *lucre* provide an interesting example of our complex attitude toward money and profit. Both words can be traced to the ancient Greek word for booty, that is money, property, or other riches that are taken as a result of war or piracy. By the time of the English Renaissance, *lucrative* and *lucre* had become two words with very different meanings. On the one hand, preachers warned their congregations against the pursuit of money and profit, which they denounced as "filthy lucre." On the other hand, teachers and business people advised the young to enter lucrative professions and trades. The young people of Renaissance England thus received a mixed message about the role that money should play in their lives.

In today's world, *lucrative* has mostly positive associations, suggesting wealth and luxury. *Lucre*, however, still suffers from the taint of ill-gotten gain. And we still receive mixed messages about money.

The Last Word

Writing

Write an imaginary story that includes three of the items listed below. Choose one item from each column.

Characters	Incidents	Conditions
• a *prosperous* business person	• trying to find *solitude*	• in a *disturbing* set of circumstances
• a *vigorous* athlete	• *endowed* with great wealth	• with *avaricious* tendencies
• a *military* officer	• walking in a *procession*	• with a *flourish*
• a *stalwart* opponent	• living in a *principality*	• in a *lucrative* enterprise
• a *dauntless* hero	• *adorned* with beautiful gems	

Speaking

Divide into groups of two or three students each. Each group should choose one of the thirteen adjectives from the Target and Related Words lists and create a short skit that demonstrates the meaning of the adjective in a colorful and original manner. The other groups should try to guess which adjective is being acted out.

Group Discussion

"In *solitude* we are least alone."—William Wordsworth
What does Wordsworth mean? Do you agree or disagree? As a class, discuss the possible interpretations of this quotation.

UNIT 10

Part A   Target Words and Their Meanings

1. appropriate (ə prō′ prē it) adj. (-āt′) v.
2. assume (ə soom′, -syoom′) v.
3. depress (di pres′) v.
4. distinctly (dis tiŋkt′ lē) adv.
5. epoch (ep′ ək) n.
6. gradually (graj′ oo wə lē) adv.
7. immense (i mens′) adj.
8. isolate (ī′ sə lāt′) v.
9. metamorphosis (met′ ə môr′ fə sis, -môr fō′ sis) n.
10. native (nāt′ iv) adj., n.
11. novel (näv′ 'l) adj., n.
12. profile (prō′ fīl) n., v.
13. reap (rēp) v.
14. remote (ri mōt′) adj.
15. renounce (ri nouns′) v.
16. sunder (sun′ dər) v.
17. thrust (thrust) n., v.
18. vary (ver ē′) v.
19. villa (vil′ ə) n.
20. yield (yēld) v., n.

Inferring Meaning from Context

For each sentence write the letter of the word or phrase that is closest to the meaning of the word or words in italics. Use context clues to help you determine the correct answer.

_____ 1. "Sincerely" is *an appropriate* closing for a business letter, but it is too formal for a friendly letter.

   a. a suitable   b. a timely   c. an old-fashioned   d. an incorrect

_____ 2. After standing for ten minutes in the same position, the model *assumed* a new stance.

   a. acclaimed   b. concealed   c. took on   d. continued

_____ 3. To examine a patient's throat, the doctor must *depress* the tongue with a flat stick.

   a. hurt   b. dislodge   c. raise   d. press down

_____ 4. After focusing our telescope on the speck of light, we could see Venus quite *distinctly* in the eastern sky.

   a. clearly   b. disturbingly   c. fuzzily   d. scrupulously

_____ 5. The flights to the moon marked the beginning of a fascinating *epoch* in American space exploration.

   a. period of time   b. colonization   c. climax   d. disaster

_____ 6. We watched as the snail moved *gradually* down the path.

   a. secretively   b. vigorously   c. little by little   d. by leaps and bounds

_____ 7. Carmen was thrilled that she had made such *an immense* improvement over her last long-jump record.

a. a large   b. a tiny   c. a sufficient   d. a routine

_____ 8. Because of the raging blizzard, the hunter was *isolated* for the night in an abandoned cabin far from civilization.

a. located   b. lost   c. close to others   d. set apart from others

_____ 9. An amazing example of *metamorphosis* occurs in nature, when a caterpillar changes into a moth or a butterfly.

a. mutual agreement   b. chemistry   c. transformation   d. isolation

_____ 10. Although *native to* Maine, Mrs. Scott moved to Iowa as a teen-ager.

a. endowed with   b. undaunted by   c. unfamiliar with
d. originally from

_____ 11. Walking on the moon was a *novel* experience in 1969.

a. new   b. fictitious   c. cynical   d. familiar

_____ 12. A *profile* of Thomas Jefferson is on one side of this nickel, and his home, Monticello, is on the other side.

a. quote   b. caricature   c. side view   d. prophecy

_____ 13. Today most farmers who grow corn *reap* their crops at harvest time with the use of machines.

a. destroy   b. plant   c. gather   d. plow

_____ 14. The mine is in a *remote* region, accessible only on foot or on horseback.

a. nearby   b. far-removed   c. suburban   d. flourishing

_____ 15. Having heard of the link between tobacco use and lung disease, George has *renounced* smoking.

a. required   b. advocated   c. given up   d. taken up

_____ 16. The American Revolution *sundered* Great Britain from its most important colony.

a. recalled   b. protected   c. expressed support for   d. separated

_____ 17. The emcee *thrust* his hand into a hat and pulled out the winning ticket.

a. waved   b. shoved   c. gently placed   d. released

_____ 18. The schedule at music camp *varies* from day to day. For example, after lunch we may have private lessons, small group rehearsals, or free time.

a. repeats   b. changes   c. continues   d. is reviewed

_____ 19. The wealthy people left the cities to relax at their *villas* in the mountains.

a. factories   b. jobs   c. country estates   d. principalities

_____ 20. A rule of safe driving is to *yield to* vehicles that have the right of way.

a. give way to   b. take from   c. ignore   d. go before

Number correct _____ (total 20)

Part B Target Words in Reading and Literature

You should now have a general idea of the meaning of each target word. Refine your understanding by examining the shades of meaning the words have in the following excerpt.

A Week on the Concord and Merrimack Rivers

Henry David Thoreau

In the following passage the nineteenth-century writer Henry David Thoreau discusses the idea of visual perspective and how a change in perspective can provide new insights into a familiar setting.

Sitting facing upstream, we studied the landscape by degrees, as one unrolls a map, rock, tree, house, hill, and meadow, **assuming** new and **varying** positions as wind and water shifted the scene, and there was variety enough for our entertainment in the **metamorphoses** of the simplest objects. Viewed from this side, the scenery appeared new to us.

5

The most familiar sheet of water, viewed from a new hilltop, **yields** a **novel** and unexpected pleasure. When we have traveled a few miles, we do not recognize the **profiles** even of the hills which overlook our **native** village; and perhaps no man is quite familiar with the horizon as seen from the hill nearest to his house, nor can he recall its outline **distinctly** when in the valley. We do not commonly know, beyond a short distance, which way the hills range which take in our houses and farms in their sweep. As if our birth has at first **sundered** things, and we had been **thrust** up through into nature like a wedge, and not until the wound heals and the scar disappears do we begin to discover where we are,

10

and that nature is one and continuous everywhere. It is an important **epoch**   15
when a person who has always lived on the east side of a mountain, and sees it
in the west, travels round and sees it in the east. Yet the universe is a sphere
whose center is wherever there is intelligence. The sun is not so central as a
person. Upon an **isolated** hilltop, in an open country, we seem to ourselves to
be standing on the boss[1] of an **immense** shield, the immediate landscape being   20
apparently **depressed** below the more **remote**, and rising **gradually** to the
horizon, which is the rim of the shield, **villas**, steeples, forests, mountains, one
above another, until they are swallowed up in the heavens. The most distant
mountains in the horizon appear to rise directly from the shore of that lake in the
woods by which we chance to be standing, while from the mountaintop, not only   25
this, but a thousand nearer and larger lakes are equally unobserved.

    Seen through this clear atmosphere, the work of the farmer, his ploughing and
reaping, have a beauty to our eyes which he has never seen. How fortunate are
we who do not own an acre of these shores, who have not **renounced** our title to
the whole. One who knew how to **appropriate** the true value of this world would   30
be the poorest person in it. The poor rich man! All he has is what he has bought.
What I see is mine. I am a large owner in the Merrimack intervals[2].

---

[1] boss: a knoblike ornament
[2] intervals: low, flat land between hills or along a river

Refining Your Understanding

For each of the following items, consider how the target word is used in the passage. Write the letter of the word or phrase that best completes each sentence.

_____ 1. The *"metamorphoses* of the simplest objects" (line 4) relates to Thoreau and his companion seeing   a. differences in the countryside between morning and evening   b. differences in the countryside because of the different directions from which they were viewing it   c. the objects changing into new forms before their eyes.

_____ 2. When Thoreau says that a view *"yields* a *novel* . . . pleasure" (lines 6-7), he is referring to   a. a familiar experience for the viewer b. a new experience for the viewer   c. a pleasure that comes from reading.

_____ 3. By using the word *epoch* (line 15), the author suggests that when a person first studies a region from a different angle,   a. that person has opened a new period in his or her life   b. a new period of world history has begun   c. the countryside itself changes.

_____ 4. The author believes that we *renounce* our title to the countryside as a whole (lines 29-30) when we   a. buy a portion of the land   b. sell land   c. don't take time to enjoy land.

_____ 5. Thoreau uses the word *appropriate* (line 30) to mean   a. "do what is right about"   b. "use good manners toward"   c. "take for oneself."

Number correct _____ (total 5)

Part C *Ways to Make New Words Your Own*
Using Language and Thinking Skills

Understanding Multiple Meanings Read the definitions of the boldfaced words that follow. Write the letter of the definition that fits each sentence.

---

assume
  a. to take on the appearance, form, or role of (v.)
  b. to take over (v.)
  c. to take upon oneself; to undertake (v.)
  d. to take for granted; to suppose (v.)

_____ 1. When the President dies, the Vice-President *assumes* office.

_____ 2. Students should *assume* responsibility for getting assignments in on time.

_____ 3. Alex was ten minutes late; the teacher *assumed* Alex would be absent.

_____ 4. George *assumed* the role of Sherlock Holmes in the school play.

---

depress
  a. to press down; to lower (v.)
  b. to lower in spirits; to make gloomy (v.)
  c. to decrease the activity of; to weaken (v.)

_____ 5. Receiving disappointing grades in math and science *depressed* Tamara.

_____ 6. The stock market has been *depressed,* causing a business slowdown.

_____ 7. *Depress* the coin return lever if you do not hear a dial tone.

---

native
  a. inborn (trait) rather than acquired (adj.)
  b. belonging to a locality or country by birth, production, or growth (adj.)
  c. a person born in a certain place or country (n.)
  d. an original inhabitant, as distinguished from an explorer, or colonist (n.)

_____ 8. The *natives* in Mexico, the Aztecs, mistook Cortez for a god.

_____ 9. A *native* of India, Dr. Patel came to the United States to study medicine.

_____ 10. Azaleas are not *native* to this area; they cannot survive the cold.

_____ 11. It is obvious, even from her doodles, that Sue possesses *native* artistic talent.

_____ 12. The *native* languages of Canada are French and English.

> **appropriate**
> a. suitable; right for the purpose (adj.)
> b. to set aside for a specific use (v.)
> c. to take improperly, as without permission (v.)

_____ 13. A percentage of the advertising budget was *appropriated* for printing costs.

_____ 14. Blue jeans are not *appropriate* attire for a job interview.

_____ 15. A banker may not *appropriate* a customer's savings account funds and use them for unsafe investments.

Number correct _____ (total 15)

Practicing for Standardized Tests

Synonyms Write the letter of the word closest in meaning to the capitalized word.

_____ 1. SUNDER: (A) fluster (B) prescribe (C) separate (D) reflect (E) join

_____ 2. DISTINCTLY: (A) apparently (B) clearly (C) secretly (D) vaguely (E) angrily

_____ 3. YIELD: (A) plant (B) flourish (C) give (D) subject (E) seize

_____ 4. RENOUNCE: (A) announce (B) reject (C) get (D) recall (E) advocate

_____ 5. THRUST: (A) disturb (B) forage (C) withdraw (D) stake (E) push

_____ 6. ISOLATE: (A) unite (B) extend (C) endow (D) set apart (E) disfigure

_____ 7. METAMORPHOSIS: (A) characteristic (B) change (C) procession (D) inertia (E) permanence

_____ 8. IMMENSE: (A) vast (B) profitable (C) avaricious (D) minimal (E) conspicuous

_____ 9. VARY: (A) change (B) score (C) adjust (D) deceive (E) convey

_____ 10. NOVEL: (A) traditional (B) wise (C) magnificent (D) wordy (E) new

Number correct _____ (total 10)

Word's Worth: metamorphosis

The Roman poet Ovid wrote a long poem called *Metamorphoses*. Ovid's witty poem chronicles the adventures and love affairs of the gods. All the tales are linked by the common theme of metamorphosis, which comes from the Greek words for change (*meta*) and form (*phosis*).

One story tells about the god Apollo, who chased the beautiful but shy Daphne. To escape, Daphne prayed to be transformed into a laurel tree. Her wish was granted, thus frustrating Apollo's amorous desires. From that day on, Apollo commemorated Daphne by bestowing laurel wreaths as prizes for poets. Gradually, the laurel came to symbolize any triumph or victory.

Spelling and Wordplay

Word Maze Find and circle each target word in this maze.

```
B  D  L  E  I  Y  S  O  O  D  A  R  M  O  R
I  Y  L  L  A  U  D  A  R  G  P  A  Y  T  E
L  E  U  B  I  R̄  T  N  U  O  P  B  L  R  N
P  D  R  O  R  L  L  D  L  E  R  Y  T  I  O
I  T  S  T  S  R  U  L  E  V  O  N  C  L  U
N  A  N  K  I  E  Y  W  L  U  P  T  N  K  N
V  I  U  Q  M  X  P  P  A  E  R  H  I  W  C
I  R  S  U  S  A  R  O  S  O  I  R  T  E  E
L  A  S  E  L  L  O  K  C  H  A  U  S  S  T
L  S  E  T  H  L  F  R  N  H  T  S  I  N  O
A  R  R  A  O  I  I  D  E  A  E  T  D  E  M
L  A  P  L  S  V  L  N  F  I  T  E  S  M  E
E  K  E  O  M  G  E  C  K  U  N  I  A  M  R
S  O  D  S  P  O  B  R  I  N  O  C  V  I  E
O  R  S  I  S  O  H  P  R  O  M  A  T  E  M
B  I  Z  K  J  Y  R  A  V  I  C  D  F  G  N
N  G  O  R  I  A  Z  R  W  R  E  D  N  U  S
```

appropriate
assume
· depress
distinctly
epoch
gradually
immense
isolate
metamorphosis
native
novel
profile
reap
remote
renounce
sunder
thrust
villa
vary
yield

Part D Related Words

A number of words are closely related to the target words you have studied. Learning these related words expands your vocabulary and helps you learn the target words more thoroughly.

1. announce (ə nouns′) v.
2. appropriateness (ə prō′ prē it nəs) n.
3. assumption (ə sump′ shən) n.
4. asunder (ə sun′ dər) adv.
5. compression (kəm presh′ ən) n.
6. denounce (di nouns′) v.
7. depression (di presh′ ən) n.
8. expression (ik spresh′ ən) n.
9. extinct (ik stiŋkt′) adj.
10. graduation (graj′ oo wā′ shən) n.
11. immensity (i men′ sə tē) n.
12. impression (im presh′ ən) n.
13. instinct (in′ stiŋkt) n.
14. isolation (ī′ sə lā′ shən, is′ ə-) n.
15. nature (nā′ chər) n.
16. novelist (näv′ ′l ist) n.
17. novelty (näv′ ′l tē) n.
18. remoteness (ri mōt′ nəs) n.

Turn to **The Suffix *-ion*** on pages 204-205 of the **Spelling Handbook**. Read the rule and complete the exercises provided.

Understanding Related Words

Using Context to Define Words   Write the definition of each italicized word by examining its context in the sentence. Then check your definitions with those in the dictionary.

1. The director of a play evaluates the *appropriateness* of the gestures and voice inflections actors use to develop their characters.

   _____

2. Because the paint was still tacky, Darren made the *assumption* that the walls had been painted earlier in the day.

   _____

3. The machine creates solid cloth by using *compression* to squeeze the cotton fibers together.

   _____

4. Zoologists are trying to breed pandas in captivity so that these lovable animals will not become *extinct*.

   _____

5. The dynamite blasted the huge boulders *asunder*.

   _____

6. The *immensity* of the air pollution problem indicates that everyone must work for a solution.

   _____

7. Shortly after their birth, the two joeys, or baby kangaroos, by *instinct* found their way to their mother's pouch.

   _____

8. Before the discovery of antibiotics, patients with scarlet fever were frequently placed in *isolation* for several weeks.

   _____

9. Henry David Thoreau obviously enjoyed the *remoteness* of his cabin on Walden Pond.

   _____

10. Pearl Buck is an American *novelist* whose stories are often set in China.

   _____

Number correct _____ (total 10)

116

Close Relatives   For each blank in the sentence below choose the appropriate word from the list.   Each word may be used only once.

announce   depression   gradually   impression   novelist
denounced   expression   graduation   novel   novelty

1. As officials _____ Mr. Wade for his wrongdoings, Mr. Wade

   proceeded to _____ to the crowd of reporters that he had
   already resigned his position.

2. From the _____ on her face, I got the _____ that

   she was suffering from _____ .

3. At the high-school _____ , the audience watched proudly as the

   seniors _____ filed into the gymnasium.

4. Writing a _____ is a _____ for any

   first-time _____ .

Number correct _____ (total 10)

Analyzing Word Parts

The Prefix *de-*   *De-* typically means "down," "away," or "from."   It is one of the most common prefixes in the English language.   In this unit the words *depress, depression,* and *denounce* are examples of words containing this prefix.

Each of the following sentences contains a *de-* word.   Use context clues and word structure to determine the italicized words' meanings.   Write the meaning of each word in the blank provided.   Check your meanings with the dictionary.

1. The hospital room was sprayed with chemicals to *decontaminate* it and kill any harmful bacteria.

   _____

2. Because Lisa's tooth hurt when she ate anything cold, the dentist suggested using a toothpaste that would help *desensitize* the tooth.

   _____

3. In a large corporation with hundreds of employees, a worker might sense a *depersonalized* atmosphere.

   _____

4. The argument grew more heated and then *degenerated* into an ugly brawl.

   _____

5. The campers all understood that if they earned three or more *demerits* for rude behavior, they would be confined to their cabins.

   _____

Number correct _____ (total 5)

Scrambled Words Unscramble the following words. You will spell five nouns from the Related Words list, all ending with *-ion*. Write the noun form in Column 1. Then write the verb form of the word in Column 2.

Example:

smeopirnis	impression	impress
	NOUNS	VERBS

1. psumtasion   _____   _____

2. iontiloas   _____   _____

3. udaionargt   _____   _____

4. nosixepres   _____   _____

5. ssiondpere   _____   _____

Number correct _____ (total 5)

Number correct in Unit _____ (total 80)

The Last Word

Writing

Use an encyclopedia or other reference books to write a short paper describing a *metamorphosis*. This metamorphosis could be one from science (the transformation of a tadpole into a frog), from literature (the myth of Narcissus), or from some other field.

Speaking

An *epoch* is a period of time characterized by noteworthy events, attitudes, or ideas. For example, the 1950's in this country included the coming of television, the baby boom, and relative economic prosperity. Prepare a speech in which you describe the present epoch. In years to come, what events, attitudes, or ideas will characterize this period in history?

Group Discussion

Depression is an emotional condition that brings feelings of hopelessness and inadequacy to people. As a class, discuss the following questions: Why do people become depressed? Does everyone experience depression at one time or another? Is depression an unavoidable state? What might a person do to help others who suffer from depression?

UNIT 11

Part A Target Words and Their Meanings

1. aggrieved (ə grēvd′) adj.
2. aversion (ə vur′ zhən) n.
3. befitting (bi fit′ iŋ) adj.
4. commentary (käm′ ən ter′ ē) n.
5. contempt (kən tempt′) n.
6. contrite (kən trīt′, kän′ trīt) adj.
7. dandy (dan′ dē) n., adj.
8. defiant (di fī′ ənt) adj.
9. frayed (frād) adj.
10. habitual (hə bich′ oo wəl) adj.
11. impertinence (im pur′ t′n əns) n.
12. indispensable (in′ dis pen′ sə b′l) adj.
13. involuntary (in väl′ ən ter′ ē) adj.
14. misdemeanor (mis′ di mēn′ ər) n.
15. offensive (ə fen′ siv) adj.
16. perplexity (pər plek′ sə tē) n.
17. rancor (raŋ′ kər) n.
18. shudder (shud′ ər) n., v.
19. suave (swäv) adj.
20. synopsis (si näp′ sis) n.

Inferring Meaning from Context

For each sentence write the letter of the word or phrase that is closest to the meaning of the word or words in italics. Use context clues to help you determine the correct answer.

_____ 1. The mother felt terribly *aggrieved* over her daughter's running away.

a. pleased   b. disturbed   c. confused   d. soothed

_____ 2. Since Ron has *an aversion to* cabbage, he politely refused when the hostess offered him some.

a. a story about   b. a preference for   c. a dislike of   d. a craving for

_____ 3. The retirement party for Ms. Chan was splendid, *a befitting* tribute to her long years of service.

a. an inappropriate   b. a boring   c. a minimized   d. a suitable

_____ 4. At the end of the newscast every evening, the anchorman gave his *commentary* on an issue of local interest.

a. remarks   b. acclaim   c. goals   d. commercial

_____ 5. The criminal's arrogant and disrespectful behavior in the courtroom showed his *contempt* for the law.

a. aspirations   b. instinct   c. admiration   d. scorn

_____ 6. Because the shoplifter was *contrite*, Judge Vallarta gave her probation instead of a jail sentence.

a. enthusiastic   b. sorrowful   c. inconspicuous   d. hostile

119

_____ 7. Uncle Charles is a *dandy;* he always wears a fresh carnation in his lapel.

    a. greedy person b. cruel person c. fancy dresser d. careless dresser

_____ 8. The teacher talked privately to the *defiant* student who upset the class.

    a. disobedient b. naive c. avaricious d. tactful

_____ 9. The *frayed* elbows on a sport coat can be repaired with patches.

    a. tight b. mended c. ragged d. offensive

_____ 10. Norman Chesterfield became famous for his *habitual* bird watching; by the time he was seventy-three, he had observed 6,220 species!

    a. constant b. appropriate c. foolish d. infrequent

_____ 11. Brian was ordered to apologize for his *impertinence* and rude behavior.

    a. graciousness b. vigor c. disrespect d. expedience

_____ 12. The efficiency and speed of a word processor have made it *an indispensable* tool for many writers.

    a. a frivolous b. a disposable c. a costly d. an essential

_____ 13. Hiccups are caused by *an involuntary* muscle contraction, over which we have no control.

    a. an intentional b. a nonbinding c. a reflex d. a harmful

_____ 14. The Puritans punished even a harmless *misdemeanor* very severely.

    a. ceremony b. minor offense c. disease d. serious crime

_____ 15. Because many people find smoking to be *offensive* and hazardous to health, smoking is now forbidden on some airlines.

    a. sophisticated b. disagreeable c. attractive d. militant

_____ 16. Imagine the *perplexity* one man experienced when he awoke in the morning to find that his house had slid fifty yards down the hill.

    a. confusion b. delight c. guilt d. permanence

_____ 17. The game ended in *rancor*, with team members arguing among themselves.

    a. temporary harmony b. jubilation c. reflection d. bitterness

_____ 18. The sudden shriek in the night made us *shudder*, but we stopped trembling when we realized it was merely the cry of a jungle bird.

    a. apprehend b. grin nervously c. shake with fear d. speak louder

_____ 19. Jerry's *suave* manner with the elegant French waiters suggested that he was much more experienced than his youthfulness indicated.

    a. confused b. dishonest c. smooth d. adequate

_____ 20. Time did not permit a detailed explanation, so Maria gave *a synopsis* of the novel *Great Expectations*.

    a. an expanse b. a brief outline c. an in-depth analysis d. a lengthy description

Number correct _____ (total 20)

Part B Target Words in Reading and Literature

You should now have a general idea of the meaning of each target word. Refine your understanding by examining the shades of meaning the words have in the following excerpt.

Paul's Case

Willa Cather

Most students when sent to the principal's office for misconduct are nervous and apologetic. Not so with Paul, the defiant young man in this Willa Cather story.

It was Paul's afternoon to appear before the faculty of the Pittsburgh High School to account for his various **misdemeanors**. He had been suspended a week ago, and his father had called at the Principal's office and confessed his **perplexity** about his son. Paul entered the faculty room **suave** and smiling. His clothes were a trifle outgrown, and the tan velvet on the collar of his open overcoat was **frayed** and worn; but for all that there was something of a **dandy** about him, and he wore an opal pin in his neatly knotted black four-in-hand[1], and a red carnation in his buttonhole. This latter adornment the faculty somehow felt was not properly significant of the **contrite** spirit **befitting** a boy under the ban of suspension.

Paul was tall for his age and very thin, with high, cramped shoulders and a narrow chest. His eyes were remarkable for a certain hysterical brilliancy, and he continually used them in a conscious, theatrical sort of way, peculiarly **offensive** in a boy.

5

10

When questioned by the Principal as to why he was there, Paul stated, politely
enough, that he wanted to come back to school. This was a lie, but Paul was
quite accustomed to lying; found it, indeed, **indispensable** for overcoming
friction. His teachers were asked to state their respective charges against him,
which they did with such a **rancor** and **aggrievedness** as evinced[2] that this was
not a usual case. Disorder and **impertinence** were among the offenses named,
yet each of his instructors felt that it was scarcely possible to put into words the
real cause of the trouble, which lay in a sort of hysterically **defiant** manner of the
boy's; in the **contempt** which they all knew he felt for them, and which he
seemingly made not the least effort to conceal. Once, when he had been
making a **synopsis** of a paragraph at the blackboard, his English teacher had
stepped to his side and attempted to guide his hand. Paul had started back with
a **shudder** and thrust his hands violently behind him. The astonished woman
could scarcely have been more hurt and embarrassed had he struck at her. The
insult was so **involuntary** and definitely personal as to be unforgettable. In one
way and another, he had made all his teachers, men and women alike,
conscious of the same feeling of physical **aversion**. In one class he **habitually**
sat with his hand shading his eyes; in another he always looked out of the
window during the recitation; in another he made a running **commentary** on the
lecture, with humorous intent.

_____
[1] four-in-hand: a necktie tied in the common way, with a slip knot
[2] evinced: to show plainly

Refining Your Understanding

For each of the following items, consider how the target word is used in the
passage. Write the letter of the word or phrase that best completes each sentence.

_____ 1. The fact that Paul's father "confessed his *perplexity* about his son" (lines
3-4) suggests that the father   a. did not like his son   b. did not
understand his son   c. wanted to help his son.

_____ 2. Paul entered the room "*suave* and smiling" (line 4), showing that   a. he
was confident in his ability to deal with the faculty   b. he was sorry
about his behavior   c. he felt self-conscious and embarrassed about his
appearance.

_____ 3. Paul found lying "*indispensable*" (line 17) because   a. it was the best way
to avoid trouble   b. he wanted to make fools of everyone   c. he
couldn't distinguish truth from falsehood.

_____ 4. "*Rancor* and *aggrievedness*" (line 19) suggest that the teachers   a. were
hostile toward Paul   b. were trying to help Paul   c. felt sorry for Paul.

_____ 5. An example of the "physical *aversion*" (line 31) Paul felt for his teachers
could be seen in   a. his shuddering reaction when his English teacher
tried to guide his hand   b. the "hysterical brilliancy" in his eyes   c. the
way he dressed for the hearing.

Number correct _____ (total 5)

Part C   Ways to Make New Words Your Own

By now you are familiar with the target words and their meanings. This section presents reinforcement activities that will help you make these words part of your permanent vocabulary.

Using Language and Thinking Skills

Finding Examples Write the letter of the situation that best demonstrates the meaning of each word.

_____ 1. **aggrieved**

a. James's mean behavior hurt the feelings of his best friend.
b. Jennifer made gravy to pour on the meat.
c. Hernando never doubts his own ability.

_____ 2. **commentary**

a. The citizens were angry about a tax increase and demanded a meeting.
b. The crowd cheered wildly when the ball went in the basket.
c. The reporter wrote an editorial about a recent scandal in city hall.

_____ 3. **contempt**

a. Raymond thought intently about the algebra problem.
b. Ms. Rollins was surprised to see a parking ticket on her car.
c. The defendant admitted that he despised his neighbor.

_____ 4. **contrite**

a. Collins had a bad habit of constantly interrupting a conversation.
b. Mr. Heiges asked his daughter to forgive his outburst of temper.
c. Diane felt proud of her recent accomplishments.

_____ 5. **dandy**

a. Martin had fashionable clothes and prided himself on his appearance.
b. Colleen always bragged that she never made a mistake.
c. Officer Luccini took great pleasure in detective work.

_____ 6. **habitual**

a. Coretta occasionally liked to go shopping with her friends.
b. The young boy tugged his ear every time he became nervous.
c. The raccoons scurried away from the garbage dump.

_____ 7. **rancor**

a. With the aid of a cane, the determined woman crossed the busy street.
b. The smell of the fresh-cut lawn made him remember the farm.
c. The citizens never forgot how brutally the dictator had treated them.

_____ 8. **shudder**

a. The little girl was embarrassed by her inability to speak clearly.
b. The strange sound in the attic made the children tremble with fear.
c. Roxanne often tripped while she was bounding up the stairs.

_____ 9. **suave**

    a. Jessica always knew how to act politely and graciously in social situations.

    b. The candidate angrily accused her opponent of distorting her record.

    c. The store manager insisted on punctuality even though he himself was often late in arriving at work.

_____ 10. **synopsis**

    a. This map shows all the hiking trails in the park, as well as the main camping area.

    b. The study group summarized the main points of the chapter.

    c. William Faulkner wrote the novel _Light in August_.

Number correct _____ (total 10)

Practicing for Standardized Tests

Antonyms Write the letter of the word whose meaning is most nearly _opposite_ that of the capitalized word.

_____ 1. AVERSION: (A) thrust (B) contempt (C) assumption (D) defiance (E) affection

_____ 2. BEFITTING: (A) unsuitable (B) appropriate (C) lucrative (D) vigorous (E) undaunted

_____ 3. DEFIANT: (A) daring (B) distinct (C) cooperative (D) rife (E) simpering

_____ 4. FRAYED: (A) remote (B) smooth (C) worn (D) fearless (E) isolated

_____ 5. IMPERTINENCE: (A) unfitness (B) depression (C) respectfulness (D) rudeness (E) graduation

_____ 6. INDISPENSABLE: (A) absolute (B) necessary (C) stalwart (D) disturbing (E) unneeded

_____ 7. INVOLUNTARY: (A) impulsive (B) native (C) intentional (D) novel (E) avaricious

_____ 8. CONTRITE: (A) flourishing (B) unapologetic (C) mistaken (D) involuntary (E) trivial

_____ 9. OFFENSIVE: (A) insulting (B) pleasant (C) annoying (D) distinguished (E) assumed

_____ 10. PERPLEXITY: (A) bewilderment (B) isolation (C) clarity (D) renouncement (E) principle

Number correct _____ (total 10)

Spelling and Wordplay

Crossword Puzzle Read each clue to determine what word will fit in the corresponding squares. There are several target words in the puzzle.

ACROSS

1. Absolutely necessary
11. Contraction of *I am*
12. Inquired
13. Boy
14. Not shut
16. Abbr. Irish
17. To crudely chop
19. The very poor
21. Abbr. California
23. See 20 Down
24. Tennis stroke
26. Abbr. Old German
27. Abbr. Station
29. Suitable
31. Cues
34. Foot digit
35. Abbr. Treasurer
36. Abbr. United Nations
37. Abbr. Rice University
38. Abbr. Indiana State University
39. Abbr. Rhode Island
40. In resistance to authority
41. Abbr. for *id est*, meaning "that is to say"
42. Abbr. Down
43. Abbr. Latin
45. Abbr. Television
46. Sounds being reflected
49. Price paid for services
50. Prefix meaning "back" or "again"
51. A continuing hatred
54. To rot
57. Abbr. American Association of Retired People
59. Series of remarks

DOWN

1. Disrespectfulness
2. Dude
3. Third person singular of be
4. Snow or water __ __ __
5. Bewilderment
6. Nickname for Edwin
7. Large body of water
8. Abbr. Block
9. Abbr. Los Angeles
10. Suffix used to form past tense of regular verbs
11. An electrically charged atom
15. Abbr. Electrical Engineer
17. Fixed, as a routine
18. Scorn
20. Archaic form of *you*
21. Sorrowful for wrongs
22. To offend or injure
25. Commonly used preposition
27. Trembled
28. Indefinite article
30. Toward
32. Prefix meaning "three"
33. Polite and polished
44. Joan of __ __ __
47. Butter substitute
48. Ma and __ __
49. To become ragged
51. A cereal grass
52. Negative word
53. Boat paddle
54. Abbr. Direct Current
55. Abbr. Centimeter
56. Morning hours
58. 3.14159265

Turn to **The Prefix *in-*** on page 198 of the **Spelling Handbook.** Read the rule and complete the exercises provided.

Part D Related Words

A number of words are closely related to the target words you have studied. Use your knowledge of the target words and of word parts to determine the meanings of these words. (For information about word parts analysis, see pages 6-12.) Learning these related words expands your vocabulary and helps you learn the target words more thoroughly.

1. averse (ə vʉrs´) adj.
2. avert (ə vʉrt´) v.
3. comment (käm´ ent) n., v.
4. contemptible (kən temp´ tə b'l) adj.
5. contrition (kən trish´ ən) n.
6. defy (di fī´) v.
7. demeanor (di mēn´ ər) n.
8. dispensable (dis pen´ sə b'l) adj.
9. dispense (dis pens´) v.
10. fray (frā) n., v.
11. habit (hab´ it) n.
12. inoffensive (in´ ə fen´ siv) adj.
13. perplex (pər pleks´) v.
14. pertinent (pʉr´ t'n ənt) adj.
15. voluntary (väl´ ən ter´ ē) adj.
16. volunteer (väl´ ən tir´) n., v., adj.

Understanding Related Words

Sentence Completion In the blank write the word from the list below that best completes each sentence. Each word may be used only once.

avert	contrition	demeanor	fray	pertinent
comment	defied	dispense	habit	volunteer

1. The student who was found guilty of cheating failed to show any

   _____ for his action.

2. Ramon was nominated for _____ of the month because he had donated more than two hours per day to working on the new library project.

3. Smoking is a bad _____ that is not easy to break.

4. Denise's old skirt had begun to _____ at the hemline.

5. The Wright brothers _____ the law of gravity.

6. Ernie's snide _____ about Betty's poor taste in clothes was rude.

7. When Mrs. Williams's wig blew off in the wind, Vern had to

   _____ his face so that she wouldn't see him smiling.

8. The machine was designed to _____ an equal amount of milk into each glass.

9. Although the point seemed minor, Mr. Gunness insisted that it was

   extremely _____ to a thorough discussion of the author's latest work.

10. The candidate's sour _____ during the debates cost him votes.

Number correct _____ (total 10)

126

Analyzing Word Parts

The Latin Root *grav* The Latin word *gravis*, meaning "heavy," provides the basis for several of our English words containing the root *grav* or *griev*. Look up the following words in your dictionary and explain their connection to "heavy."

1. grave (adj.): _____

2. grieve: _____

3. aggravate: _____

4. aggrieve: _____

5. grievous: _____

Number correct _____ (total 5)

Number correct in Unit _____ (total 60)

The Last Word

Writing

Try your hand at being an editor. Rewrite each sentence by replacing the italicized phrases with one of the words from the list below.

aversion	commentary	defiant	indispensable	rancor
befitting	contrite	habitual	involuntary	synopsis

Example:
Original: The participants in the discussion made many comments *that had little or nothing to do with the topic.*
Revision: The participants in the discussion made many *irrelevant* comments.

1. *Bitter and hateful feelings* dominated the relationship between the two brothers.

   _____

2. Rachel's *humble and penitent* behavior convinced her mother that she was sincerely sorry for what she had done.

   _____

   _____

3. The announcer's *series of observations* made the game much more enjoyable.

   _____

4. Because time was running short, Alvaro gave only a *thumbnail sketch* of the program to members of his group.

   _____

   _____

5. Wood products are an *absolutely essential* element of Oregon's economy.

_____

6. The students complained that their participation in the school cleanup was *not the result of their free will*.

_____

_____

7. The runner's stretching exercises had become a *routine and predictable* part of her fitness program.

_____

_____

8. Lu soon acquired a reputation for a *hostile, rebellious* attitude.

_____

9. Roy could not understand Bob's *intentional avoidance of* all forms of exercise.

_____

10. The retirement reception held for the popular physics teacher certainly was a *suitable and proper* tribute to his years of service.

_____

Speaking and Discussion

A *suave* person knows how to behave in all kinds of social settings. He or she knows how to treat other people in a gracious and tactful way. Discuss how a suave person would respond to the following situations:

1. A classmate comes to school with a large blob of shaving cream on his ear.
2. At a dinner party, a nervous guest accidentally drops a plate of spaghetti.
3. In driver's education class, a student driver confuses the gas pedal and the brake—in the middle of heavy traffic.
4. A struggling basketball player mistakenly scores the winning basket for the other team.

Word's Worth: dandy

"A dandy is a clothes-wearing man, a man whose trade, office, and existence consist in the wearing of clothes." — Thomas Carlyle, 1831

The word *dandy* came into use in England in the early 1880's to describe a type of fashionably dressed man. If you had been a dandy in that period, you would have worn pointed shoes, silk stockings, a narrow-waisted greatcoat, and laced French cuffs. You would also have sported a long, powdered wig adorned with a ribbon in back. For the finishing touch, to be truly in style, you would have had an exquisite beauty mark painted on your face. Today, although the clothing style has changed, we still use the word *dandy* to describe the very fashionably dressed.

UNIT 12:   Review of Units 9–11

Part A   Review Word List

Unit 9 Target Words

1. absolutely	11. militia
2. adorn	12. peerless
3. assemblage	13. principality
4. avaricious	14. procession
5. dauntless	15. prosperous
6. disfigure	16. rife
7. disturb	17. simper
8. endow	18. solitude
9. flourish	19. stalwart
10. lucrative	20. vigorous

Unit 9 Related Words

1. absolute	8. military
2. adornment	9. peer
3. avarice	10. perturb
4. disfigurement	11. proceed
5. endowment	12. solitary
6. invigorate	13. undaunted
7. militant	14. vigor

Unit 10 Target Words

1. appropriate	11. novel
2. assume	12. profile
3. depress	13. reap
4. distinctly	14. remote
5. epoch	15. renounce
6. gradually	16. sunder
7. immense	17. thrust
8. isolate	18. vary
9. metamorphosis	19. villa
10. native	20. yield

Unit 10 Related Worlds

1. announce	10. graduation
2. appropriateness	11. immensity
3. assumption	12. impression
4. asunder	13. instinct
5. compression	14. isolation
6. denounce	15. nature
7. depression	16. novelist
8. expression	17. novelty
9. extinct	18. remoteness

Unit 11 Target Words

1. aggrieved	11. impertinence
2. aversion	12. indispensable
3. befitting	13. involuntary
4. commentary	14. misdemeanor
5. contempt	15. offensive
6. contrite	16. perplexity
7. dandy	17. rancor
8. defiant	18. shudder
9. frayed	19. suave
10. habitual	20. synopsis

Unit 11 Related Words

1. averse	9. dispense
2. avert	10. fray
3. comment	11. habit
4. contemptible	12. inoffensive
5. contrition	13. perplex
6. defy	14. pertinent
7. demeanor	15. voluntary
8. dispensable	16. volunteer

Inferring Meaning from Context

For each sentence write the letter of the word or phrase that is closest to the meaning of the word or words in italics.

_____ 1. Because my uncle has *an aversion to* meat, we eat vegetarian meals when he comes to visit.

    a. a taste for   b. an instinct about   c. a dislike for

    d. an assumption about

_____ 2. Shirley proved how *dauntless* she was when she hurried up the stairs alone to discover the source of the strange sounds.

    a. deficient   b. avaricious   c. brave   d. suave

_____ 3. The *defiant* workers said they would remain on strike until their demands for better working conditions were met.

    a. tired   b. depressed   c. avaricious   d. rebellious

_____ 4. The signing of the Declaration of Independence was the beginning of an important *epoch* in American history.

    a. assemblage   b. profile   c. period of time   d. government

_____ 5. The banker claims that our savings will *flourish* if we follow his advice.

    a. sunder   b. disperse   c. grow vigorously   d. decrease gradually

_____ 6. Because the patient had a contagious disease, he was kept *in isolation*.

    a. in comfort   b. apart from others   c. overnight   d. for observation

_____ 7. The investment of time and effort in our invention turned out to be very *lucrative* because the invention sold rapidly when it was made available to the public.

    a. immense   b. profitable   c. befitting   d. expensive

_____ 8. Enrique's *native* language was Spanish, but he became fluent in English after living in the United States.

    a. second   b. original   c. favorite   d. distinct

_____ 9. As a quarterback, Douglas was *peerless*; no one else could lead the team so effectively.

    a. without equal   b. novel   c. injury prone   d. adequate

_____ 10. When she realized she had made a wrong turn, Mia's *perplexity* became so great that she ran through a red light.

    a. solitude   b. confusion   c. boldness   d. tedium

_____ 11. Kindness and understanding can soothe even a person filled with sarcasm and *rancor*.

    a. vigor   b. humor   c. contrition   d. bitterness

_____ 12. There is *a remote* chance that Sylvia will beat the odds and be able to raise enough money to attend summer camp.

    a. a slight   b. a very good   c. a disturbing   d. an extinct

_____ 13. Everyone was whispering about Superintendent Dahl's dismissal, and gossip was *rife* throughout the school.
a. widespread b. malicious c. spoken d. limited

_____ 14. The internationally acclaimed athlete believed that *vigorous* daily exercise and a high-protein diet were the keys to her success.
a. gradual b. varied c. isolated d. energetic

_____ 15. The accident occurred because the bus driver did not *yield* the right of way to the turning car, but continued into the intersection at full speed.
a. refuse b. deny c. give d. give a warning of

Number correct _____ (total 15)

Using Review Words in Context

Using context clues, determine which word from the list below fits logically in each blank. Then write the word in the blank. Each word will be used only once.

announced	commentary	demeanor	immense	rife
appropriate	contemptible	disturbed	misdemeanor	vigor
avaricious	dauntless	endowed	proceeded	yielded

Nellie Bly

Elizabeth Cochrane's newspaper career began in 1885 with a letter to the editor. She had written an indignant reply to an editorial criticizing career women. The editor liked her writing so much, he eventually hired the eighteen year old as a reporter. She chose her pen name, Nellie Bly, after a Stephen Foster song.

Although Nellie Bly had a slight build and a pleasant _____ , she was _____ with incredible drive and _____ . She poured this vitality into her reporting, first at the *Pittsburgh Dispatch* and later at the New York *World*. Bly shunned articles on fashion and the arts, subjects considered to be _____ for female writers of that period. Instead she preferred to report on city slums, factories, and corruption.

To investigate the care of the mentally _____ , Bly posed as an insane person and had herself committed to an asylum. Her stories of the brutal and _____ treatment of the patients there led to major reforms. Bly had herself arrested and jailed for a _____ , then reported on the suffering of women prisoners. This became her method—become an insider at a place, witness firsthand the conditions, and then provide a growing readership with rich, you-are-there _____ .

The factory conditions in New York City _____ some of Bly's best articles. This was a domain that was _____ with corruption. Several times Bly exposed the cruelty of factory bosses, _____ men concerned only with their wallets.

Not all of Bly's assignments were so serious. In 1889 the New York *World* _____ that Bly would travel around the world in an attempt to outdo Phineas Fogg, the fictional character in the Jules Verne novel *Around the World in Eighty Days*. Bly journeyed across the Atlantic and the Mediterranean. She _____ through the Middle East and the Orient, traveling by ships, trains, horses, and rickshaws. She finally returned home to New York in seventy-two days to an _____ celebration. The _____ spirit of Nellie Bly had captured the imagination of the nation.

Number correct _____ (total 15)

Part B   *Review Word Reinforcement*

Using Language and Thinking Skills

Finding the Unrelated Word   Write the letter of the word that is not related in meaning to the other words in the set.

_____ 1. a. rife b. widespread c. narrow d. rampant

_____ 2. a. gracious b. defiant c. polite d. suave

_____ 3. a. villa b. manor c. mansion d. apartment

_____ 4. a. sundered b. frightened c. petrified d. alarmed

_____ 5. a. impertinent b. offensive c. contemptible d. contrite

_____ 6. a. rancor b. period c. epoch d. age

_____ 7. a. courageous b. dauntless c. reluctant d. brave

_____ 8. a. yielding b. stalwart c. absolute d. firm

_____ 9. a. befitting b. appropriate c. lucrative d. suitable

_____ 10. a. involuntary b. uncontrollable c. unconscious d. invigorating

Number correct _____ (total 10)

Practicing for Standardized Tests

Synonyms   Write the letter of the word whose meaning is closest to that of the capitalized word.

_____ 1. AVERSION: (A) dislike (B) attachment (C) distinction
(D) assumption (E) interval

_____ 2. BEFITTING: (A) unsuitable (B) defiant (C) appropriate
(D) accommodating (E) yielding

_____ 3. CONTRITE: (A) contemptible (B) ingenious (C) grotesque
(D) repentant (E) unapologetic

_____ 4. DISFIGURE: (A) adorn   (B) scar   (C) engulf   (D) brandish
(E) depress

_____ 5. DISTURB: (A) acclimate   (B) dignify   (C) reap   (D) avert
(E) bother

_____ 6. FLOURISH: (A) die   (B) conceal   (C) endow   (D) aspire   (E) thrive

_____ 7. IMMENSE: (A) frayed   (B) dandy   (C) huge   (D) inconspicuous
(E) lucrative

_____ 8. REAP: (A) harvest   (B) sunder   (C) renounce   (D) engulf   (E) plant

_____ 9. RENOUNCE: (A) acclaim   (B) abandon   (C) repeat   (D) maintain
(E) prescribe

_____ 10. VIGOROUS: (A) suave   (B) competent   (C) sophisticated
(D) energetic   (E) simpering

Number correct _____ (total 10)

Antonyms   Write the letter of the word whose meaning is most nearly _opposite_
that of the capitalized word.

_____ 1. APPROPRIATE: (A) unsuitable   (B) befitting   (C) avaricious
(D) contrite   (E) rife

_____ 2. CONTEMPT: (A) scorn   (B) offense   (C) admiration   (D) defiance
(E) avariciousness

_____ 3. DAUNTLESS: (A) defiant   (B) brave   (C) stalwart   (D) fearful
(E) suave

_____ 4. GRADUALLY: (A) virtually   (B) suddenly   (C) efficiently
(D) tactfully   (E) scrupulously

_____ 5. INDISPENSABLE: (A) inconspicuous   (B) central   (C) remote
(D) unnecessary   (E) independent

_____ 6. PROSPEROUS: (A) needy   (B) prominent   (C) native
(D) simpering   (E) lucrative

_____ 7. RANCOR: (A) concealment   (B) majesty   (C) renouncement
(D) sophistication   (E) good will

_____ 8. REMOTE: (A) reproachful   (B) distant   (C) nearby   (D) habitual
(E) contrite

_____ 9. SOLITUDE: (A) isolation   (B) remoteness   (C) perplexity
(D) companionship   (E) competence

_____ 10. SUAVE: (A) tactful   (B) admirable   (C) majestic   (D) peerless
(E) coarse

Number correct _____ (total 10)

133

Analogies Write the letter of the word pair that best expresses a relationship similar to that expressed in the original pair.

_____ 1. PRINCE : PRINCIPALITY ::   (A) king : kingdom   (B) native : country
(C) dinosaur : epoch   (D) villager : villa   (E) soldier : militia

_____ 2. NATIVE : FOREIGNER ::   (A) outline : synopsis   (B) citizen : alien
(C) doctor : disease   (D) banker : bank   (E) stove : appliance

_____ 3. ADORN : CROWN ::   (A) teach : education   (B) laugh : wit
(C) punish : innocence   (D) isolate : assembly   (E) offend : insult

_____ 4. ELEPHANT : IMMENSE ::   (A) butterfly : stalwart   (B) cat :
contemptuous   (C) bee : solitary   (D) dog : dauntless   (E) mouse : small

_____ 5. RENOUNCE : GIVE UP ::   (A) destroy : construct   (B) refuse : take
C) aggrieve : sadden   (D) puzzle : solve   (E) consider : decide

Number correct _____ (total 5)

Spelling and Wordplay

Fill-ins Spell the target word correctly in the blanks to the right of its definition.

1. change of form or character: m _ t _ m _ _ _ _ _ _ _

2. to harvest: r _ _ _ _

3. saddened: a _ _ _ _ e _ _ _

4. disrespect: i _ p _ _ _ _ _ _ _ _

5. necessary: i n _ _ _ _ _ _ _ _ _ l _

6. polite and polished: s _ _ _ _ _

7. to mar: d _ s _ _ _ _ _ _

8. suitable; to set aside for a specific use: a p _ _ _ _ _ _ _ _ _

9. greedy: a _ _ r _ _ _ _ _

10. country house or estate: v _ _ _ _

Number correct _____ (total 10)

Part C Related Word Reinforcement

Sentence Completion Write the word from the list below that best completes the meaning of each sentence. Each word may be used only once.

avarice	denounced	extinct	metamorphosis	perplexed
contemptible	disfigurement	inoffensive	novelty	vigor

1. Conservationists work hard to protect wildlife and make sure that rare species do not become _____ .

2. Harold was afraid that the scars from the accident would cause a _____ of his face, but the surgeon said that a thin white line along the chin would be the only permanent damage.

3. The parents were disturbed by their little boy's _____ ; whenever he met people, he asked them for money.

4. Patrick became _____ when everyone gave him different advice.

5. Mountain climbing requires great _____ ; one must prepare for it through strenuous conditioning.

6. We all change our personalities somewhat in different circumstances, but few of us undergo a _____ as complete as that of Dr. Jekyll.

7. Winston Churchill _____ the evils of Hitler and his Nazi party.

8. Although the employees thought Mr. Imeldo's habit of shaking their hands every morning was a little odd, they agreed it was _____ .

9. Once the _____ of riding in the new car wore off, we began to see it as just a form of transportation.

10. The prosecutor argued that the defendant committed a _____ crime and that only a guilty verdict would serve the cause of justice.

Number correct _____ (total 10)

Reviewing Word Structures

The Word Parts -ary, dis-, ex-, per-, and pro- Form a new word by substituting one of the word parts listed below for a word part in each of the following words. Write the new word in the blank.

-ary   dis-   ex-   per-   pro-

Example: renounce, __pronounce__

1. solitude, _____

2. disturb, _____

3. distinct, _____

4. depression, _____

5. remote, _____

Number correct _____ (total 5)

Number correct in Unit _____ (total 90)

135

Vocab Lab 3

FOCUS ON: *Medicine*

The following words pertain to the field of medicine. Learn them and incorporate them into your active vocabulary.

anesthesiologist (an′ əs thē′ zē äl′ ə jist) n. a doctor who specializes in the use of agents that block pain or produce temporary unconsciousness. • The *anesthesiologist* assured the patient that, although she would be awake during the operation, she would feel no pain.

antibiotic (an′ tē bī ät′ ik, -tī-, -bē-) n. a drug that destroys or slows the growth of bacteria or other microorganisms. • The doctor advised the patient to continue taking the *antibiotic* until all symptoms of the infection were gone.

carcinogen (kär sin′ ə jən) n. a cancer-producing substance. • Because ultraviolet radiation is a powerful *carcinogen,* people who receive too much exposure to the sun are susceptible to skin cancer.

chemotherapy (kem′ ō ther′ ə pē, kē′ mō-) n. the prevention or treatment of infection or disease by the use of chemical agents, or drugs. • *Chemotherapy* is often used to treat certain types of cancer.

endocrine (en′ də krin) adj. relating to a gland that produces secretions that are carried by the blood to other parts of the body, whose functions they regulate. • The *endocrine* glands secrete hormones that regulate the body's growth rate.

geriatrics (jer′ ē at′ riks) n. the branch of medicine dealing with the problems and diseases of old age. • As the aged population grows, *geriatrics* will become an increasingly important medical speciality.

hemophiliac (hē′ mə fil′ ē ak) n. a person with the inherited bleeding disease hemophilia, in which the blood does not clot normally. • A *hemophiliac* could bleed to death from even a tiny scratch.

immunology (im′ yoo näl′ ə jē) n. the branch of medicine dealing with the body's response to disease. • *Immunology* studies suggest that emotions play a part in a person's resistance to disease.

microbiology (mī′ krō bī äl′ ə jē) n. the branch of biology dealing with microscopic forms of life such as bacteria and viruses. • *Microbiology* has helped scientists develop cures for the diseases microorganisms cause.

orthopedics (ôr′ thə pē′ diks) n. the branch of medicine dealing with the treatment of bone and joint problems. • Sports specialists have training in *orthopedics.*

pathology (pə thäl′ ə jē, pa-) n. the branch of medicine dealing with the nature, causes, development, and diagnosis of disease. • *Pathology* studies showed that the patient was suffering from tuberculosis.

placebo (plə sē′ bō) n. a harmless substance prescribed as if it were a medicine. • The physician humored the hypochondriac by prescribing a *placebo.*

psychosomatic (sī′ kō sō mat′ ik) adj. referring to the influence of the mind on the body. • When the doctor could find no organic cause for the headaches, he concluded that they were *psychosomatic.*

136

residency (rez′ i dən sē) n. a period of advanced training in a medical or surgical specialty at a hospital.　● After Debra completes her *residency* in psychiatry, she plans to work at the state mental institution.

schizophrenia (skit′ sə frē′ nē ə, skiz′ ə-) n. a serious mental disorder characterized by a loss of contact with reality.　● A patient suffering from *schizophrenia* may hear imaginary voices and see things that don't actually exist.

Sentence Completion　Complete each sentence by using one of the focus words.

_____ 1. The hospital report from the department of ? stated that the cancer had spread beyond its original site.

_____ 2. The ? explained to the child that he would fall asleep peacefully before the surgeon removed his tonsils.

_____ 3. The woman suffering from ? seemed out of touch with reality and sometimes expressed inappropriate emotions.

_____ 4. If the ? glands secrete too many or too few of their hormones, the body cannot function as it should.

_____ 5. Scientists working in the field of ? study organisms such as bacteria, molds, fungi, protozoa, viruses, and yeasts.

_____ 6. Certain food dyes may be ?, since they cause cancer in laboratory animals.

_____ 7. Every clinic that provides medical care to elderly patients should be staffed by specialists in the field of ?.

_____ 8. The laboratory test was positive for strep throat, so the doctor prescribed a (an) ?.

_____ 9. The rapid development of new drugs enables a physician to change a cancer patient's ? treatment when an old drug becomes ineffective.

_____ 10. After completing his ? in pediatrics, Dr. Perez immediately established his own medical practice.

_____ 11. Dr. Astrup, a specialist in ?, diagnosed Jane's problem as curvature of the spine and gave her a back brace to wear.

_____ 12. In a clinical test of the effectiveness of aspirin in preventing heart disease, half the patients were given a (an) ? that looked just like aspirin.

_____ 13. Because Steve was a ?, he was careful not to cut himself.

_____ 14. ? studies indicate that allergies may result from a breakdown in the body's immune system.

_____ 15. When Aaron developed a bad stomachache before the big vocabulary test but had not eaten anything unusual, he knew it must be a (an) ? illness.

Number correct _____ (total 15)

FOCUS ON: *Denotative and Connotative Meaning*

Here's some food for thought. List as many words as you can that mean "things to eat." *Chow, grub, nourishment, edibles, sustenance, victuals,* and *rations* are a few that might come to mind. All these words have the literal, or **denotative,** meaning "food," and can be substituted for the word *food* in a sentence. However, each word also carries extra baggage, its social, emotional, and personal associations. These associated, or **connotative** meanings, determine which synonym is appropriate for a particular situation.

For example, you probably would use the word *nourishment* if you wanted to talk about food that specifically provides energy necessary for life and growth. This word has a somewhat formal connotation, so it's not likely that you would use it in discussing a lunch menu with your friends. However, you might use *nourishment* in just such a situation to create an ironic effect. You would be making ironic use of a connotative meaning if, instead of asking your junk-food-loving friend what she brought for lunch, you asked, "What's the *nourishment* for the day?" In contrast, *chow* and *grub* are slang words used to refer to any type of meal. It would not be accurate to use *chow* or *grub* interchangeably with *nourishment.*

The speakers of a language generally agree about the connotations of most words. However, each person also has a unique point of view or set of experiences that give a word individualized shades of meaning. For example, the word *motorboat* probably would have positive connotations for a fisherman, but negative ones for an environmentalist who is concerned with pollution of the waterways.

Connotative Meanings in Dictionaries

Dictionaries usually include both denotative and connotative meanings. The definition of the word is its denotative meaning. However, most dictionaries also list connotative meanings in the discussion of synonyms, as in the following definition of *beautiful* from *Webster's New World Dictionary.* Note that the connotations of the synonyms give each a distinctly different shade of meaning.

> **beau·ti·ful** (byo͞ot′ə fəl) *adj.* having beauty; very pleasing to the eye, ear, etc. —**beau′ti·ful·ly** *adv.* —**beau′ti·ful·ness** *n.* **SYN.** —**beautiful** is applied to that which gives the most pleasure and suggests that the thing that delights one comes close to one's ideal; **lovely** refers to that which delights by causing one to feel affection or warm admiration; **handsome** is used of that which attracts by its pleasing proportions, elegance, etc. and suggests a masculine quality; **pretty** implies daintiness or gracefulness and suggests a feminine quality; **comely** applies to persons only and suggests a wholesome attractiveness rather than great beauty; **fair** suggests beauty, esp. of complexion or features, that is fresh, bright, or perfect; **good-looking** generally equals either **handsome** or **pretty**; **beauteous,** a poetical synonym for **beautiful,** is now often used in a joking or belittling way —**ANT·** ugly

An awareness of connotations is important in both reading and writing. This is particularly true of poetry. For example, read the stanza from Robert Frost's poem "Stopping by Woods on a Snowy Evening" shown below:

The woods are lovely, dark and deep.
But I have promises to keep,
And miles to go before I sleep,
And miles to go before I sleep.

Now refer to the dictionary entry for the word *beautiful*. Why do you think Robert Frost used *lovely* rather than one of the other synonyms for *beautiful* in his poem? Perhaps he was looking for a word that would help create the mood of longing, resignation, and nostalgia that he wanted to convey. The word *lovely* has emotional connotations that suggest this depth of feeling.

Connotations are important not only in poetry, but in everyday prose as well. If you were writing a letter to a friend to clarify a minor misunderstanding, which synonym would you choose to complete the following sentence?

I think you _?_ what I said. (misinterpreted, distorted)

The connotations of the word *misinterpreted* suggest only that your friend did not understand you correctly. On the other hand, the word *distorted* suggests that he or she purposefully twisted your words. Therefore, *misinterpreted* is the appropriate word.

Being aware of both the denotative and connotative meanings of words will increase your ability to communicate your own ideas accurately and to understand and appreciate how others use language.

Using Connotations   You make use of the connotations of words when you express different points of view regarding a situation or condition. For example, I may say that my brother is *assertive*, but that yours is a *bully*—in order to cast my brother in a more positive light. Complete the following sentences by choosing words that have unfavorable connotations. Use a thesaurus or dictionary if you wish.

1. We are daring, but they are _____

2. We are conservative, but they are _____

3. We are deliberate, but they are _____

4. We are trusting, but they are _____

5. We are individualistic, but they are _____

6. We are thrifty, but they are _____

7. We are interested, but they are _____

8. We are self-confident, but they are _____

9. We are good-humored, but they are _____

10. We are efficient, but they are _____

11. We are casual, but they are _____

12. We are relaxed, but they are _____

13. We are well-nourished, but they are _____

14. We are persistent, but they are _____

15. We are affectionate, but they are _____

Number correct _____ (total 15)

Number correct in Vocab Lab _____ (total 30)

UNIT 13

Part A   Target Words and Their Meanings

1. adapt (ə dapt′) v.
2. agent (ā′ jənt) n.
3. buffer (buf′ ər) n.
4. component (kəm pō′ nənt) n., adj.
5. comprise (kəm prīz′) v.
6. conductivity (kän′ duk tiv′ ə tē) n.
7. constant (kän′ stənt) adj., n.
8. convert (kän′ vərt) n. (kən vʉrt′) v.
9. density (den′ sə tē) n.
10. discharge (dis′ chärj) n. (dis chärj′) v.
11. element (el′ ə mənt) n.
12. evaporation (i vap′ ə rā′ shən) n.
13. index (in′ deks) n., v.
14. monitor (män′ ə tər) n., v.
15. organism (or′ gə niz′m) n.
16. property (präp′ ər tē) n.
17. salinity (sə lin′ ə tē) n.
18. sediment (sed′ ə mənt) n.
19. system (sis′ təm) n.
20. technology (tek näl′ ə jē) n.

Inferring Meaning from Context

For each sentence write the letter of the word or phrase that is closest to the meaning of the word or words in italics. Use context clues to help you.

_____ 1. Most scientists believe that the dinosaurs became extinct because they could not *adapt* to a drastic change in the earth's climate.

a. adjust   b. incline   c. aspire   d. escape

_____ 2. Scientists constantly seek to identify cancer-causing *agents*; then scientists tell people how to limit exposure to these elements.

a. results   b. discoveries   c. experiments   d. factors

_____ 3. The small country acted as *a buffer* between the rival countries that surrounded it, preventing them from crossing each others' borders and encouraging them to reconcile their differences peacefully.

a. something that is invisible   b. something that acts unwisely   c. something that encourages hostility   d. something that lessens conflict

_____ 4. All of the *components* of an internal-combustion engine must function smoothly for the engine to run.

a. parts   b. sediments   c. complications   d. impediments

_____ 5. Most scientific experiments *comprise* three main parts: the hypothesis, the method, and the results.

a. include   b. predict   c. deliver   d. compare

_____ 6. To increase the electric current the system could deliver, the engineers improved the *conductivity* of the electrical wiring.

a. total length   b. transmitting capacity   c. color   d. condensation

140

7. Despite the many changes Dan had gone through in the last five years, his sense of humor remained *constant.*

   a. practical   b. lucrative   c. unchanged   d. unpredictable

8. When Nicole arrived in London, she immediately *converted* her American money to British currency.

   a. abandoned   b. preferred   c. changed   d. offered

9. The *density* of trees in the forest was so great that the leaves formed a solid green canopy, blocking out all the light.

   a. crowdedness   b. size   c. spaciousness   d. variety

10. The *discharge* of exhaust from the faulty muffler on Mr. Allen's car forced nearby pedestrians to gasp for breath.

    a. trace   b. release   c. disapproval   d. problem

11. All of the *elements* of Leslie's architectural design worked together to create a feeling of spaciousness and tranquility.

    a. ideals   b. impediments   c. consequences   d. basic parts

12. If it is boiled long enough, water will eventually disappear due to *evaporation.*

    a. changing to ice   b. pollution   c. changing to vapor   d. changing to salt

13. The consumer price *index* indicates whether the average price for goods has increased or decreased.

    a. prediction for the future   b. system of checks and balances
    c. number showing a length of time   d. number used as a measure

14. The bank used a television camera to *monitor* the daily transactions of customers and tellers.

    a. watch   b. ventilate   c. explain   d. prevent

15. The peculiar *organism* we found crawling near the water looked like a cross between a jellyfish and an octopus.

    a. violent monster   b. transplanted organ   c. living thing
    d. mechanism

16. Three *properties* of oxygen gas are its lack of color, odor, and taste.

    a. characteristics   b. alternatives   c. ideals   d. applications

17. The *salinity* of Great Salt Lake makes the water impossible to drink but also makes floating in it easy.

    a. stealthiness   b. remoteness   c. saltiness   d. freshness

18. After drinking the beverage, Kevin was disturbed to find *sediment* in the bottom of the glass.

    a. chemicals used in experiments   b. material rising to the top   c. dirt settled on the bottom   d. mixtures of liquids

_____ 19. Lonny's *system* for organizing his notes seemed haphazard, but it was actually very logical.

a. continuity   b. capability   c. calculations   d. method

_____ 20. Through her extensive course work dealing with the theory, structure, and function of computers, Roberta became highly trained in the *technology* of those machines.

a. dignity   b. purchasing   c. brand names   d. science

Number correct _____ (total 20)

Part B   *Target Words in Reading and Literature*

You should now have a general idea of the meaning of each target word. Refine your understanding by examining the shades of meaning the words have in the following excerpt.

How Salty Is the Ocean?

Donald G. Klim

The vitality of an ocean and the marine life in it depends on a complex balance between internal conditions and the surrounding environment. One of the most critical factors in maintaining this complex balance is an ocean's saltiness, or salinity.

Salinity is an important seawater characteristic commonly measured by oceanographers the world over. This information, along with that of temperature and depth, enables physical oceanographers to calculate water **densities** at different depths, which, in turn, provides information about deep ocean currents and also about the behavior of underwater sound waves. Biological oceanographers use the data to predict the location of schools of fish and to maintain proper living conditions for marine **organisms** in holding tanks and aquariums.

5

It is curious that salinity, the total amount of salts dissolved in a given-sized water sample, has not been directly measured for about seventy years! Instead, **properties** related to salinity have been measured and then used to estimate the salinity. The Joint Panel on Oceanographic Tables and Standards noted in 1964 that "chlorinity, electrical **conductivity**, and refractive **index** measurements are all being **converted** to salinity by inadequate tables of doubtful origin."

Before methods of salinity determination could be perfected, it was important to understand exactly why the oceans are salty. Although seawater contains nearly all the elements known, six major components (chlorine, sodium, sulfate, magnesium, calcium, and potassium) make up 99 percent of the salts in seawater. The other 1 percent is composed of minor **components** and trace **elements**. The major and minor components of seawater generally **comprise** nearly constant ratios of the total salt.

The average salinity of the oceans has remained fairly **constant** for over 600 million years, for the oceans are a steady-state **system**, with salts and water constantly added and subtracted in such a way that there is no net gain or loss. Water inflow from precipitation and river **discharge** is thus balanced by outflow due to **evaporation**. Salts are added through processes such as river outflow and volcanic action, but equal amounts of salts are removed from the system through **agents** such as biological uptake,[1] by sea spray that is carried inland, and by adsorption[2] onto clay particles and **sediments**.

What, however, is the importance of salinity? To organisms **adapted** to life in a saltwater environment, its importance is obvious, but it also has important consequences for the physical aspects of the ocean as well. Salt acts as a **buffer** that maintains the oceans at a fairly constant alkaline pH[3] of 8.2 so that they do not become either too acid or too alkaline. This buffering action is particularly important in light of the current pollution of the oceans by humans. Accurate determination and **monitoring** of salinity is thus an important part of modern **technology**.

10

15

20

25

30

35

---

[1] uptake: absorption of salts from the water by marine organisms, which require salt as a nutrient
[2] adsorption: adhesion of the molecules of a gas, liquid, or dissolved substance to a surface
[3] pH: literally, potential of hydrogen, a measure on a 14-point scale of the acidity or alkalinity of a solution (0–7=acid, 7=neutral, 7–14=alkaline)

Refining Your Understanding

For each of the following items, consider how the target word is used in the passage. Write the letter of the word or phrase that best completes each sentence.

_____ 1. When scientists measure *salinity* (line 1), they determine the
a. variation of temperature   b. carbon dioxide content   c. salt content.

_____ 2. The word *properties* (line 11) is used to refer to   a. pieces of land
b. characteristics   c. possessions.

_____ 3. "The Joint Panel . . . noted . . . that 'chlorinity, electrical *conductivity*, and refractive *index* measurements are all being *converted* to salinity by inadequate tables of doubtful origin'" (lines 12–14). From this passage it should be inferred that the degree of salinity in our oceans
a. may not be accurately known   b. is decreasing because of pollution
c. is accurately determined by a direct measurement of the salt dissolved in a water sample.

_____ 4. Words such as *constant* (line 22) and "steady-state *system*" (line 23) suggest that the ocean shows   a. stress   b. the results of technology
c. little change.

_____ 5. If salt is a *buffer* (line 33), it acts to   a. conceal   b. cancel out
c. keep things in balance.

Number correct _____ (total 5)

Part C   *Ways to Make New Words Your Own*

This section presents a variety of reinforcement activities that will help you make these words part of your permanent vocabulary.

Using Language and Thinking Skills

Understanding Multiple Meanings   Read the definitions following the boldfaced target word and then the sentences that use the word. Write the letter of the definition that applies to each sentence.

---

property
a. a thing or things owned (n.)
b. a specific piece of land or real estate (n.)
c. characteristic or essential quality (n.)
d. movable articles used as part of a stage setting (often shortened to *props*) (n.)

_____ 1. One of the easily identifiable *properties* of gold is its heavy weight.

_____ 2. The refugee fleeing from his homeland claimed that all the *property* he had was on his back.

_____ 3. David built and managed the *properties* for the sophomore class play.

_____ 4. When the chemical compound is heated, its physical *properties* change.

_____ 5. Mr. and Mrs. Jones want to build their house on the *property* next to the school.

_____ 6. Printed across the backs of the track uniforms was the statement: "*Property* of the athletic department."

> **agent**
> a. a person or thing that brings about a certain result; factor (n.)
> b. a person empowered to act for or in the place of another (n.)

_____ 7. Air pressure is one *agent* in the making of a storm.

_____ 8. Mr. Lyon, an *agent* of the French government, met with British officials to discuss trade matters.

_____ 9. Bees enable plants to flower by serving as *agents* of pollination.

> **monitor**
> a. a student chosen to assist a teacher (n.)
> b. a flesh-eating lizard of Africa and Australia (n.)
> c. a small warship used for coastal bombardment (n.)
> d. a receiver used to view the picture being picked up by a television camera (n.)
> e. to watch, observe, or check for a special purpose (v.)

_____ 10. The security guard watched the *monitor* closely to ensure that no one was in any part of the locked building.

_____ 11. The federal agents were told to *monitor* every action and conversation of the suspected spy.

_____ 12. Because Charlie was *monitor* for the week, he was responsible for distributing the tests.

_____ 13. Its crew ready for action, the *monitor* cruised close to the shoreline.

_____ 14. The zoo-keeper told us that *monitors* are so named because they warn other creatures that crocodiles are near.

_____ 15. The television camera operator studied the *monitor* intently.

Number correct _____ (total 15)

Practicing for Standardized Tests

Synonyms Write the letter of the word whose meaning is closest to that of the capitalized word.

_____ 1. ADAPT: (A) avert (B) convert (C) concede (D) acclimate (E) expand

_____ 2. BUFFER: (A) shield (B) agent (C) element (D) system (E) trouble

_____ 3. COMPRISE: (A) exclude (B) include (C) agree (D) thrust (E) enable

_____ 4. CONVERT: (A) remain (B) sunder (C) solidify (D) transform (E) comprise

_____ 5. SEDIMENT: (A) system (B) monitor (C) settlings (D) villa (E) property

Number correct _____ (total 5)

Antonyms Write the letter of the word whose meaning is most nearly *opposite* that of the capitalized word.

_____ 1. CONSTANT: (A) variable (B) offensive (C) steady (D) competent (E) liable

_____ 2. DENSE: (A) compact (B) scattered (C) constant (D) tight (E) rancorous

_____ 3. DISCHARGE: (A) dispense (B) expel (C) release (D) defy (E) load

_____ 4. ELEMENT: (A) sieve (B) component (C) whole (D) fundamental (E) property

_____ 5. EVAPORATION: (A) discharge (B) density (C) sediment (D) disappearance (E) condensation

Number correct _____ (total 5)

Spelling and Wordplay

Word Maze Find and circle the target words in this maze.

```
A F O R G A N I S M B T E
C O M P R I S E H E J N V
O O C O N S T A N T P E A
M O N I T O R U B S R G P
P K A D A P T P H Y O A O
O W J B U F F E R S P S R
N P D I S C H A R G E A A
E L E M E N T D Z H R L T
N Q T X E D N I C K T I I
T D E N S I T Y V Q Y N O
T N E M I D E S V I W I N
C O N V E R T Z B D T T X
Y F T E C H N O L O G Y C
```

adapt
agent
buffer
component
comprise
conductivity
constant
convert
density
discharge
element
evaporation
index
monitor
organism
property
salinity
sediment
system
technology

146

Part D   Related Words

A number of words are closely related to the target words you have studied. Use your knowledge of the target words and of word parts to determine the meanings of these words. (For information about word parts analysis, see pages 6–12.) If you are unsure of any definitions, use your dictionary. Learning these related words expands your vocabulary and helps you learn the target words more thoroughly.

1. adaptable (ə dap′ tə b′l) adj.
2. adaptation (ad′ əp tā′ shən) n.
3. agency (ā′ jən sē) n.
4. conducive (kən doo′ siv, -dyoo′-) adj.
5. conduct (kän′ dukt) n. (kən dukt′) v.
6. conversion (kən vur′ zhən, -shən) n.
7. deduce (di doos′, -dyoos′) v.
8. dense (dens) adj.
9. elemental (el′ ə men′ t′l) adj.
10. elementary (el′ ə men′ tər ē, -trē) adj.
11. evaporate (i vap′ ə rāt′) v.
12. organ (ôr′ gən) n.
13. organic (ôr gan′ ik) adj.
14. proprietor (prə prī′ ə tər) n.
15. saline (sā′ līn, -lēn) adj.
16. systematic (sis′ tə mat′ ik) adj.
17. technician (tek nish′ ən) n.
18. technological (tek′ nə läj′ i k'l) adj.

Understanding Related Words

Definitions from Context   Write the definition of each italicized word after examining its context. Then check your definitions with those in the dictionary.

1. The lawyer presented the *elemental* facts of the case and asked the jurors to remember this essential information as the trial progressed.

_____

2. Mr. Alonso was proud of his children's *conduct* at the restaurant and rewarded them with a dessert of their choice.

_____

3. When Jan bought the shop, she became its *proprietor*.

_____

4. Aretha was *systematic* in learning her part for the play; first she read her lines from the script, then she memorized them, and finally she recited her part to her sister.

_____

5. Tony's *adaptable* nature made it easier for him to adjust to his new home in the unfamiliar city.

_____

6. Because Kyle was such an expert medical *technician,* he was often asked to teach others about the equipment and his experimental methods.

_____

_____

7. Noticing that the lights were out, the doors were locked, and the Wilsons' car was not in the driveway, Sheila *deduced* that the Wilsons were not home.

_____

8. In a hydroelectric plant, water power is used to operate the turbines that produce electricity. This *conversion* of energy goes on every minute of the day.

_____

9. The liver is a vital *organ* of the body, playing an important role in metabolism and helping to manufacture red blood cells.

_____

_____

10. After 5:00 p.m. the crowds on the streets seemed to *evaporate*; people disappeared into the subways to catch their commuter trains.

_____

_____

Number correct _____ (total 10)

Sentence Completion   Complete each sentence with the correct word from the Related Words list on page 147.

1. At first the exam seemed _____ to Mario, but he soon discovered that it was very challenging.

2. Mr. Troy's illness was an _____ one; his gallbladder was not functioning properly.

3. The _____ undergrowth made it difficult for the inexperienced hikers to retrace their steps; they lost their way just as the sun slipped behind the mountain.

4. Gina spread her blanket on the sandy beach and tried to do her Spanish homework, but she found that the playful atmosphere was not

_____ to study.

5. The doctor at the clinic told Charlie to gargle with a (an) _____ solution, which, though unpleasantly salty, eased the pain of Charlie's sore throat.

6. Alicia's _____ approach helped her solve the mystery before her less methodical classmates did.

7. Linda had gained the _____ skill to be a first-rate engineer even though she lacked experience in the workplace.

8. Marcus, Jonathan, and Sharon visited the employment _____ every Monday and Friday afternoon in their search for interesting and well-paying summer jobs.

9. The Meades were dismayed to hear of their guest's _____ to vegetarianism; they had just barbecued steak for dinner.

10. The chameleon's ability to change color to blend in with its surroundings shows a remarkable _____ to the environment.

Number correct _____ (total 10)

Turn to **The Prefix *com-*** on pages 195-196 of the **Spelling Handbook.** Read the rule and complete the exercises provided.

Analyzing Word Parts

The Latin Root *duc* This root comes from the Latin word *ducere,* meaning "to lead" or "to bring." The related words *conducive, conduct,* and *deduce* also come from this Latin word, as do words such as *conductor* and *reduction.* Using your knowledge of this Latin root and of word parts, match each of the following words with its correct definition.

a. conducive   c. conductor   e. reduction
b. conduct   d. deduce

_____ 1. (adj.) helpful in bringing about

_____ 2. (n.) the way one acts; (v.) to escort; to guide

_____ 3. (v.) to trace the course or origin of; to figure out by logical reasoning

_____ 4. (n.) person who guides; leader of a musical ensemble

_____ 5. (n.) the act of lessening, as in size, amount, value, or price

Number correct _____ (total 5)

Number correct in Unit _____ (total 75)

Word's Worth: element

Element comes from the Latin word *elementum,* meaning "rudiment" or "first principle." Ancient people thought that all matter on the earth was either an element or a combination of elements. Medieval scientists recognized four elements: earth, water, air, and fire. Our knowledge of matter has advanced considerably since medieval times. Today, the International Union of Pure and Applied Chemistry recognizes one hundred and four chemical elements that compose all matter. These elements are themselves composed of more elementary, atomic particles.

The Last Word

Writing

How *adaptable* are you to change? Write a brief essay discussing an adaptation you have had to make to something new or different (for example, a new school, another town, or a different climate). Was it easy or difficult for you to adapt to the change? What are the advantages and/or disadvantages of having to adapt to something new or different?

Speaking

Choose an *organ* in the human body (for example, the heart or liver), and research its function. Then explain to the class the function of the organ, how it works, and what would happen to the body if something went wrong with the organ.

Group Discussion

The quality of our environment is vital to our quality of life. In order to maintain environmental quality, the land, the oceans, and the air need to be protected. As a class, discuss the following questions, which relate to the environment:

1. How are resources such as land, oceans, and air sometimes endangered by humans?
2. Is one of these resources more important to protect than the others? Why?
3. What are some ways in which we can *monitor* these resources and protect them from misuse?

UNIT 14

Part A Target Words and Their Meanings

1. abolish (ə bäl′ ish) v.
2. accordingly (ə kôrd′ iŋ lē) adv.
3. accustomed (ə kus′ təmd) adj.
4. candid (kan′ did) adj.
5. constrain (kən strān′) v.
6. derive (di rīv′) v.
7. despotism (des′ pə tiz′m) n.
8. dictate (dik′ tāt) v.
9. dispose (dis pōz′) v.
10. entitle (in tīt′′l) v.
11. evince (i vins′) v.
12. impel (im pel′) v.
13. institute (in′ stə toot′, -tyoot) n., v.
14. invariably (in ver′ ē ə blē, -var′-) adv.
15. prudence (prood′′ns) n.
16. pursuit (pər soot′, -syoot′) n.
17. self-evident (self-ev′ ə dənt) adj.
18. transient (tran′ shənt) adj., n.
19. tyranny (tir′ ə nē) n.
20. usurpation (yoo′ sər pā′ shən, -zər-) n.

Inferring Meaning from Context

For each sentence write the letter of the word or phrase that is closest to the meaning of the word or words in italics. Use context clues to help you.

_____ 1. The senator assured his constituents that he would try to *abolish* hunger.
   a. reinstate   b. differentiate between   c. approve   d. do away with

_____ 2. Few people showed interest in purchasing the company's latest flavor of ice cream; *accordingly*, the company decided to stop making it.
   a. therefore   b. irresponsibly   c. technically   d. admittedly

_____ 3. Because Ellen always liked summer weather, she found it easy to become *accustomed to* the warm, dry climate of Arizona.
   a. annoyed with   b. uncomfortable in   c. used to
   d. knowledgeable of

_____ 4. Sharon appreciated Jack's *candid* opinion of her paper even though she was uncertain about how to respond to the criticism.
   a. frank   b. brief   c. possessive   d. mild

_____ 5. Although the sounds made by the oboist resembled a honking goose, we *constrained* our laughter because we did not want to embarrass him.
   a. perpetuated   b. held back   c. ridiculed   d. made apparent

_____ 6. The drug insulin, prescribed for many diabetics, is *derived* from the pancreas of such animals as sheep and cows.
   a. monitored   b. assumed   c. raised   d. taken

151

_____ 7. *Despotism* does not allow for basic liberties, such as freedom of speech, because the ruler does not tolerate disagreement.

a. Government by a small group   b. Democracy   c. Self-government
d. Rule by a tyrant

_____ 8. The store manager *dictated* the procedures that her workers were to follow.

a. abolished   b. ridiculed   c. appreciated   d. gave orders about

_____ 9. Without specific goals, most people are *disposed* to waste time.

a. monitored   b. assumed   c. raised   d. inclined

_____ 10. The coupon indicated that Juan *was entitled to* a discount on his next purchase of groceries.

a. had a right to   b. was mistaken about   c. had bought
d. had been denied

_____ 11. The novelist's first published work *evinced* a talent rarely seen in the early stages of a writing career.

a. obviously lacked   b. clearly showed   c. never included
d. exaggerated

_____ 12. Religious intolerance *impelled* the Pilgrims to leave England.

a. forced   b. determined   c. compromised   d. requested

_____ 13. Today the hospital *instituted* a new regulation: all visitors are now required to sign in before being admitted to patients' rooms.

a. eliminated   b. debated   c. initiated   d. controlled

_____ 14. Whenever we order a pizza over the telephone, we are *invariably* asked to give our telephone number.

a. rarely   b. without warning   c. sometimes   d. always

_____ 15. *Prudence* was one of Mr. Kendall's attributes as a banker; customers knew their money was handled properly.

a. Conceitedness   b. Sound judgment   c. Wealth
d. Official privilege

_____ 16. In *pursuit of* her goals, Angela tried hard to maintain a grade-point average that would enable her to get accepted into college.

a. the changing of   b. an attempt to determine   c. an attainment of
d. an attempt to reach

_____ 17. Uncle Charlie likes to argue about even *self-evident* knowledge, such as the fact that the earth is round or that the sun sets in the west.

a. controversial   b. ideal   c. commonly accepted   d. unimportant

_____ 18. Colin learned that success can be *transient*; two days after he won the bicycle championship, the congratulations diminished and most people had forgotten about the race.

a. temporary   b. not real   c. astonishing   d. constant

_____ 19. Throughout history, acts of *tyranny* have been met with acts of rebellion.
a. lawful behavior   b. royal duty   c. cruel use of power
d. popular approval

_____ 20. The new leader declared himself emperor for life after he was certain
that his enemies lacked the power to challenge his *usurpation*.
a. unlawful taking of power   b. desire to rule   c. wise behavior
d. supreme fairness

Number correct _____ (total 20)

Part B   Target Words in Reading and Literature

You should now have a general idea of the meaning of each target word. Refine your
understanding by examining the shades of meaning the words have in the following excerpt.

Declaration of Independence

Thomas Jefferson

In this excerpt from the Declaration of Independence, *Thomas Jefferson
outlines the fundamental beliefs of the American Revolutionaries.*

When, in the course of human events, it becomes necessary for one people to
dissolve the political bands which have connected them with another, and to
assume, among the powers of the earth, the separate and equal station to
which the laws of nature and of nature's God **entitle** them, a decent respect to
the opinions of mankind requires that they should declare the causes which   5
impel them to the separation.

---

[1] unalienable rights: rights that cannot be taken away or transferred (Currently, *inalienable* is the
preferred form of the word)

We hold these truths to be **self-evident**—That all men are created equal; that they are endowed by their Creator with certain unalienable rights;[1] that among these are life, liberty, and the **pursuit** of happiness. That, to secure these rights, governments are instituted among men, **deriving** their just powers from the consent of the governed; that, whenever any form of government becomes destructive of these ends, it is the right of the people to alter or to **abolish** it, and to **institute** a new government, laying its foundation on such principles, and organizing its powers in such form, as to them shall seem most likely to effect their safety and happiness. **Prudence**, indeed, will **dictate** that governments long established should not be changed for light and **transient** causes; and, **accordingly**, all experience hath shown that mankind are more **disposed** to suffer, while evils are sufferable, than to right themselves by abolishing the forms to which they are **accustomed**. But, when a long train of abuses and **usurpations**, pursuing **invariably** the same object, **evinces** a design to reduce them under absolute **despotism**, it is their right, it is their duty, to throw off such government, and to provide new guards for their future security. Such has been the patient sufferance[2] of these colonies; and such is now the necessity that **constrains** them to alter their former systems of government. The history of the present King of Great Britain[3] is a history of repeated injuries and usurpations, all having, in direct object, the establishment of an absolute **tyranny** over these States. To prove this, let facts be submitted to a **candid** world.

10

15

20

25

---

[2] sufferance: endurance
[3] present King of Great Britain: George III (1760–1820)

Refining Your Understanding

For each of the following items, consider how the target word is used in the passage. Write the letter of the word or phrase that best completes each sentence.

_____ 1. When Jefferson uses the word *entitle* (line 4), he suggests that "the separate and equal station" is something people should regard as a. a right b. an obligation c. a desire.

_____ 2. The statement that governments *derive* "their just powers from the consent of the governed" (lines 10–11) means that a. citizens get their power from the government b. a government gets its power from the citizens c. both citizens and government must be in agreement on the subject of power.

_____ 3. Instead of using the word *prudence* (line 15), Jefferson might have used a. common sense b. sense of indignation c. religion.

_____ 4. The use of *disposed* (line 17) suggests that, rather than overthrow a government, most citizens a. want to suffer b. try to avoid suffering c. are inclined to suffer.

_____ 5. The meaning of *constrains* (line 24) in this passage is a. forces b. prevents c. imprisons.

Number correct _____ (total 5)

Part C   Ways to Make New Words Your Own
Using Language and Thinking Skills

Finding the Unrelated Word Write the letter of the word that is not related in meaning to the other words in the set.

_____ 1. a. frank b. shy c. open d. candid

_____ 2. a. despotism b. tyranny c. dictatorship d. democracy

_____ 3. a. impel b. stop c. hinder d. restrain

_____ 4. a. establish b. institute c. abolish d. install

_____ 5. a. enable b. entitle c. allow d. obligate

_____ 6. a. temporary b. permanent c. fleeting d. transient

_____ 7. a. prudence b. discretion c. carelessness d. caution

_____ 8. a. sometimes b. constantly c. invariably d. always

_____ 9. a. show b. evince c. conceal d. demonstrate

_____ 10. a. usual b. accustomed c. common d. rare

Number correct _____ (total 10)

Practicing for Standardized Tests

Analogies Write the letter of the word pair that best expresses a relationship similar to that expressed in the original pair.

_____ 1. DESPOTISM : GOVERNMENT :: (A) gentleness : violence (B) baseball : game (C) painting : canvas (D) leader : followers (E) novel : poem

_____ 2. PURSUIT : WITHDRAWAL :: (A) dusk : dawn (B) images : pictures (C) editors : writers (D) dancing : music (E) punishment : crime

_____ 3. TYRANT : DICTATE :: (A) president : elect (B) restaurant : patronize (C) school : teach (D) servant : serve (E) bravery : risk

_____ 4. TRANSIENT : TEMPORARY :: (A) routine : extraordinary (B) proud : snobbish (C) lukewarm : boiling (D) warm-blooded : cold-blooded (E) nervous : anxious

_____ 5. INSTITUTE : INSTITUTIONAL :: (A) evidence : self-evident (B) variation : invariable (C) despotism : despotic (D) church : irreligious (E) flower : plastic

_____ 6. IMPEL : URGE :: (A) dictate : request (B) abolish : inhibit (C) pursue : capture (D) derive : obtain from (E) guffaw : giggle

_____ 7. ENTITLE : BOOK :: (A) dream : sleep (B) pretend : honesty (C) run : track (D) mail : letter (E) hire : job

_____ 8. CONSTRAIN : MOVEMENT :: (A) lie : dishonesty (B) usurp : power (C) dictate : cooperation (D) evince : obscurity (E) abolish : rejection

9. ACCUSTOMED : HABITUAL :: (A) faithful : disloyal   (B) colorless : pale   (C) reliable : undependable   (D) prejudiced : tolerant   (E) enlightened : distorted

_____ 10. TRUTH : SELF-EVIDENT ::   (A) circle : square   (B) arctic : frozen   (C) addition : additional   (D) fitness : lazy   (E) noise : soothing

Number correct _____ (total 10)

Spelling and Wordplay

Crossword Puzzle

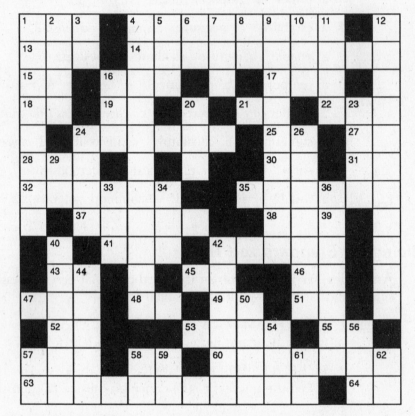

ACROSS

1. _ _ _ wood (one word)
4. To familiarize
13. _ _ _ de Janeiro
14. Holds back
15. Abbr. United Nations
16. To play a part
17. Creative work
18. Abbr. Delaware
19. Abbr. Commanding Officer
21. Not out
22. _ _ _ and feather
24. To deduce or infer from
25. Abbr. South Dakota
27. Abbr. Long Playing
28. Prefix meaning "new"
30. Initials of main character in "The Death of Ivan Ilych"
31. Chemical symbol for tantalum
32. Frank and honest
35. Tyrannical ruler
37. A council of churches
38. Abbr. Notary Public
40. Chemical symbol for uranium
41. Hen's product
42. Engine
43. Abbr. Intransitive Verb
45. _ _ and behold
46. Abbr. Shortstop
47. Objective case of *he*
48. Abbr. Year
49. Abbr. Connecticut
51. Chemical symbol for europium

52. Initials of painter Nicolas Poussin
53. Boxing abbr. for *Technical Knockouts*
55. In case that
57. Same as 16 Down
58. Slang for *hello*
60. To give a title to
63. Evident without proof
64. Archaic form of *you*

DOWN

1. Careful management
2. Clothes _ _ _ _ (one word)
3. _ _ - yo
4. In a fitting way
5. Narrow collapsible bed
6. Abbr. Credit Note
7. To employ
8. Abbr. State
9. Temporary
10. Boat paddle
11. Catcher's glove
12. Unlawful seizures of power
16. High card
20. Climbing plant
23. Lowest female voice
24. Puts on
26. To get rid of

29. Abbr. Each
33. Coloring agent
34. A canine
36. A chase
40. To demonstrate a point
42. Ridiculed
44. To push forward
50. A sound
54. Abbr. Station
56. To soar
57. As far _ _
58. That man
59. Abbr. Intravenous
61. That thing
62. Abbr. Electrical Engineering

Part D   Related Words

A number of words are closely related to the target words you have studied. Use your knowledge of the target words and of word parts to determine the meanings of these words. (For information about word parts analysis, see pages 6–12.) If you are unsure of any definitions, use your dictionary. Learning these related words expands your vocabulary and helps you learn the target words more thoroughly.

1. abolition (ab′ ə lish′ ən) n.
2. accordance (ə kôrd′′ns) n.
3. compel (kəm pel′) v.
4. constraint (kən strānt′) v.
5. despot (des′ pət, -pät) n.
6. despotic (də spät′ ik) adj.
7. dictator (dik′ tāt ər, dik tāt′-) n.
8. dispel (dis pel′) v.
9. entitlement (in tīt′′l mənt) n.
10. expel (ik spel′) v.
11. institution (in′ stə too′ shən, -tyoo′-) n.
12. invincible (in vin′ sə b′l) adj.
13. prudent (prood′′nt) adj.
14. pursuance (pər soo′ əns, -syoo′-) n.
15. repel (ri pel′) v.
16. restrain (ri strān′) v.
17. restraint (ri strānt′) n.
18. transition (tran zish′ ən, -sish-) n.
19. tyrannical (ti ran′ i k'l, tī-) adj.
20. usurp (yoo surp′, -zurp′) v.
21. variable (ver′ ē ə b'l, var′-) adj., n.

Turn to **Doubling the Final Consonant** on pages 202–203 of the **Spelling Handbook**. Read the rule and complete the exercises provided.

Understanding Related Words

Sentence Completion   Write the letter of the word that best completes the meaning of each sentence.

_____ 1. Our state university is considered one of the finest public __?__ of its kind.
   a. institutions   b. constraints   c. despots   d. accordances
   e. entitlements

_____ 2. As the club president stepped down and was replaced by the newly elected president, club members hoped for a trouble-free __?__ of power.
   a. abolition   b. entitlement   c. index   d. accordance   e. transition

_____ 3. In __?__ with the new tax law, some people will be required to pay income tax on their social security benefits.
   a. restraint   b. accordance   c. constraint   d. institution
   e. entitlement

_____ 4. Everyone found it difficult to __?__ themselves from devouring the luscious dessert.
   a. expel   b. dispel   c. repel   d. restrain   e. impel

_____ 5. Joseph Stalin's _?_ actions caused great suffering and hardship throughout the Soviet Union.

a. exquisite   b. suave   c. despotic   d. self-evident   e. prudent

_____ 6. Food prices are _?_ because they are extremely sensitive to changes in supply and demand.

a. disposable   b. candid   c. involuntary   d. elemental   e. variable

_____ 7. Mr. Jones, the store owner, became known for his _?_ behavior; after several months most of his employees had quit.

a. tyrannical   b. self-evident   c. transient   d. accustomed
e. prudent

_____ 8. My aunt's _?_ investments paid unusually high dividends.

a. candid   b. tyrannical   c. variable   d. prudent   e. accustomed

_____ 9. As First Consul of France, Napoleon attempted to _?_ all powers of government for himself.

a. institute   b. repel   c. dispel   d. entitle   e. usurp

_____ 10. Various _?_ are placed upon prisoners who are granted parole.

a. variables   b. constraints   c. despots   d. dictators   e. pursuances

Number correct _____ (total 10)

Analyzing Word Parts

The Latin Root _pel_ The target word _impel_ comes from the Latin word _pellere_, meaning "to drive." The following related words also come from this Latin word: _compel, dispel, expel,_ and _repel._ Carefully read the definition of each word, then read the sentences below. Write the word that best completes each sentence. Each word may be used only once.

compel: to force or oblige to do something
dispel: to scatter and drive away; to disperse
expel: to drive out by force; to eject
impel: to push, drive, or move forward; propel
repel: to drive back or force back; to reject

_____ 1. The enthusiastic cheers of the crowd can sometimes _?_ runners to even greater speeds.

_____ 2. The threat of punishment cannot always _?_ obedience to the law.

_____ 3. Police arrived to _?_ the crowd of curious onlookers that had gathered at the scene of the accident.

_____ 4. The Heimlich maneuver is designed to _?_ any object that might get caught in one's windpipe.

5. The general was uncertain whether his troops could _?_ another attack.

Number correct _____ (total 5)

Number correct in Unit _____ (total 60)

The Last Word

Writing

According to Jefferson's Declaration of Independence, all citizens are *entitled* to "life, liberty, and the pursuit of happiness." Add a fourth item to Jefferson's list of "unalienable rights." Then write a paragraph in which you explain why all citizens are entitled to that right.

Speaking

Candor is a quality valued by many people. However, others believe that honesty is not always the best policy, especially with regard to the feelings of others. Students should divide themselves into two groups to debate the advantages and disadvantages of being *candid*.

Group Discussion

"Liberty exists in proportion to wholesome *restraint*."—Daniel Webster

As a class, discuss the meaning of Webster's quotation. Do you agree that some form of restraint is necessary in order for liberty to exist? Explain why or why not. What would the world be like if there were a total absence of restraint?

Word's Worth: derive

Derive, in its oldest meaning, suggests altering something radically, even changing the geography of a region. It comes from the Latin *derivare*, "to change the course of a river." When we derive something, we are drawing it away from its source. But as we use the word today, we are probably not thinking of a change as radical as that of redirecting a river.

UNIT 15

Part A   Target Words and Their Meanings

1. abstract (ab strakt′, ab′strakt) adj., n., v.
2. assertion (ə sʉr′ shən) n.
3. deplorable (di plôr′ ə b′l) adj.
4. devotion (di vō′ shən) n.
5. exile (eg′ zīl, ek′ sīl) n., v.
6. faculty (fak′′l tē) n.
7. fidelity (fə del′ ə te, fī-) n.
8. humane (hyo͞o mān′, hyo͝o-, yo͞o-) adj.
9. immaculate (i mak′ yə lit) adj.
10. implement (im′ plə mənt) n., (-ment′) v.
11. incognito (in′ käg nēt′ ō, in käg ni tō) adv., adj., n.
12. inevitably (in ev′ ə tə blē) adv.
13. ingratitude (in grat′ ə to͞od′, -tyo͞od′) n.
14. intolerable (in täl′ ər ə b′l) adj.
15. monosyllable (män′ ə sil′ ə b′l) n.
16. ostentation (äs′ tən tā′ shən) n.
17. perception (pər sep′ shən) n.
18. regulation (reg′ yə lā′ shən) n.
19. sensibility (sen′ sə bil′ ə tē) n.
20. sieve (siv) n.

Inferring Meaning from Context

For each sentence write the letter of the word or phrase that is closest in meaning to the word or words in italics. Use context clues to help you determine the correct answer.

_____ 1. Some people find higher-level mathematics too *abstract* and lacking in practical, down-to-earth uses.

a. theoretical   b. amusing   c. difficult to remember   d. absorbing

_____ 2. In presenting an argument, one makes *an assertion* and then defends it.

a. an attribute   b. an introduction   c. a mistake   d. a declaration

_____ 3. The inspector was shocked by the *deplorable* state of the kitchen and ordered the restaurant closed.

a. wretched   b. exciting   c. depleted   d. improved

_____ 4. The health-care worker, who voluntarily assisted at the local clinic, was praised for her *devotion* to the community.

a. adaptation   b. constraint   c. dedication   d. demonstration

_____ 5. After the battle of Waterloo, Napoleon was *exiled to* the island of St. Helena, where he remained a prisoner until his death in 1821.

a. banished to   b. secluded from   c. invited to   d. cherished by

_____ 6. Ray's remarkable *faculty for* playing the violin was discovered when he was five years old; at that age he could already play concertos.

a. plan for   b. happiness in   c. educated group for   d. aptitude for

_____ 7. Leo's _fidelity_ toward his friends is well known; he always supports them.
   a. efficiency   b. loyalty   c. indifference   d. aversion

_____ 8. The _humane_ treatment of prisoners of war is required by the rules of the Geneva Convention.
   a. critical   b. merciful   c. objective   d. artistic

_____ 9. The _immaculate_ condition of the house convinced the Millers that the previous owner had taken excellent care of it.
   a. freshly painted   b. tasteful   c. staid   d. spotless

_____ 10. Charlie found that the hoe was the most useful _implement_ for weeding.
   a. time-saver   b. skill   c. method   d. tool

_____ 11. Because the young king wanted to see what his kingdom was really like, he traveled around _incognito_ so that no one would recognize him.
   a. cautiously   b. as a common thief   c. in disguise   d. quietly

_____ 12. With only one gallon left, we knew that we would _inevitably_ run out of gas sometime in the next forty miles.
   a. practically   b. possibly   c. certainly   d. constantly

_____ 13. Henry showed his _ingratitude_ for the gift by carelessly tossing it on the table and turning to open the next box.
   a. ungratefulness   b. appreciation   c. perception   d. devotion

_____ 14. Leanne decided that the noise in her apartment building had become _intolerable_ and complained to the manager about it.
   a. elemental   b. beneficial   c. self-evident   d. unbearable

_____ 15. The word _oh_ is an example of a _monosyllable_.
   a. blended word   b. one-syllable word   c. signal word   d. half-syllable

_____ 16. Modest Greg surprised everyone by his _ostentation_ at the party.
   a. showing off   b. seriousness   c. shyness   d. devotion

_____ 17. A dog has such keen _perception_ that it can detect some sounds that people cannot hear.
   a. restraint   b. awareness   c. intelligence   d. eyesight

_____ 18. The hospital strictly enforced its _regulation_ that visitors not be allowed after 9:00 P.M.
   a. rule   b. proposal   c. feature   d. informal request

_____ 19. Matt had the _sensibility_ to understand his friend's concerns.
   a. correction   b. agility   c. insensitivity   d. sensitivity

_____ 20. Chef LeBrier washed the spinach carefully and placed it in a _sieve_, letting the water drain before making the salad.
   a. disposal   b. wedge   c. bag   d. container with holes

Number correct _____ (total 20)

Part B   Target Words in Reading and Literature

You should now have a general idea of the meaning of each target word. Refine your understanding by examining the shades of meaning the words have in the following excerpt.

Lord Jim

Joseph Conrad

Lord Jim is a fascinating novel about a man who is haunted by the memory of a youthful act of cowardice. Jim wanders from place to place, trying to stay ahead of his cowardly reputation, which is passed on from sailor to sailor at the various seaports. The following passage describes this interesting wanderer.

He was an inch, perhaps two, under six feet, powerfully built, and he advanced straight at you with a slight stoop of the shoulders, head forward, and a fixed from-under stare which made you think of a charging bull. His voice was deep, loud, and his manner displayed a kind of dogged **self-assertion** which had nothing aggressive in it. It seemed a necessity, and it was directed apparently as much at himself as at anybody else. He was spotlessly neat, appareled in **immaculate** white from shoes to hat, and in the various Eastern ports where he got his living as ship chandler's[1] water clerk he was very popular.

5

---

[1] ship chandler: a retail dealer in provisions, supplies, and equipment for ships

A water clerk need not pass an examination in anything under the sun, but he must have ability in the **abstract** and demonstrate it practically. His work consists in racing under sail, steam, or oars against other water clerks for any ship about to anchor, greeting the captain cheerily, forcing upon him a card—the business card of the ship chandler—and on his first visit on shore piloting him firmly but without **ostentation** to a vast, cavern-like shop which is full of things that are eaten and drunk on board ship; where you can get everything to make the ship seaworthy and beautiful, from a set of chain hooks for the cable to a book of gold leaf for the carvings of the stern; and where the commander is received like a brother by a ship chandler he has never seen before. There is a cool parlor, easy-chairs, bottles, cigars, writing **implements,** a copy of harbor **regulations,** and a warmth of welcome that melts the salt of a three months' passage out of a seaman's heart. The connection thus begun is kept up, as long as the ship remains in harbor, by the daily visits of the water clerk. To the captain he is faithful like a friend and attentive like a son, with the patience of Job[2], the unselfish **devotion** of a woman, and the jollity of a boon[3] companion. Later on, the bill is sent in. It is a beautiful and **humane** occupation. Therefore, good water clerks are scarce. When a water clerk who possesses ability in the abstract has also the advantage of having been brought up to the sea, he is worth to his employer a lot of money and some humoring. Jim had always good wages and as much humoring as would have bought the **fidelity** of a fiend. Nevertheless, with **ingratitude** he would throw up the job suddenly and depart. To his employers the reasons he gave were obviously inadequate. They said "Confounded fool!" as soon as his back was turned. This was their criticism of his exquisite **sensibility.**

To the white men in the waterside business and to the captains of ships he was just Jim—nothing more. He had, of course, another name, but he was anxious that it should not be pronounced. His **incognito,** which had as many holes as a **sieve,** was not meant to hide a personality but a fact. When the fact broke through the incognito he would leave suddenly the seaport where he happened to be at the time and go to another—generally farther east. He kept to seaports because he was a seaman in **exile** from the sea, and had ability in the abstract, which is good for no other work but that of a water clerk. He retreated in good order towards the rising sun, and the fact followed him casually but **inevitably.** Thus, in the course of years he was known successively in Bombay, in Calcutta, in Rangoon, in Penang, in Batavia—and in each of these halting places was just Jim the water clerk. Afterwards, when his keen **perception** of the **intolerable** drove him away for good from seaports and white men, even into the virgin forest, the Malays of the jungle village, where he had elected to conceal his **deplorable faculty,** added a word to the **monosyllable** of his incognito. They called him Tuan Jim: as one might say—Lord Jim.

---

[2] Job: an Old Testament figure whose devotion God tested by imposing a series of trials and tribulations
[3] boon: merry

Refining Your Understanding

For each of the following items, consider how the target word is used in the passage. Write the letter of the word or phrase that best completes each sentence.

_____ 1. Conrad's use of *immaculate* (line 7) suggests Jim was   a. fussy about his appearance   b. very religious   c. carelessly dressed.

_____ 2. "The unselfish *devotion* of a woman" (line 25) indicates that Jim   a. wished he had been married   b. was attractive to women   c. tried to do whatever he could to help ship captains.

_____ 3. When the author describes a water clerk's job as *humane* (line 26), he suggests that this line of work   a. is suitable for humans   b. deals in human kindness   c. concerns itself with fighting cruelty.

_____ 4. His *incognito* (line 37) was   a. a name he chose because he didn't like his real name   b. a nickname others gave him   c. a false name intended to hide his shameful past.

_____ 5. As Jim moved on, "the fact followed him casually but *inevitably*" (line 44) means that   a. he could not stop committing shameful deeds   b. word of what he had done always followed him   c. word of his casual attitude got around.

Number correct _____ (total 5)

Part C   Ways to Make New Words Your Own

By now you are familiar with the target words and their meanings. This section presents a variety of reinforcement activities that will help you make these words part of your permanent vocabulary.

Using Language and Thinking Skills

Finding Examples   Write the letter of the situation that best demonstrates the meaning of each word.

_____ 1. **ingratitude**
   a. The retiring executive expressed her appreciation for the gifts she received at her farewell party.
   b. Wayne loved to tell stories about his childhood fights with his brother.
   c. Angelo never thanked his friends for their assistance.

_____ 2. **ostentation**
   a. The rowdy young women were quarreling loudly at the back of the restaurant.
   b. Lisa usually sat at the back of the classroom to avoid being seen by others.
   c. Denise wore her fur coat and jewels to the corner grocery store.

164

_____ 3. **humane**

    a. The Barrons sometimes leave their dog locked up in the car, even on hot summer days.

    b. The citizens of New Canaan approved funding for shelters to be built for the homeless.

    c. Rich's older brother teaches psychology at the university.

_____ 4. **devotion**

    a. Rita endured bad weather and traveled great distances to watch every game of her favorite soccer team.

    b. Hannah complained loudly about the prospect of Saturday chores.

    c. Colin took pleasure in entertaining his friends with jokes and tricks.

_____ 5. **immaculate**

    a. After the baseball team trooped through the kitchen with their muddy shoes, they were ordered to leave the house.

    b. Raphael's newly washed and waxed car was the pride of the neighborhood.

    c. Leonardo da Vinci left many sculptures unfinished.

_____ 6. **abstract**

    a. The two magnets moved together with a clicking sound.

    b. Patricia carefully listened to the difficult explanation of the theory of relativity.

    c. Darrell did not show up for work in the morning and left no explanation.

_____ 7. **incognito**

    a. The detective traveled in disguise so that he would not be recognized.

    b. Secret ballots are an essential part of democracy.

    c. When the hubcap fell off the car on the highway, the driver did not even notice.

_____ 8. **sieve**

    a. Vegetables should be carefully washed and drained in the strainer.

    b. When Grandma startled the thief by banging a cast-iron pan, he left.

    c. If you give Hank good directions, he will not get lost.

_____ 9. **implement**

    a. Kathy went next door to borrow a hammer.

    b. The accident slowed traffic in both directions.

    c. The children attentively watched the musician on the brightly lit stage.

_____ 10. **inevitable**

    a. Jose hoped to make the baseball team this year.

    b. If you guess, you may be able to choose the right answer.

    c. When the apples get ripe enough, those that are not picked will fall from the tree.

Number correct _____ (total 10)

Practicing for Standardized Tests

Synonyms   Write the letter of the word whose meaning is closest to that of the capitalized word in the exercises that follow.

_____ 1. EXILE: (A) defiance   (B) banishment   (C) finale   (D) immigration
(E) accommodation

_____ 2. FIDELITY: (A) technology   (B) nonfiction   (C) finance
(D) devotion   (E) ingratitude

_____ 3. HUMANE: (A) cruel   (B) tedious   (C) kind   (D) exquisite
(E) constrained

_____ 4. IMPLEMENT: (A) instrument   (B) agent   (C) impediment
(D) virtue   (E) epoch

_____ 5. INCOGNITO: (A) ideal   (B) disguised   (C) routine   (D) scrupulous
(E) picturesque

_____ 6. INEVITABLE: (A) perceptible   (B) invisible   (C) adaptable
(D) preventable   (E) unavoidable

_____ 7. INTOLERABLE: (A) irreproachable   (B) satisfactory   (C) frayed
(D) unbearable   (E) assertive

_____ 8. PERCEPTION: (A) contempt   (B) prudence   (C) awareness
(D) density   (E) abstraction

_____ 9. REGULATION: (A) rule   (B) institution   (C) irregularity
(D) transition   (E) abolition

_____ 10. SIEVE: (A) plug   (B) strainer   (C) acid   (D) retainer   (E) gasket

Number correct _____ (total 10)

Antonyms   Write the letter of the word whose meaning is most nearly opposite that of the capitalized word.

_____ 1. ABSTRACT: (A) magnificent   (B) sufficient   (C) inevitable
(D) concrete   (E) theoretical

_____ 2. ASSERTION: (A) declaration   (B) prescription   (C) tolerance
(D) perception   (E) denial

_____ 3. DEPLORABLE: (A) deceptive   (B) admirable   (C) offensive
(D) regrettable   (E) tedious

_____ 4. DEVOTION: (A) infidelity   (B) loyalty   (C) humanity   (D) cynicism
(E) virtue

_____ 5. FACULTY: (A) assertion   (B) fidelity   (C) inability   (D) talent
(E) provision

_____ 6. IMMACULATE: (A) tattered   (B) majestic   (C) dandy   (D) filthy
(E) spotless

_____ 7. INGRATITUDE: (A) aversion   (B) competence   (C) finesse
(D) contempt   (E) appreciation

_____ 8. MONOSYLLABLE: (A) word   (B) syllable   (C) sounds
(D) polysyllable   (E) regulation

_____ 9. OSTENTATION: (A) majesty   (B) perception   (C) splendor
(D) recognition   (E) inconspicuousness

_____ 10. SENSIBILITY: (A) fidelity   (B) insensitivity   (C) awareness
(D) agility   (E) judgment

Number correct _____ (total 10)

Spelling and Wordplay

Word Maze   Find and circle each target word in this maze.

```
A I N E V I T A B L Y B D C N L
H J R X C M W Y T I N E E H O I
Q U C F B P Z E B O V L P M I M
K C M Q G L A V I O E B L S T Z
E O D A P E X T T D I A O D A N
T S R U N M P I U L N L R Y L O
A I Y L T E O T U W C L A B U I
L E A W C N I Z A R O Y B F G T
U V Z R M T O K H E G S L I E A
C E E F A C U L T Y N O E D R T
A P O R N V X A S K I N X E D N
M Q G H O I J M P Q T O I L N E
M N O I T R E S S A O M L I U T
I N T O L E R A B L E C E T F S
G O Z S E N S I B I L I T Y O O
T C A R T S B A F V N J G P E P
```

abstract   faculty   incognito   ostentation
assertion   fidelity   inevitably   perception
deplorable   humane   ingratitude   regulation
devotion   immaculate   intolerable   sensibility
exile   implement   monosyllable   sieve

Part D   Related Words

A number of words are closely related to the target words you have studied. Learning these related words expands your vocabulary and helps you learn the target words more thoroughly.

1. abstraction (ab strak′ shən) n.
2. assertive (ə sur′ tiv) adj.
3. deplore (di plôr′) v.
4. devote (di vōt′) v.
5. devotee (dev′ ə tē′, -tā′) n.
6. gracious (grā′ shəs) adj.
7. humanity (hyoo man′ ə tē, hyoo, yoo-) n.
8. implementation (im′ plə mən tā′ shən) n.
9. infidelity (in′ fə del′ ə tē) n.
10. intolerance (in täl′ ər əns) n.
11. ostentatious (äs′ tən ta′ shəs) adj.
12. perceive (pər sēv′) v.
13. perceptible (pər sep′ tə b'l) adj.
14. perceptive (pər sep′ tiv) adj.
15. regulate (reg′ yə lāt′) v.
16. sensible (sen′ sə b'l) adj.
17. tolerable (täl′ ər ə b'l) adj.
18. tolerate (täl′ ə rāt′) v.

Understanding Related Words

Close Relatives For each sentence or group of sentences below, determine which two words of the same root belong in the blanks.

devote, devotee human, humane sensibility, sensible
fidelity, infidelity perceptible, perceptive

1. Jonathan was a _____ of the rock group, and he

   would _____ most of his spare time to listening to their tapes and attending their performances.

2. Patrick Henry's _____ to the cause of freedom was unquestioned by his revolutionary friends. Loyalists to King George, however,

   accused him of _____ to the crown.

3. Jane was a _____ person who thought Kate was acting unwisely; however, her blunt advice to Kate showed little regard for Kate's

   fragile _____ .

4. To fear danger is only _____ , but Ramon cast aside his fear in

   his _____ effort to rescue the boy from the fire.

5. Although Anne's disappointment in not winning the game was not

   _____ to most of her friends, Brad was such a _____ person that he knew immediately that she was upset.

Number correct _____ (total 10)

Turn to **Words with *ie* and *ei*** on pages 205-206 of the **Spelling Handbook.** Read the rule and complete the exercises provided.

168

Analyzing Word Parts

The Prefix *mono-* *Mono-* is a prefix meaning "one," "alone," or "single." For each word in the list below, combine *mono* with the word's root (defined in parentheses) to determine the word's meaning. Match each word in the list with its appropriate definition.

monocle (*ocu* = "eye")   monophonic (*phon* = "sound")
monogamy (*gam* - "marry")   monopoly (*pol* - "to sell")
monograph (*graph* = "write")   monochromatic (*chrom* = "color")
monolith (*lith* = "stone")   monotheism (*the* = "god")
monologue (*log* = "word")   monotone (*ton* = "sound")

_____ 1. a book or long article on a single subject

_____ 2. a repetition of sounds without change of key or pitch

_____ 3. an eyeglass for one eye

_____ 4. the state of being married to one person at a time

_____ 5. exclusive possession or control of something

_____ 6. designating sound reproduction that uses a single channel to carry sound

_____ 7. the doctrine or belief that there is only one God

_____ 8. a single large block or piece of stone

_____ 9. having one color

_____ 10. a part in a play in which one character speaks alone

Number correct _____ (total 10)

Number correct in Unit _____ (total 75)

Word's Worth: humane

In the Middle Ages the word *humane* simply meant "human." It referred to any characteristics of humanity, good or bad. Gradually, however, the word took on a more specialized meaning. It was used to identify only the most noble characteristics of humanity: kindness, compassion, generosity, and mercy. The first Humane Society, established in England in 1774, was formed to put those noble characteristics into action. The original Humane Society rescued drowning victims from the sea and taught lifesaving techniques. Later, other humane societies were organized to ensure that children and animals were treated with kindness and protected from cruelty.

The Last Word

Writing

Intolerance can take many forms. It can have racial, religious, ethnic, or political motivations, or it can be the result of a peer group that refuses to accept individuals who are not the same as other members of the group. Think of an example of intolerance that you have witnessed. Write a description of that situation and its negative effects.

Speaking

In a speech, give a description of a well-known person, a fictional character, or a historical figure. In your description, focus on one of the character traits or descriptive terms listed below. Do not name the person in your talk; see if the class can guess who it is.

assertive   gracious
humane   sensible

Group Discussion

As a class, discuss a contemporary social problem that has *deplorable* consequences. What factors have contributed to the origin of this problem? What steps can be taken to solve it? Is there anything that the class can do as a whole to contribute to the solution?

UNIT 16: Review of Units 13–15

Part A Review Word List

Unit 13 Target Words

1. adapt
2. agent
3. buffer
4. component
5. comprise
6. conductivity
7. constant
8. convert
9. density
10. discharge
11. element
12. evaporation
13. index
14. monitor
15. organism
16. property
17. salinity
18. sediment
19. system
20. technology

Unit 13 Related Words

1. adaptable
2. adaptation
3. agency
4. conducive
5. conduct
6. conversion
7. deduce
8. dense
9. elemental
10. elementary
11. evaporate
12. organ
13. organic
14. proprietor
15. saline
16. systematic
17. technician
18. technological

Unit 14 Target Words

1. abolish
2. accordingly
3. accustomed
4. candid
5. constrain
6. derive
7. despotism
8. dictate
9. dispose
10. entitle
11. evince
12. impel
13. institute
14. invariably
15. prudence
16. pursuit
17. self-evident
18. transient
19. tyranny
20. usurpation

Unit 14 Related Words

1. abolition
2. accordance
3. compel
4. constraint
5. despot
6. despotic
7. dictator
8. dispel
9. entitlement
10. expel
11. institution
12. invincible
13. prudent
14. pursuance
15. repel
16. restrain
17. restraint
18. transition
19. tyrannical
20. usurp
21. variable

Unit 15 Target Words

1. abstract
2. assertion
3. deplorable
4. devotion
5. exile
6. faculty
7. fidelity
8. humane
9. immaculate
10. implement
11. incognito
12. inevitably
13. ingratitude
14. intolerable
15. monosyllable
16. ostentation
17. perception
18. regulation
19. sensibility
20. sieve

Unit 15 Related Words

1. abstraction
2. assertive
3. deplore
4. devote
5. devotee
6. gracious
7. humanity
8. implementation
9. infidelity
10. intolerance
11. ostentatious
12. perceive
13. perceptible
14. perceptive
15. regulate
16. sensible
17. tolerable
18. tolerate

Inferring Meaning from Context

For each sentence write the letter of the word or phrase that is closest in meaning to the word or words in italics.

_____ 1. Many students at our school wanted to *abolish* the dress code.
a. dispose of   b. dictate   c. reinstate   d. monitor

_____ 2. Charles did not easily *adapt to* travel; he found it very difficult.
a. return to   b. adjust to   c. convert   d. institute

_____ 3. Few people agreed with his *assertion* that success is simply a matter of good luck.
a. assumption   b. ostentation   c. declaration   d. discharge

_____ 4. The rope *constrained* the vicious dog.
a. held back   b. impelled   c. disposed   d. punished

_____ 5. Curt's piano teacher was *candid* when she discussed his chances for a music scholarship.
a. devoted   b. intolerable   c. frank   d. adaptable

_____ 6. Patrick's sports collection *comprises* old baseball cards, tattered programs, autographs, and newspaper clippings.
a. implements   b. monitors   c. includes   d. glorifies

_____ 7. The renowned Japanese tradition of courtesy can be partially explained by the *density* of the population in Japan.
a. prudence   b. sparseness   c. crowdedness   d. buffer

_____ 8. The book had landed in a mud puddle and was in *deplorable* shape.
a. sensible   b. tolerable   c. fair   d. wretched

_____ 9. The lawyer's eloquent persuasiveness *evinced* his impressive command of the language.
a. rudely dictated   b. obviously prevented   c. clearly showed
d. quickly dispelled

_____ 10. The animal shelter gave *humane* treatment to lost and abandoned pets.
a. kind   b. immaculate   c. ostentatious   d. tyrannical

_____ 11. The jockey *impelled* the racehorse to faster and faster speeds.
a. entitled   b. talked   c. deplored   d. drove

_____ 12. Even if Hitler had defeated Russia, his ruthless ambition would have *inevitably* led to his eventual defeat.
a. candidly   b. doubtfully   c. certainly   d. assertively

_____ 13. The doctor admitted Suzanne to the hospital so that he could *monitor* her condition more closely.
a. constrain   b. document   c. watch   d. institute

_____ 14. Esther's keen *perception* allowed her to recognize subtle shades of color that other people did not notice.
a. awareness   b. pursuit   c. adaptation   d. conversion

_____ 15. During the summer the influx of tourists gave the resort town a sense of prosperity; unfortunately, that feeling was *transient*, fading at the end of each summer.
a. transmitted   b. self-evident   c. temporary   d. constant

Number correct _____ (total 15)

Using Review Words in Context

Using context clues, determine which word from the list fits logically in each blank. Write the word in the blank. Each word may be used once.

abolish   conducted   element   prudent
accustomed   constrained   expel   repel
adapt   convert   instituted   system
compelled   derived   monitor   tolerate
conducive   dispelling   perception   transition

A Healthy Laugh

Did you know that an average four year old feels _____ to chuckle, giggle, or laugh almost five hundred times a day? As that child grows older, however, he or she will become _____ to laughing less. By the time the _____ to adulthood is completed, the average person laughs only fifteen times a day. Many adults, unfortunately, don't seem to realize that laughter is _____ to good health. Many people hold back laughter, feeling _____ by the mistaken belief that frequent laughter may be seen as a sign of immaturity.

Psychologists believe that laughter is an essential _____ of mental health. A good sense of humor may not be enough to eliminate or _____ problems, but it can help reduce them to a manageable size. When you find the humor in difficult situations, you can _____ pain or embarrassment to amusement, releasing negative feelings and _____ tension. Your sense of humor helps you to _____ to the challenges and frustrations of life. It also makes it easier for you to _____ your own limitations. Most importantly, humor improves your _____ of yourself and builds self-esteem.

Research _____ recently provides interesting evidence about the effects of laughter. One study showed a strong connection between laughter and problem-solving abilities. One group in the study saw a comedy film before they were asked to solve a difficult mathematical problem; the other viewed a math film. The subjects who saw the comedy film did significantly better, perhaps because laughter made them more relaxed and clear-headed.

Laughter benefits the body as well as the mind. A hearty laugh allows you to breath in more oxygen and _____ more carbon dioxide, which helps relax the body. Some experts believe that laughter releases endorphins—the body's natural painkillers—inside the brain. Laughter also stimulates your immune _____ thus releasing antibodies that fight off or _____ infection. Norman Cousins, a famous editor and writer, has written an eloquent book about the healing effects of laughter; he claims that his recovery from life-threatening illness was partially _____ from his daily regimen of Marx Brothers movies. To take advantage of laughter's healing potential, hospitals have even _____ laughter-therapy programs to help patients recover from serious illness. Perhaps one day doctors will find a way to _____ your sense of humor as well as your blood pressure. The next time you feel bad, a healthy dose of laughter may be your most _____ choice of medicine.

Number correct _____ (total 20)

Part B Review Word Reinforcement

Using Language and Thinking Skills

Matching Ideas Write the word from the list below that best matches the idea or situation described in each sentence.

| agent | components | dispose | index | sieve |
| buffer | derive | incognito | self-evident | usurpation |

_____ 1. Rubber tires were mounted all the way around the pier to protect the boats from hitting the wood.

_____ 2. The rock crushing machine contained a screen that sifted out the desired size of rock pieces for gravel.

_____ 3. Many books have an alphabetized listing of names and subjects and the pages on which they appear.

_____ 4. Mara's stereo system has seven main parts.

_____ 5. Mark Twain's *The Prince and the Pauper* tells of a prince who changed places with a commoner so that the prince could travel throughout his kingdom without being recognized.

_____ 6. David McBride represents several insurance companies in the local area.

174

_____ 7. Domingo finally had to get rid of several of his beautiful model ships because he was running out of space in his apartment.

_____ 8. When the young girl was asked if she wanted to go to the circus, she smiled broadly, making her answer obvious to all of us.

_____ 9. The scientist patiently explained how his theory could be traced to an accidental discovery he made three years ago.

_____ 10. The guerrilla troops overthrew the existing government and took control of the country.

Number correct _____ (total 10)

Practicing for Standardized Tests

Synonyms Write the letter of the word whose meaning is closest to that of the capitalized word.

_____ 1. ACCUSTOMED: (A) unusual (B) cultural (C) variable
(D) sensible (E) habitual

_____ 2. BUFFER: (A) cushion (B) medicine (C) edge (D) implement
(E) counter

_____ 3. CONVERT: (A) evince (B) transform (C) repel (D) constrain
(E) institute

_____ 4. DESPOTISM: (A) humanism (B) technology (C) proprietorship
(D) tyranny (E) entitlement

_____ 5. DICTATE: (A) perceive (B) request (C) command (D) dispel
(E) discharge

_____ 6. DISPOSE: (A) avoid (B) incline (C) convert (D) impel
(E) disorganize

_____ 7. ELEMENT: (A) organism (B) soil (C) component (D) mixture
(E) refinement

_____ 8. INTOLERABLE: (A) deplorable (B) inevitable (C) acceptable
(D) careless (E) variable

_____ 9. REGULATION: (A) rule (B) conversion (C) uniform
(D) abstraction (E) courtesy

_____ 10. SYSTEM: (A) language (B) argument (C) institute (D) faculty
(E) method

Number correct _____ (total 10)

Antonyms Write the letter of the word whose meaning is most nearly opposite that of the capitalized word.

_____ 1. ABSTRACT: (A) theoretical (B) specific (C) general (D) constant (E) candid

_____ 2. DEVOTION: (A) fidelity (B) disagreement (C) insensitivity (D) gratitude (E) infidelity

_____ 3. EVAPORATION: (A) condensation (B) salinity (C) conversion (D) discharge (E) usurpation

_____ 4. HUMANE: (A) mental (B) tolerable (C) cruel (D) bored (E) prudent

_____ 5. IMMACULATE: (A) scrupulous (B) immature (C) adaptable (D) filthy (E) ostentatious

_____ 6. INGRATITUDE: (A) laziness (B) rudeness (C) thanklessness (D) praise (E) appreciation

_____ 7. PRUDENCE (A) recklessness (B) assertiveness (C) compromise (D) constraint (E) wisdom

_____ 8. PURSUIT: (A) tolerance (B) avoidance (C) chase (D) revelation (E) pressure

_____ 9. OSTENTATION: (A) expense (B) variable (C) wealth (D) prominence (E) inconspicuousness

_____ 10. TYRANNY: (A) dictatorship (B) despotism (C) democracy (D) cruelty (E) fidelity

Number correct _____ (total 10)

Analogies Write the letter of the word pair that best expresses a relationship similar to that expressed in the original pair.

_____ 1. TRANSIENT : PERMANENT :: (A) timely : recent (B) transporting : traveling (C) momentary : enduring (D) cooked : boiled (E) candid : frank

_____ 2. FACULTY : TEACHER :: (A) Egypt : pyramid (B) bricklayer : mason (C) doctor : surgeon (D) juror : jury (E) team : pitcher

_____ 3. USURP : THRONE :: (A) crown : president (B) overthrow : government (C) argue : lawyer (D) file : cabinet (E) eat : restaurant

_____ 4. IMMACULATE : SOILED :: (A) constant : habitual (B) flawless : flawed (C) impure : immodest (D) white : yellow (E) autumnal : wintry

_____ 5. TYRANNY : DESPOTISM :: (A) government : democracy (B) cruelty : power (C) dictator : freedom (D) domination : democracy (E) assertion : claim

Number correct _____ (total 5)

Spelling and Wordplay

Word Pyramid The word part *-ment* comes from the Latin word *mentium*. It indicates a product, means, action, or state. Build a word pyramid by following the code.

MENT

— — — MENT
3 5 3

— — — — MENT
11 3 2 4

— — — MENT — —
3 5 3   5 1

— — — — — MENT
4 6 9 5 3

— — — — — MENT — — — — —
4 6 9 5 3   1 12 4 8 7

CODE
A D E I L M N O P R S T Y
1 2 3 4 5 6 7 8 9 10 11 12 13

Number correct _____ (total 5)

Use four of your pyramid words to match the definitions below. Write the word to the left of the appropriate definition.

_____ 1. A tool or utensil

_____ 2. The act of carrying out or putting into effect

_____ 3. Matter that settles to the bottom of a liquid

_____ 4. Any or all of four basic substances—earth, air, fire, and water

Number correct _____ (total 4)

Part C   Related Word Reinforcement

Using Related Words

Correct Usage For each sentence, decide whether or not the word in italics is used correctly. Write **C** if it is used correctly within the context of the sentence; write **I** if it is used incorrectly.

_____ 1. As the water *evaporated*, the water level in the pan rose.

_____ 2. The *saline* taste in the water was an unmistakable sign that the water came from the ocean.

_____ 3. As the fog became more *dense*, we began to see clearly.

_____ 4. Ricardo's statements were so *assertive* that few people disagreed with him.

_____ 5. Putting files in alphabetical order is a *systematic* approach.

_____ 6. Craig followed a *sensible* budget; he spent money whenever the urge came upon him.

_____ 7. The young man chose a stylish pair of glasses, also known as a *monocle*.

_____ 8. Mrs. Issaks, the *proprietor*, had operated the corner store for fifteen years.

_____ 9. Kidney transplants are one of the most common kinds of *organ* transplants.

_____ 10. A college coach may be fired if his or her recruitment policies are not in strict *accordance* with the rules.

_____ 11. Vicki showed that she was a true *devotee* of the candidate by abandoning his campaign at the first sign of trouble.

_____ 12. Purple banners and flags in every window made our truck somewhat *ostentatious*.

_____ 13. A *technician* seldom if ever deals with the practical applications of science.

_____ 14. Jessica exercised *restraint* by avoiding ice cream when she was on her diet.

_____ 15. The snowstorm made the road signs *perceptible*.

Number correct _____ (total 15)

Reviewing Word Structures

The Word Parts *duc*, *pel*, and *mono-* Each of these word parts creates a family of related words. Several of the words that can be made from each word part are listed below. Add two more words containing the same word part to each set; then define these added words. Use a dictionary if necessary.

duc   conducive   conduct   conductivity   deduce

1. _____ Definition: _____

_____

2. _____ Definition: _____

_____

pel　　dispel　　compel　　impel　　expel　　repel

3. _____ Definition: _____

_____

4. _____ Definition: _____

_____

mono-　　monocle　　monogamy　　monopoly　　monosyllable

5. _____ Definition: _____

_____

6. _____ Definition: _____

_____

Number correct _____ (total 6)

Number correct in Unit _____ (total 100)

Vocab Lab 4

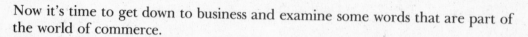

FOCUS ON: Business

Now it's time to get down to business and examine some words that are part of the world of commerce.

appraisal (ə prā′ z'l) n. an expert's estimate of the value or price of something. • The art critic's *appraisal* set the value of the painting at less than we had expected.

arbitration (är′ bə trā′ shən) n. a method of settling disputes in which both sides agree to accept the decision of an impartial third party. • Union and management could not come to an agreement and had to resort to *arbitration* to settle the strike.

assets (as′ ets) n. the resources of a business that have exchange value, such as cash, stock, buildings, land, machinery, good will, and reputation. • The XYZ Company has *assets* worth over a billion dollars.

audit (ô′ dit) n. a formal examination of financial records to verify their correctness. • Ms. Jones, a Certified Public Accountant, does an *audit* of the bank's books twice a year.

cash flow (kash flō) n. the passage of money into and out of a business enterprise. • The *cash flow* at Arnie's Hardware doubled during the busy Christmas season.

Dow-Jones average (dou jōnz av′ rij) n. an index of the average price of selected stocks and bonds. Four averages are computed: (1) thirty industrial stocks, (2) twenty transportation stocks, (3) fifteen utility stocks, and (4) an overall average for the sixty-five stocks that make up the first three averages. The advances and declines are given in points. • In a period of exceptionally good business growth, the *Dow-Jones average* showed a thirty-point increase in one day.

entrepreneur (än′ trə prə noor′, -nur′) n. a person expecting to make a profit who organizes, manages, and accepts the risk of starting a business. • J.C. Penney, an extremely successful *entrepreneur*, started as a clerk in a general store and headed 1,612 stores when he retired in 1946.

equity (ek′ wət ē) n. the value of property after subtracting everything that is owed against it in the form of mortgages and liens. • The *equity* in our house goes up each time we make a mortgage payment.

inventory (in′ vən tôr′ ē) n. an itemized list of the goods or property of an individual or company. • We spent three days taking an *inventory* of all the goods in the store in preparation for the Fourth of July sale.

liability (lī′ ə bil′ ə tē) n. the debts owed by an individual or company. • Enrique's greatest financial *liability* is the mortgage on his home.

merger (mur′ jər) n. a combination of two or more companies in which one company absorbs the other(s) or a new firm is formed. • The *merger* of Apex Laundry, Barber Laundry, and Capitol Laundry created a new company, the ABC Laundry.

retail (rē′ tāl) n. the sale of goods in small quantities directly to the consumer. • Goods sold at *retail* are more expensive than those sold wholesale because the price includes the expenses of the retailer, the wholesaler, and the manufacturer.

shareholder (sher′ hōl′ dər) n. someone who owns a share or shares of stock in a business. • As a *shareholder* in the utility company, I receive a yearly cash dividend based on the profits of the company.

subsidy (sub′ sə dē) n. a grant of money, usually by the government, to assist an enterprise that would benefit the public.
  • Many farmers receive a *subsidy* from the federal government to regulate crop production.

wholesaler (hōl′ sāl′ ər) n. a merchant who sells goods in large quantities to retailers, who in turn sell the goods to consumers at higher prices. • Our food cooperative store buys produce in bulk from a local *wholesaler*.

Sentence Completion Fill in the blanks with the most appropriate word or phrase.

1. The accountant prepared a list of the company's assets, including accounts receivable, property valuation, and an _____ of goods in the company warehouse.

2. Because the _____ sold his goods to only a few retail stores, his records were not very complicated, and it took his accountant only a few hours to do the biannual _____ .

3. The fire that destroyed our garage added to our _____ and decreased the _____ in our property.

4. The _____ of the butcher shop and the produce market into a one-stop food store attracted more customers and doubled the _____ of the individual businesses.

5. Even though my aunt is not a _____ in a publicly held company, she reads the daily report of the _____ because she thinks it is a good indicator of the state of the economy.

Number correct _____ (total 10)

Matching Write the focus word from the list below in the blank next to the situation it best describes.

appraisal   arbitration   entrepreneur   retail   subsidy

_____ 1. a realtor determining the value of house to be sold

_____ 2. a person starting up his or her own business

_____ 3. hiring a judge to settle a dispute

_____ 4. receiving a grant from the U.S. government

_____ 5. selling shoes to the public

Number correct _____ (total 5)

FOCUS ON: Etymology

By the time you finish this book, you will have added approximately seven hundred new words to your vocabulary—quite a feat. What you may not realize, however, is that each word is a living thing with its own life history. *Etymology,* the study of the origins and development of words, comes from the Greek words *etymon,* meaning "true sense of a word," and *ology,* meaning "the study of." Becoming familiar with the history of words can have several beneficial effects on your vocabulary development. Often, learning the origin of a word will lead to an understanding of several other words with related or similar backgrounds. In addition, word etymologies provide clues to the history of a language by showing the influences, such as conquest or colonization, that a culture has undergone. Finally, since the meanings of words change with time, a word's history may provide an interesting story that extends your understanding of the current meaning.

Tracing the Past

You don't have to participate in an archaeological dig or comb the dusty archives of the library to discover the etymology of a word. You need only a dictionary and a little curiosity. For example, look at this partial dictionary entry for the word *life* shown below.

> **life** (lif) *n., pl.* **lives** [ME. < OE. *lif,* akin to ON. *lif,* life, G. *leib,* body < IE. base **leibh-,* to live, whence L. *(cae)lebs,* unmarried, orig., living alone (cf. CELIBATE)] **1.** that property of plants and animals which makes it possible for them to take in food, get energy from it, grow, adapt themselves to their surroundings, and reproduce their kind: it is the quality that distinguishes a living animal

The etymology is the part of the entry that appears in brackets. The languages from which a word is derived are represented by abbreviations that are explained in the introduction to a dictionary. The symbol means "derived from" and shows the chronological order in which a word passed from one language into another.

The etymology for *life* tells you that the word *life* appeared in the same form in Middle English and was derived from the Old English word *lif.* This word, in turn, was related to the Old Norse word *lif,* which also meant "life," and to the German word *leib,* which meant "body." All of these words are descendants of the reconstructed Indo-European base **leibh-,* meaning "to live" (the asterisk indicates that this base is hypothetical, since the speakers of Indo-European left no records). Finally, the entry lists a Latin word, *caelebs,* derived from this same base, which means "unmarried," or "living alone," and a cross-reference to another modern English word, *celibate,* descended from it.

The Family Tree

From this etymology you can infer that today's English has evolved from earlier periods and that English is related to several other languages. A look at other etymologies will reveal that English has borrowed numerous words from its relatives. Further investigation will show that many of our words are taken from the names of people and places. Finally, the interesting deviations that some meanings have undergone is proof that English is an ever-changing language.

Historical Look-alikes Many modern English words bear a strong resemblance to their ancestors. Study the original forms and Old English versions of the words below. Write the modern equivalent in the blank. Check your answer against a dictionary etymology.

Original Word	Old English	Modern English
1. papyrus (L.)	papire	_____
2. febris (L.)	fefer	_____
3. butyrum (L.)	butere	_____
4. skinn (ON.)	skynn	_____
5. uggligr (ON.)	ugli	_____
6. schola (L.)	scol	_____
7. stringere (L.)	streng	_____
8. rectus (L.)	riht	_____
9. candela (L.)	candel	_____
10. doctour (OF.)	doctur	_____

Number correct _____ (total 10)

People and Places Use your dictionary to learn the person or place from which each of the following words is derived. Write the name in the blank.

1. America _____

2. atlas _____

3. bedlam _____

4. canary _____

5. cardigan _____

6. denim _____

7. jeans _____

8. nicotine _____

9. sandwich _____

10. tangerine _____

Number correct _____ (total 10)

Number correct in Vocab Lab _____ (total 40)

Units 1-8 *Standardized Vocabulary Test*

The following questions test your comprehension of words studied in the first half of the book. Test questions have been written in a way that will familiarize you with the typical standardized test format. As on most standardized vocabulary tests, questions are divided into the following categories: **antonyms, analogies,** and **sentence completion**.

Antonyms

Each question below consists of a word in capital letters followed by five words that are lettered. In the blank write the letter of the word that is most nearly *opposite* in meaning to the word in capital letters. Since some of the questions require you to distinguish fine shades of meaning, consider all the choices before deciding which is best.

_____ 1. SCRUPULOUSLY: (A) conscientiously (B) carefully (C) dishonestly (D) clumsily (E) religiously

_____ 2. STAID: (A) dignified (B) playful (C) settled (D) hasty (E) sensitive

_____ 3. CYNICAL: (A) immoral (B) musical (C) hopeful (D) skeptical (E) loud

_____ 4. ACCLAIM: (A) criticism (B) compliment (C) applause (D) accommodation (E) incompetence

_____ 5. STEALTH: (A) absence (B) secrecy (C) robbery (D) openness (E) noise

_____ 6. THRIVE: (A) bloom (B) throb (C) flourish (D) revive (E) fail

_____ 7. DEMORALIZE: (A) discourage (B) disorganize (C) evaluate (D) encourage (E) depress

_____ 8. IRONY: (A) sarcasm (B) sincerity (C) absurdity (D) drama (E) sweetness

_____ 9. TEDIOUS: (A) boring (B) agile (C) tearful (D) tactful (E) exciting

_____ 10. SUFFICIENT: (A) inefficient (B) adequate (C) inadequate (D) abundant (E) undesirable

_____ 11. AGILITY: (A) gracefulness (B) cleverness (C) stupidity (D) clumsiness (E) harshness

_____ 12. MILITANT: (A) aggressive (B) moderate (C) mindless (D) combative (E) peaceable

_____ 13. PROMINENT: (A) noticeable (B) insignificant (C) busy (D) poor (E) modern

_____ 14. TACT: (A) insensitivity (B) delicacy (C) sensibility (D) intelligence (E) anger

_____ 15. INCONSPICUOUS: (A) modest (B) inconsistent (C) faint (D) noticeable (E) trusting

_____ 16. FERVENT: (A) fiery (B) incomprehensible (C) festive (D) devout (E) unfeeling

_____ 17. PROFOUND: (A) wise (B) scanty (C) conservative (D) shallow (E) educated

_____ 18. PERPETUATE: (A) destroy (B) preserve (C) prepare (D) permit (E) describe

_____ 19. DENY: (A) admit (B) conceal (C) detain (D) permit (E) contradict

_____ 20. APPREHEND: (A) seize (B) comprehend (C) appreciate (D) discharge (E) assist

Number correct _____ (total 20)

Analogies

Each question consists of a pair of words followed by five pairs of words. In the blank write the letter of the pair that *best* expresses a relationship similar to that expressed in the original pair.

_____ 1. MECHANIZATION : EFFICIENCY :: (A) invention : inventor (B) organization : productivity (C) rules : cheating (D) system : confusion (E) adage : saying

_____ 2. OFFICER : MILITARY :: (A) lawyer : jury (B) minister : clergy (C) church : prayer (D) official : director (E) lieutenant : commander

_____ 3. DISCUSSION : CONSENSUS :: (A) satire : irony (B) money : bank (C) training : fitness (D) foresight : hindsight (E) brain : tree

_____ 4. ANCESTOR : DESCENDANT :: (A) forefather : successor (B) uncle : grandfather (C) heredity : ancestry (D) family : tree (E) parent : parentage

_____ 5. SMILE : SHEEPISHLY :: (A) gaze : skyward (B) perpetuate : forever (C) believe : doubtfully (D) laugh : heartily (E) admit : admittedly

_____ 6. ASSUAGE : SOOTHE :: (A) sharpen : cut (B) practice : perform (C) intensify : diminish (D) impede : assist (E) calm : relieve

_____ 7. MEAGER : SLIGHT :: (A) adequate : insufficient (B) scant : sparse (C) generous : stingy (D) first : next (E) pink : red

_____ 8. SUFFRAGE : VOTER :: (A) advocacy : lawyer (B) forefather : son (C) subject : king (D) committee : member (E) army : military

_____ 9. ETERNAL : MORTAL :: (A) collective : combined (B) wintry : autumnal (C) permanent : temporary (D) timeless : perpetual (E) prior : previous

_____ 10. PREDATOR : PREY :: (A) conqueror : winner (B) criminal : lawbreaker (C) mission : missionary (D) terrorist : victim (E) unicorn : beast

_____ 11. TEDIOUS : TEDIUM :: (A) admirable : virtue (B) boring : boredom (C) mortal : immortality (D) majestic : royalty (E) fragrant : flower

_____ 12. FINESSE : TACT :: (A) diplomacy : rudeness (B) food : hunger (C) expertise : research (D) skill : competence (E) agility : awkwardness

_____ 13. PRECIPITATION : SLEET :: (A) baking : oven (B) exercise : running (C) teacher : instruction (D) acclimatization : climate (E) contraction: extension

_____ 14. ROADBLOCK : IMPEDIMENT :: (A) question : curiosity (B) flour : wheat (C) decade : century (D) automobile : vehicle (E) airplane : airport

_____ 15. CYCLE : RECURRENT :: (A) diet : thin (B) terrain : hilly (C) luxury : necessary (D) perfume : fragrant (E) prominence : inconspicuous

Number correct _____ (total 15)

Sentence Completion

Each sentence below has one or two blanks. Each blank indicates that something has been omitted. Beneath the sentence are five words or sets of words that are lettered. In the blank at the left of each sentence, write the word or set of words that *best* fits the meaning of the sentence.

_____ 1. As the dentist explained the benefits of enduring the _?_ of wearing braces, Jamie remained calm with a (an) _?_ expression on his face.
(A) interval . . . stunned (B) ordeal . . . deadpan (C) expediency . . . secretive (D) irony . . . grotesque (E) menace . . . ingenious

_____ 2. It was the _?_ of the Capulet family that Romeo was not a proper _?_ for Juliet.
(A) misconception . . . mortal (B) semblance . . . advocate (C) unity . . . cynic (D) consensus . . . suitor (E) stereotype . . . project

_____ 3. The white shark we encountered while we were scuba diving was a(n) _?_ to our safety.
(A) predator (B) menace (C) urgency (D) prey (E) expediency

_____ 4. When the hecklers began to _?_ the speaker, he tore up his notes and walked off the stage _?_.
(A) isolate . . . recalled (B) defy . . . dignified (C) fluster . . . stunned (D) adorn . . . vigorous (E) renounce . . . encompassed

_____ 5. With great _?_ Lisa managed to avoid the controversial topic at the _?_ dinner party she attended.
(A) panic . . . characteristic   (B) liability . . . tedious   (C) finesse . . . exquisite   (D) despair . . . ancestral   (E) acclaim . . . competent

_____ 6. Although the palm reader did not _?_ disaster for Bob in the future, she did warn him to _?_ danger.
(A) foretell . . . anticipate   (B) acclaim . . . apprehend   (C) assuage . . . seize   (D) impede . . . dispute   (E) convey . . . extend

_____ 7. Carol's _?_ solution to the problem saved everyone much time and effort.
(A) inconspicuous   (B) grateful   (C) ingenious   (D) quaint   (E) majestic

_____ 8. Walking by the fountain, we jumped in on a sudden _?_, obviously without _?_.
(A) dare . . . virtue   (B) dispute . . . irony   (C) adage . . . stealth
(D) whim . . . forethought   (E) misconception . . . agility

_____ 9. The shy hero _?_ his accomplishments by _?_ saying that anyone could have done what he did.
(A) demoralized . . . urgently   (B) preserved . . . unmercifully
(C) minimized . . . sheepishly   (D) ennobled . . . grotesquely
(E) brandished . . . craftily

_____ 10. The child pulled her brother's hair and was _?_ by her parents for her _?_ behavior.
(A) secluded . . . exquisite   (B) accommodated . . . dependent
(C) reproached . . . mischievous   (D) encompassed . . . staid
(E) impeded . . . moral

Number correct _____ (total 10)

Number correct in Units 1–8 test _____ (total 45)

The following questions test your comprehension of words studied in the second half of the book. As on most standardized vocabulary tests, questions are divided into the following categories: **antonyms, analogies,** and **sentence completion**.

Antonyms

Each question below consists of a word in capital letters, followed by five lettered words. Choose the word that is most nearly *opposite* in meaning to the word in capital letters. Since some of the questions require you to distinguish fine shades of meaning, consider all the choices before deciding which is best.

_____ 1. FIDELITY: (A) ferocity (B) disloyalty (C) finality
(D) trustworthiness (E) honesty

_____ 2. VIGOROUS: (A) assertive (B) grateful (C) offensive (D) inactive
(E) forceful

_____ 3. IMPEL: (A) compel (B) impose (C) devote (D) restrain (E) assist

_____ 4. PROSPEROUS: (A) comfortable (B) lucky (C) unsuccessful
(D) untitled (E) improper

_____ 5. STALWART: (A) strong (B) stale (C) undaunted (D) fearful
(E) beautiful

_____ 6. CANDID: (A) entitled (B) evasive (C) transient (D) offensive
(E) straightforward

_____ 7. RENOUNCE: (A) abandon (B) accept (C) announce (D) yield
(E) discontinue

_____ 8. AVARICIOUS: (A) greedy (B) enthusiastic (C) generous
(D) miserly (E) conservative

_____ 9. ELEMENT: (A) whole (B) subdivision (C) part (D) universe
(E) chemical

_____ 10. ISOLATE: (A) separate (B) intimidate (C) seclude (D) interpret
(E) join

_____ 11. DEVOTION: (A) truth (B) assertion (C) indifference (D) faithfulness
(E) emotion

_____ 12. LUCRATIVE: (A) unprofitable (B) evil (C) beneficial
(D) influential (E) untimely

_____ 13. REAP: (A) obtain (B) gather (C) repair (D) spend (E) forget

_____ 14. NOVEL: (A) common (B) bookish (C) inconspicuous (D) fresh
(E) frayed

_____ 15. TYRANNY: (A) despotism   (B) beauty   (C) regulation   (D) exile
(E) freedom

_____ 16. IMMACULATE: (A) impure   (B) guiltless   (C) glorious
(D) miniature   (E) imminent

_____ 17. PEERLESS: (A) friendless   (B) dauntless   (C) unequaled
(D) ordinary   (E) visible

_____ 18. DISTINCTLY: (A) definitely   (B) discretely   (C) vaguely
(D) distantly   (E) extraordinarily

_____ 19. PERPLEX: (A) confuse   (B) aggrieve   (C) propose   (D) react
(E) clarify

_____ 20. DEFIANT: (A) averse   (B) disobedient   (C) pertinent
(D) accustomed   (E) compliant

Number correct _____ (total 20)

Analogies

Each question consists of a pair of words followed by five pairs of words. In the
blank write the letter of the pair that _best_ expresses a relationship similar to that
expressed in the original pair.

_____ 1. PRUDENT : PRUDENCE ::   (A) pertinent : impertinence   (B) air :
atmosphere   (C) averse : aversion   (D) water : evaporation
(E) careless : accident

_____ 2. AVARICIOUS : GENEROUS ::   (A) vicious : fierce   (B) humane :
honorable   (C) profane : crude   (D) greedy : unselfish
(E) crafty : cunning

_____ 3. DEPRESS : PEDAL ::   (A) perform : stage   (B) increase : inflation
(C) throw : pitcher   (D) compress : compression   (E) release : brake

_____ 4. EPOCH : ERA ::   (A) second : instant   (B) decade : century
(C) youth : age   (D) minute : hour   (E) present : past

_____ 5. PRINCIPALITY : EMPIRE ::   (A) town : village   (B) state : country
(C) land : territory   (D) neighborhood : section   (E) city : suburb

_____ 6. DEPLORABLE : ACCEPTABLE ::   (A) miserable : wretched
(B) comfortable : pleasant   (C) depressed : cheerless   (D) intolerable :
bearable   (E) reasonable : just

_____ 7. AGENT : ACTOR ::   (A) proprietor: property   (B) lawyer : client
(C) banker : investment   (D) employee : employer
(E) psychiatrist : doctor

_____ 8. INDEX : BOOK ::   (A) suit : tailor   (B) lawyer : court
(C) solution: detective   (D) card catalog : library   (E) map : graph

_____ 9. SALINITY : SALT ::   (A) afterthought : impulse   (B) thinking : action
(C) gold : silver   (D) chemist : chemistry   (E) insanity : insane

_____ 10. PEERLESS : ORDINARY :: (A) incredible : remarkable
(B) routine : mediocre   (C) moist : wet   (D) uncommon : common
(E) faultless : flawless

_____ 11. IMPLEMENT : GARDENER :: (A) hammer : nail   (B) utensil : fork
(C) surgeon : knife   (D) instrument : musician   (E) flowers : garden

_____ 12. METAMORPHOSIS : TRANSFORMATION :: (A) conversion : change
(B) alteration : permanence   (C) critic : critique
(D) continuity : interruption   (E) prescription : pharmacy

_____ 13. CONDUCT : ELECTRICITY :: (A) gold : sell   (B) sound : music
(C) invent : device   (D) pump : gasoline   (E) heat : fire

_____ 14. REAP : HARVEST :: (A) ignite : explode   (B) sow : plant   (C) save :
spend   (D) buy : sell   (E) realize : dream

_____ 15. RANCOR : HATRED :: (A) impediment : asset   (B) camera :
photograph   (C) synopsis : summary   (D) sleeve : shirt   (E) cellar : attic

Number correct _____ (total 15)

Sentence Completion

Each sentence below has one or two blanks. Each blank indicates that
something has been omitted. Beneath the sentence are five words or sets of words
that are lettered. In the blank write the letter of the word or set of words that
best fits the meaning of the sentence.

_____ 1. The caterpillar's _?_ into a butterfly took place abruptly, not _?_.
(A) procession . . . inevitably   (B) arrangement . . . generally
(C) metamorphosis . . . gradually   (D) dissolution . . . absolutely
(E) assemblage . . . consequently

_____ 2. Harry's _?_ complaining day after day was _?_ to those around him.
(A) contemptible . . . appropriate   (B) habitual . . . offensive
(C) self-evident . . . indispensable   (D) simpering . . . lucrative   (E) suave
. . . conducive

_____ 3. Sarah was _?_ in diamonds, a designer gown, and a full-length mink coat;
her _?_ was difficult to overlook.
(A) presented . . . idealism   (B) concealed . . . perception   (C) befitting
. . . naivete   (D) intolerable . . . appropriateness   (E) adorned . . .
ostentation

_____ 4. In the monkey house, two apes showed such hostility and _?_ to each
other that they had to be separated.
(A) remoteness   (B) prudence   (C) aversion   (D) demeanor
(E) conductivity

_____ 5. The _?_ pioneers were _?_ in their attempt to withstand the hardships of
the trip west.
(A) militant . . . avaricious   (B) contrite . . . contemptible   (C) stalwart
. . . dauntless   (D) dispensable . . . vigorous   (E) suave . . . prosperous

6. The dictator established a(an) _?_ by _?_ the power of other officials.
(A) tyranny . . . usurping   (B) technology . . . repelling   (C) assemblage
. . . perturbing   (D) demeanor . . . endowing   (E) immediacy . . .
centralizing

7. Jana and her dog hiked to a(n) _?_ area far from the congestion
of the city.
(A) extinct   (B) remote   (C) immediate   (D) continuous
(E) peripheral

8. The Renaissance was a(n) _?_ when the arts and sciences _?_.
(A) concept . . . collided   (B) epoch . . . flourished   (C) atmosphere . . .
revolted   (D) technology . . . prospered   (E) principality . . . limited

9. Joel wished the world were a perfect _?_ where everyone prospered; he
realized that this was a(n) _?_, not a reality.
(A) epoch . . . utility   (B) organism . . . buffer   (C) Utopia . . . ideal
(D) system . . . mission   (E) exposition . . . impulse

10. The company _?_ huge profits after its invention of the popular toy.
(A) deleted   (B) dedicated   (C) imitated   (D) reaped   (E) adapted

Number correct _____ (total 10)

Number correct in Units 9–16 test _____ (total 45)

SPELLING HANDBOOK

Knowing the meanings of words is essential to using language correctly. However, another important skill is knowing how to spell the words you use.

Almost everyone has at least some problems with spelling. If you have trouble spelling, you might be encouraged to know that many people like you have learned to spell by following these suggestions:

1. **Proofread everything you write.** Everyone occasionally makes errors caused by carelessness or haste. By carefully reading through what you have written, you will catch many of your errors.

2. **Look up difficult words in a dictionary.** If you are not sure about the spelling of a word, don't guess. Take the time to look up the word.

3. **Learn to look at the letters in a word.** Learn to spell a word by examining various letter combinations contained in the word. Note the prefix, suffix, or double letters. Close your eyes and visualize the word. Then write the word from memory. Look at the word again to check your spelling.

4. **Pronounce words carefully.** It may be that you misspell certain words because you do not pronounce them correctly. For example, if you write *probly* instead of *probably,* it is likely that you are mispronouncing the word. Learning how to pronounce words, and memorizing the letter combinations that create the sounds, will improve your spelling.

5. **Keep a list of your own "spelling demons."** Although you may not think about it, you *do* correctly spell most of the words that you use. It is usually a few specific words that give you the most trouble. Keep a list of the words you have trouble spelling, and concentrate on learning them.

6. **Use memory helps, called mnemonic devices, for words that give you trouble.** *Stationery* has *er* as in *letter*; there is *a rat* in *separate; Wednesday* contains *wed.*

7. **Learn and apply the rules given in this section.** Make sure you understand these rules. Then practice using them until they become automatic.

Words with Prefixes

The Addition of Prefixes

A prefix is a group of letters added to the beginning of a word to change its meaning. When a prefix is added to a base word, the spelling of the word remains the same. (For further information about word parts, see pages 6–12.)

in- + dependent = independent in- + credulous = incredulous

un- + sung = unsung   extra- + ordinary = extraordinary

fore- + father = forefather   re- + design = redesign

A prefix can be added to a root as well as to a word. A root is a word part that cannot stand alone; it must be joined to other parts to form a word. A root can be joined with many different prefixes to form words with different meanings. **However, the spelling of the prefix and the root remains the same.**

pro- + ject = project in- + ject = inject

com- + pose = compose im- + pose = impose

Exercise A Add the prefixes as indicated and write each new word.

1. pre- + serve = _____

2. in- + conspicuous = _____

3. re- + source = _____

4. in- + efficient = _____

5. mono- + syllable = _____

6. dis- + engage = _____

7. un- + daunted = _____

8. mis- + conception = _____

9. re- + call = _____

10. in- + vincible = _____

Number correct _____ (total 10)

Exercise B Complete each sentence with two words from the following list that have the same root.

announcement	denounced	disturbing	perturbed
appreciate	depreciated	exceeding	preceding
conceded	depress	expressed	preserve
conserve	dispel	extinquish	retained
contained	distinquishes	impelled	succeeded

193

1. During his vacation Mr. Minkus was _____ by the

   _____ noise emanating from the hotel room next to his.

2. In order to _____ the wildlife refuge, environmentalists

   developed a way to _____ the natural resources of the area.

3. The instructions in the automobile manual were _____ in a

   straightforward manner, stating that one should _____ the
   clutch first before attempting to change gears.

4. Being an excellent salesperson, Irene _____ in

   _____ all previous sales records.

5. The fire academy curriculum _____ between those firefighters

   who _____ blazes and those who provide medical care.

6. The rare book, which _____ some of John Donne's early

   poems, still _____ its original gold-leaf cover.

7. Terri tried to _____ the rumor that certain people

   felt _____ to believe.

8. Josh finally _____ the election to his opponent and thanked his

   supporters for all their support _____ the election.

9. In a public _____ broadcast over radio and television, the police

   commissioner _____ the kidnapping attempt.

10. We do not _____ the fact that our house has

    _____ in value.

Number correct _____ (total 20)

The Prefix *ad-*

When some prefixes are added to certain words, the spelling of the prefix
changes. The prefix *ad-* changes in the following cases to create a double
consonant:

ac- before *c*	*al-* before *l*	*ar-* before *r*
af- before *f*	*an-* before *n*	*as-* before *s*
ag- before *g*	*ap-* before *p*	*at-* before *t*

Examples:

ad- + clamation = acclamation   *ad-* + prehension = apprehension

ad- + fect = affect   *ad-* + range = arrange

ad- + gression = aggression   *ad-* + sure = assure

ad- + locate = allocate   *ad-* + tributable = attributable

ad- + nounce = announce

Exercise Add the prefix *ad-* to each of the roots or base words below. Change the spelling of the prefix as appropriate.

1. *ad-* + mire = _____

2. *ad-* + commodation = _____

3. *ad-* + sembly = _____

4. *ad-* + cordance = _____

5. *ad-* + sumption = _____

6. *ad-* + vocate = _____

7. *ad-* + gravate = _____

8. *ad-* + propriateness = _____

9. *ad-* + next = _____

10. *ad-* + suagement = _____

11. *ad-* + custom = _____

12. *ad-* + liance = _____

13. *ad-* + front = _____

14. *ad-* + sertive = _____

15. *ad-* + preciation = _____

Number correct _____ (total 15)

The Prefix *com-*

The spelling of the prefix *com-* does not change when it is added to roots or words that begin with the letters *m*, *p*, or *b*.

com- + mon = common   *com-* + pression = compression
com- + bat = combat   *com-* + municate = communicate

The prefix *com-* changes to *con-* when added to roots or words that begin with the letters *c, d, g, j, n, q, s, t,* and *v*.

com- + current = concurrent   *com-* + tinual = continual
com- + nection = connection   *com-* + verge = converge

The prefix *com-* changes to *col-* when added to roots or words that begin with the letter *l*, creating a double consonant.

com- + lect = collect   *com-* + lide = collide

The prefix *com-* changes to *cor-* before *r* to create a double consonant.

com- + rode = corrode   *com-* + rupt = corrupt

Exercise Add the prefix *com-* to each of the roots or base words below. Change the spelling of the prefix as appropriate and write the word.

1. *com-* + sequence = _____

2. *com-* + pel = _____

3. *com-* + duct = _____

4. *com-* + lection = _____

5. *com-* + cept = _____

6. *com-* + vince = _____

7. *com-* + tain = _____

8. *com-* + league = _____

9. *com-* + sent = _____

10. *com-* + junction = _____

11. *com-* + laborate = _____

12. *com-* + rection = _____

13. *com-* + straint = _____

14. *com-* + relate = _____

15. *com-* + mercial = _____

16. *com-* + bine = _____

17. *com-* + prise = _____

18. *com-* + quest = _____

19. *com-* + prehension = _____

20. *com-* + gress = _____

Number correct _____ (total 20)

The Prefix ex-

The spelling of the prefix *ex-* does not change when joined to vowels or to the consonants *p, t, h,* or *c.*

ex- + pert = expert   ex- + clamation = exclamation
ex- + tinct = extinct   ex- + it = exit
ex- + haust = exhaust   ex- + ample = example

Exception: *Ex-* becomes *ec-* before *c* in the word *eccentric.*
The prefix *ex-* changes to *ef-* before *f.*

ex- + fort = effort   ex- + fect = = effect

The prefix *ex-* changes to *e-* before most other consonants.

ex- + ject = eject   ex- + rase = erase
ex- + merge = emerge   ex- + lection = election

No common English words begin with the letters *exs.* When the prefix *ex-* is joined to roots that begin with the letter *s,* the *s* is dropped.

ex- + sert = exert   ex- + sist = exist

Exercise Find the misspelled word in each group. Write the word correctly.

_____ 1. elate
         expedition
         examination
         ellaborate

_____ 2. exercise
         exel
         exorbitant
         exit

_____ 3. expound
         exspect
         external
         expire

_____ 4. evolve
         evasive
         eplicit

_____ 5. exquisite
         excursion
         exvacuate
         enormous
         effusive

_____ 6. expediency
         eceed
         extreme
         evince

_____ 7. erode
         exuberant
         exmit
         exalt

_____ 8. extinguish
         exvaporation
         expel
         extract

_____ 9. erupt
         efface
         efhibit
         experiment

_____ 10. exficient
         evolve
         examine
         expanse

Number correct _____ (total 10).

The Prefix *in-*

The spelling of the prefix *in-* does not change except in the following cases:

(a) The prefix *in-* changes to *im-* before *m*, *p*, or *b*.

in- + mediacy = immediacy   *in-* + pression = impression
in- + mensity = immensity   *in-* + balance = imbalance

(b) The prefix *in-* changes to *il-* before *l* to create a double consonant.

in- + lustrate = illustrate   *in-* + legal = illegal

(c) The prefix *in-* changes to *ir-* before *r* to create a double consonant.

in- + rigate = irrigate   *in-* + resistible = irresistible

Exercise Find the misspelled word in each group. Write the word correctly.

_____ 1. ingenuity invigorate increase imcredible	_____ 6. intolerance impel inmaculate implement
_____ 2. inpend independent inertia impede	_____ 7. inport inherit intend inopportune
_____ 3. infidelity imstinct inject immune	_____ 8. immortality imstitution inconspicuous indefinite
_____ 4. irresponsible imreproachable inefficient imperfect	_____ 9. imminent illiterate irdebted irreparable
_____ 5. illogical ilmature immodest ingratitude	_____ 10. invincible inevitable ilvariably illusion

Number correct _____ (total 10)

Words with Suffixes

Words Ending in *y*

A suffix is a group of letters added to the end of a word that changes the word's meaning.

When a suffix is added to a word ending in *y* preceded by a consonant, the *y* is usually changed to *i*.

rely + *-ance* = reliance   utility + *-es* = utilities
defy + *-ed* = defied   primary + *-ly* = primarily

Exceptions:

(a) When *-ing* is added, the *y* does not change.

rely + *-ing* = relying   justify + *-ing* = justifying

try + *-ing* = trying   carry + *-ing* = carrying

(b) In some one-syllable words the *y* does not change.

dry + *-ness* = dryness   shy + *-ness* = shyness

When a suffix is added to a word ending in *y* preceded by a vowel, the *y* usually does not change.

array + *-ed* = arrayed   player + *-er* = player

enjoy + *-able* = enjoyable   joy + *-ful* = joyful

Exceptions: day + *-ly* = daily   gay + *-ly* = gaily

Exercise A In these sentences find each misspelled word and write the correct spelling on the line following the sentence. There may be more than one misspelled word in each sentence.

1. For centuries varyous Italian principalityes have been famous for their wines.

   _____

2. It was obvious that most people sympathyzed with Mary's sensibilitys.

   _____

3. At the assemblie the basketball coach discussed the need for a unified defense.

   _____

4. The judge decreed that the monopolyes on foreign trade were illegal.

   _____

5. Expediency in twentieth-century technology has raised the curiositys of many.

   _____

6. In order to promote their candidacys, the nominees preyed on the whims of their constituencies.

   _____

7. Thomas's liabilityes were magnified by the stealthiness of his enemy.

   _____

Number correct _____ (total 10)

Exercise B Add the suffixes indicated and write the word.

1. responsibility + *-es* = _____

2. dignify + *-ed* = _____

3. ancestry + *-al* = _____

4. crafty + *-ness* = _____

5. envy + *-able* = _____

6. military + -ly = _____

7. annoy + -ed = _____

8. horrify + -ing = _____

9. imply + -ed = _____

10. efficiency + -es = _____

11. controversy + -al = _____

12. sly + -ness = _____

13. prey + -ing = _____

14. convey + -ance = _____

15. mercy + -ful = _____

16. pay + -able = _____

17. witty + -ly = _____

18. plenty + -ful = _____

19. gratify + -ing = _____

20. unify + -ed = _____

Number correct _____ (total 20)

The Final Silent e

When a suffix beginning with a vowel is added to a word ending in a silent e, the e is usually dropped.

increase + -ed = increased   aspire + -ing = aspiring

evolve + -es = evolves   precipitate + -ion = precipitation

extreme + -ist = extremist   argue + -able = arguable

When a suffix beginning with a consonant is added to a word ending in a silent e, the e is usually retained.

spite + -ful = spiteful   amaze + -ment = amazement

extreme + -ly = extremely   shame + -less = shameless

subtle + -ty = subtlety   exquisite + -ness = exquisiteness

Exceptions:

true + -ly = truly   whole + -ly = wholly

argue + -ment = argument   awe + -ful = awful

Exercise A In these sentences find each misspelled word and write the correct spelling on the line following the sentence.

1. Susan acclimateed herself to the indisputable fact that the forcast called for rain on Saturday.

_____

2. Jacob's thriving busyness enabled him to exceed all precedeing attempts to control the market.

_____

3. The Adamsons were gratful that the bank had accommodateed their loan application.

_____

4. The seizeure of the stolen merchandise impeded the thief's original plan.

_____

5. "Maintain your composure dureing the fire drill," Mr. Ortiz announceed in an appropriatly loud voice.

_____

6. Evaporateion caused the salinity of the solution to increase.

_____

7. The principal's secretary calculated that Patricia had accumulated nineteen absencees during her four years in high school.

_____

8. After pursuing a career as a computer analyst for more than nine years, Trina was entitld to the success she finally enjoyed.

_____

9. The arrangement of silk flowers looked convinceingly real.

_____

10. As the tide receded and atmosphereic conditions worsened, four boats retreated to the shores of the isolated island.

_____

11. Beauty was able to look beyond the grotesquness of the Beast to see his kindness.

_____

12. A menaceing cloud minimized our view of the sun.

_____

13. Marie assumed that Ernie's rudeness was precipitated by the fact that his credibileity had been challenged.

_____

14. The remotness of the Frankels's home gave visitors a sense of foreboding.

_____

15. Tony had been considered immensely avariceious until he donated a large portion of his inheritance to charity.

_____

Number correct _____ (total 20)

Exercise B Add the suffixes indicated and write the new word.

1. dilapidate + -ed = _____

2. absolute + -ly = _____

3. prime + -er = _____

4. emerge + -ence = _____

5. rove + -ing = _____

6. immense + -ity = _____

7. engage + -es = _____

8. compete + -ent = _____

9. grate + -ful = _____

10. profile + -es = _____

11. overtake + -en = _____

12. comprise + -es = _____

13. advocate + -ed = _____

14. virtue + -ous = _____

15. institute + -ion = _____

16. prescribe + -er = _____

17. agile + -ity = _____

18. admire + -able = _____

19. depreciate + -ing = _____

20. irresponse + -ible = _____

Number correct _____ (total 20)

Doubling the Final Consonant

Before adding a suffix beginning with a vowel to a word of two or more syllables, double the final consonant only if both of the following conditions exist:

1. The word ends with a single consonant preceded by a single vowel.
2. The word is accented on the second syllable.

im-pel′ + -ed = im-pelled′   re-fer′ + -al = re-fer′-ral
pro-pel′ + -er = pro-pel′-ler   per-mit′ + -ing = per-mit′-ting
com-mit′ + -ed = com-mit′-ted   de-ter′ + -ence = de-ter′-rence

Note in the examples above that the syllable accented in the new word is the same syllable that was accented before adding the suffix.

If the newly formed word is accented on a different syllable, the final consonant is not doubled.

re-fer′ + -ence = ref′-er-ence   pre-fer′ + -ence = pref′-er-ence

Exercise Each word below is divided into syllables. Determine which syllable in each word is accented and insert the accent mark. Add the suffix indicated, noting if the accent moves to a different syllable. Then write the new word. Repeat this process with the second suffix indicated.

Example: e mit′t-*ed* = *emitted* + -*ing* = *emitting*

1. com mit′ + -*al* = _____ + -*ing* = _____

2. gov′ ern + -*ed* = _____ + -*or* = _____

3. re pel′ + -*ing* = _____ + -*ent* = _____

4. be gin′ + *er* = _____ + -*ing* = _____

5. vis′ it + -*ed* = _____ + -*or* = _____

6. dis pel′ + -*ed* = _____ + -*ing* = _____

7. oc cur′ + -*ed* = _____ + -*ence* = _____

8. a bet′ + -*ed* = _____ + -*ing* = _____

9. ed′ it + -*ed* = _____ + -*or* = _____

10. pre fer′ + -*ed* = _____ + -*ence* = _____

11. e quip′ + -*ed* = _____ + -*ing* = _____

12. in hib′ it + -*ed* = _____ + -*ing* = _____

13. con fer′ + -*ing* = _____ + -*ence* = _____

14. in fer′ + -*ed* = _____ + -*ence* = _____

15. ben′ e fit + -*ed* = _____ + -*ing* = _____

16. e mit′ + -*ed* = _____ + -*ing* = _____

17. re mit′ + -*ing* = _____ + -*ance* = _____

18. dif′ fer + -*ed* = _____ + -*ent* = _____

19. de liv′ er + -*ed* = _____ + -*able* = _____

20. ex hib′ it + -*ed* = _____ + -*or* = _____

Number correct _____ (total 20)

Words Ending in *ize* or *ise*

The suffix -*ize* is added to base words to form verbs meaning "to make or become."

sympathy + -*ize* = sympathize (to become sympathetic)
satire + -*ize* = satirize (to make into a satire)

The -*ise* ending is less common. It is usually part of the base word itself rather than a suffix.

surprise   devise   advertise   despise

Exercise Decide whether -*ize* or -*ise* should be added to each word or letter group. Then write the complete word.

1. author _____   11. telev _____

2. central _____   12. custom _____

3. compr _____   13. conc _____

4. merchand _____   14. exerc _____

5. organ _____   15. real _____

6. comprom _____   16. critic _____

7. general _____   17. immortal _____

8. disgu _____   18. rev _____

9. superv _____   19. human _____

10. ideal _____   20. surm _____

Number correct _____ (total 20)

The Suffix -*ion*

The -*ion* suffix changes verbs to nouns.

evaporate + -*ion* = evaporation   discuss + -*ion* = discussion
calculate + -*ion* = calculation   express + -*ion* = expression
distract + -*ion* = distraction   transit + -*ion* = transition

In the examples above, -*ion* is either added directly to the verb form, or the final *e* is dropped before -*ion* is added.

Other forms of the -*ion* suffix include -*tion*, -*ation* and -*sion*. Some verbs, when made into nouns, reflect these variant spellings.

convert + -*ion* = conversion   adapt + -*ion* = adaptation
subtract + -*ion* = subtraction   deride + -*ion* - derision

In the case of words that do not adhere to regular spelling patterns, you must memorize their spellings.

Exercise A Add -*ion* to each of the following words. Then write the new word. Refer to your dictionary for those words that have irregular spellings.

1. abstract _____   5. compress _____

2. assert _____   6. proclaim _____

3. provide _____   7. regulate _____

4. abolish _____   8. appreciate _____

9. devote _____   13. subscribe _____

10. implement _____   14. usurp _____

11. expand _____   15. isolate _____

12. ventilate _____

Number correct _____ (total 15)

Exercise B Each of the following nouns is formed by adding a variation of the *-ion* suffix to a verb. Write the verb form of each word. Use a dictionary when needed.

1. assumption _____   9. prescription _____

2. graduation _____   10. sophistication _____

3. anticipation _____   11. preservation _____

4. seclusion _____   12. depreciation _____

5. apprehension _____   13. evolution _____

6. depression _____   14. designation _____

7. acclimation _____   15. precipitation _____

8. projection _____

Number correct _____ (total 15)

Other Spelling Problems

Words with *ie* and *ei*

When the sound is long *e(ē)*, it is spelled *ie* except after *c*. If the vowel combination sounds like a long *a(ā)*, spell it *ei*.

i **before** *e*

believe	brief	chief
fierce	grief	niece
relieve	thief	yield

except after *c*

ceiling	deceit	deceive
perceive	receipt	receive

or when sounded as *a*

neighbor   reign   weigh

Exceptions:

either	weird	seize	financier
neither	species	leisure	

You can remember these words by combining them into the following sentence: *Neither financier seized either weird species of leisure.*

Exercise A In these sentences find each misspelled word and write the correct spelling on the line following the sentence.

1. The feirce storm continued covering the town with snow, and the weather forecast gave no promise of relief.

   _____

2. The receipt caused Joel to think that the proprietor had decieved him.

   _____

3. Joy replaced grief when the princess learned that the arrow had not peirced the prince's heart.

   _____

4. Neither of the tourists understood why his luggage had been siezed.

   _____

5. Sally's neice had a weird habit of repeating everything said to her.

   _____

6. Tara cannot percieve of a more leisurely afternoon than one spent on a beach.

   _____

7. To achieve the desired look, the contractor lowered the apartment cieling.

   _____

8. We were releived that Andy's shriek was one of delight rather than one of pain.

   _____

9. The sleigh made a breif stop as it traveled over the Alaskan frontier.

   _____

10. Please retrieve the newspaper from the nieghbor's yard before the rain begins.

   _____

Number correct _____ (total 10)

Exercise B Fill in the blanks with *ie* or *ei*.

1. y _ _ l d

2. c o n c _ _ _ t

3. b r _ _ f

4. w _ _ r d

5. s l _ _ _ g h

6. s h r _ _ _ _ k

7. b e l _ _ _ f

8. _ _ g h t

9. s h _ _ _ l d

10. p _ _ _ _ r

11. f _ _ l d

12. h a n d k e r c h _ _ _ f

13. c o n c _ _ v e

14. n _ _ g h b o r

15. l _ _ s u r e

Number correct _____ (total 15)

206

Words with the "Seed" Sound

One English word ends in *sede*:

supersede

Three words end in *ceed*:

exceed   proceed   succeed

All other words ending in the sound of "seed" are spelled *cede*:

accede   concede   precede   recede   secede

Exercise A In these sentences find each misspelled word and write the correct spelling on the line following the sentence.

1. Angela had to conceed that her biology experiment had not succeeded.

_____

2. Upon hearing of the king's death, the prince acceded to the throne and immediately interceded in the quarrel between his two ministers.

_____

3. The preceeding statement made by the president superseded all others.

_____

4. The senator seceded from the political party and proseded to vote independently.

_____

5. The flood waters finally receeded and we proceeded with the clean-up.

_____

6. Denise was excedingly happy when she learned that the student council had succeeded in obtaining more student parking spaces.

_____

7. The announcer conceded that he had misread the previous announcement, but he promised to read a correction on all succeding broadcasts.

_____

8. As the disagreement proceeded, Marty felt he had no recourse but to acceed to his opponent's wishes.

_____

9. All preceding versions of the computer were superceded by the latest model.

_____

10. After his soliloquy the actor reseded from the front of the stage, and the audience broke into a round of applause that far exceeded their responses to preceding acts of the play.

_____

Number correct _____ (total 10)

207

Exercise B Put a check by the five correctly spelled words below.

1. supersede _____
2. intersede _____
3. seceed _____
4. excede _____
5. recede _____

6. proceed _____
7. succede _____
8. concede _____
9. precede _____
10. acsede _____

Number correct _____ (total 10)

The Letter c

When the letter *c* has a *k* sound, it is usually followed by the vowels *a*, *o*, or *u* or by any consonant except *y*.

*ca*lendar   *co*mmunity   *cu*riosity   *cl*uster

When the letter *c* has an *s* sound, it is usually followed by an *e*, an *i*, or a *y*.

avari*ce*   prin*ci*pal   bi*cy*cle

Exercise A Decide if the *c* in each word below has a *k* or an *s* sound. Write *K* or *S* in the blank.

1. craft _____
2. resourceful _____
3. conserve _____
4. projection _____
5. evince _____
6. faculty _____
7. incredible _____
8. sophisticated _____
9. mercy _____
10. cognizant _____

11. renounce _____
12. excessive _____
13. menace _____
14. perceptible _____
15. process _____
16. picturesque _____
17. creditable _____
18. constrain _____
19. central _____
20. dictate _____

Number correct _____ (total 20)

Exercise B Write the missing letter or letters in each word.

1. acc __ imate
2. c __ escendo
3. anc __ stral
4. prec __ pitate
5. forec __ st

6. c __ inic __ l
7. magnific __ nt
8. c __ rc __ mstantial
9. antic __ pation
10. rec __ ll

208

11. misc __ nc __ ption

12. c __ llec __ ion

13. c __ nsent

14. epoc __

15. distinc __ ly

16. sc __ upulously

17. prominenc __

18. c __ ndidac __

19. c __ ndid

20. c __ nc __ pt

Number correct _____ (total 20)

The Letter g

When the letter *g* has a sound as in the word *go*, it is usually followed by the vowels *a*, *o*, *u*, or by any consonant except *y*.

*g*ather   *g*overn   en*g*ulfment   ma*g*nify

When the letter *g* has a *j* sound, it is usually followed by an *e*, an *i*, or a *y*.

assua*g*ement   ri*g*id   *g*ymnasium

Exceptions: *g*iggle   *g*ill   *g*irl   *g*ive   *g*ift   *g*et

Exercise A   Decide if the *g* in each word below has a *j* sound or a sound as in the word *go*. Write **J** or **Go** in the blank.

1. degree _____

2. ingenious _____

3. aggression _____

4. ego _____

5. gypsy _____

6. ambiguity _____

7. gradually _____

8. gesture _____

9. allegedly _____

10. submerge _____

11. enigma _____

12. fragile _____

13. pragmatic _____

14. gauze _____

15. ghastly _____

Number correct _____ (total 15)

Exercise B   Write the missing letter in each word.

1. g __ atitude

2. heritag __ s

3. urg __ ncy

4. ag __ lity

5. disting __ ish

6. reg __ lation

7. forag __

8. dig __ ity

9. org __ nism

10. wedg __

11. recog __ ition

12. ag __ nt

13. g __ nerally

14. discharg __

15. technolog __ cal

Number correct _____ (total 15)

Spelling Review

Exercise A Add the prefix or suffix indicated and write the new word.

1. *in-* + credible = _____

2. *ad-* + climate = _____

3. *de-* + tain = _____

4. satire + *-ize* = _____

5. *pre-* + serve = _____

6. appreciate + *-ion* = _____

7. *ex-* + ficient = _____

8. *in-* + responsible = _____

9. *dis-* + engage = _____

10. dignify + *-ing* = _____

11. avarice + *-ious* = _____

12. prescribe + *-ion* = _____

13. grotesque + *-ly* = _____

14. *com-* + relate = _____

15. *ad-* + vocate = _____

16. *com-* + veyance = _____

17. *in-* + mediate = _____

18. *ad-* + tribute = _____

19. arrange + *-ment* = _____

20. *ex-* + pression = _____

Number correct _____ (total 20)

Exercise B Three of the words in each row follow the same spelling pattern. Circle the word that does not follow that pattern.

1. immense   invigorate   inconspicuous   inefficient

2. sophistication   regulation   evaporation   composition

3. merciful   preyed   novelties   various

4. memorize   devise   generalize   satirize

5. eject   exceed   expansion   extinct

210

6. perceive   relief   deceit   receive

7. remoteness   isolation   extremity   maturity

8. evolution   expansion   seclusion   conversion

9. agent   emerge   organism   technology

10. precede   exceed   accede   concede

11. collection   composure   competence   combustion

12. committal   reference   preferring   remittance

13. apprehension   accommodation   admirable   attributable

14. rudeness   resource   demoralize   preserve

15. fancy   contrive   candor   dictate

Number correct _____ (total 15)

Exercise C In these sentences find each misspelled word and write the correct spelling on the line following the sentence.

1. We were advized not to exceed our limitasions.

_____

2. After witnessing Doug's carless mistake, it was difficult to sympathyze with him.

_____

3. The fabric was sewn into an exquisitly provocative evening gown that capturred the elegance of the festivitys.

_____

4. The new club president had a unifing influence on the membership.

_____

5. The scar left by Jim's bicycle accident remained noticable for a few years.

_____

6. Before boarding an airplane for the first time, Agnes had great apprehention.

_____

7. Joanna's two nieces and three nephewes sent her get-well cards.

_____

8. Al dennounced his peers by pointing out their faults.

_____

9. The availability of irigation made the region good for farming.

_____

10. A large varyety of butterflies congregated on the grass outside the school.

   _____

11. The continueus stream of trafic made it virtually impossible to cross the street.

   _____

12. Atmosphereic conditions were such that a tornado was likly to occurr in a matter of hours.

   _____

13. The young girl regreted haveing lost several peices of her puzzle.

   _____

14. Even though it was not our responsibilitie to take care of the pet canary, we felt sorry that it had flown away.

   _____

15. Please exsamine your test booklet before proceding.

   _____

16. Lisa's adtempt to mediate between her two friends ended in complete failure.

   _____

17. The principle attributed the sucess of the fund-raiseer to the students' determinasion.

   _____

18. Jason could not percieve any differents between the identical twins.

   _____

19. Angie relied too heavyly on her brother's advise.

   _____

20. Do you recall the types of exercizes in that training program?

   _____

Number correct _____ (total 35)

Number correct in Handbook _____ (total 410)

Commonly Misspelled Words

abbreviate	description	intelligence	realize
accidentally	desirable	knowledge	recognize
achievement	despair	laboratory	recommend
all right	desperate	lightning	reference
altogether	dictionary	literature	referred
amateur	different	loneliness	rehearse
analyze	disappear	marriage	repetition
anonymous	disappoint	mathematics	representative
answer	discipline	medicine	restaurant
apologize	dissatisfied	minimum	rhythm
appearance	efficient	mischievous	ridiculous
appreciate	eighth	missile	sandwich
appropriate	eligible	misspell	schedule
argument	eliminate	mortgage	scissors
arrangement	embarrass	municipal	separate
associate	emphasize	necessary	sergeant
awkward	enthusiastic	nickel	similar
bargain	environment	ninety	sincerely
beginning	especially	noticeable	sophomore
believe	exaggerate	nuclear	souvenir
bicycle	exhaust	nuisance	specifically
bookkeeper	experience	obstacle	success
bulletin	familiar	occasionally	syllable
bureau	fascinating	occur	sympathy
business	February	opinion	symptom
calendar	financial	opportunity	temperature
campaign	foreign	outrageous	thorough
candidate	fourth	parallel	throughout
certain	fragile	particularly	together
changeable	generally	permanent	tomorrow
characteristic	government	permissible	traffic
column	grammar	persuade	tragedy
committee	guarantee	pleasant	transferred
courageous	guard	pneumonia	truly
courteous	gymnasium	politics	Tuesday
criticize	handkerchief	possess	twelfth
curiosity	height	possibility	undoubtedly
cylinder	humorous	prejudice	unnecessary
dealt	imaginary	privilege	vacuum
decision	immediately	probably	vicinity
definitely	incredible	pronunciation	village
dependent	influence	psychology	weird

Commonly Confused Words

The following section lists words that are commonly confused and misused. Some of these words are homonyms, words that sound similar but have different meanings. Study the words in this list and learn how to use them correctly.

accent (ak′ sent) n.—stress in speech or writing
ascent (ə sent′) n.—act of going up
assent (ə sent′) n.—consent; v.—to accept or agree

accept (ək sept′, ak-) v.—to agree to something or receive something willingly
except (ik sept′) v.—to omit or exclude; prep.—not including

adapt (ə dapt′) v.—to adjust, to make fitting or appropriate
adept (ə dept′) adj.—proficient
adopt (ə däpt′) v.—to choose as one's own, to accept

affect (ə fekt′) v.—to influence, to pretend
affect (af′ ekt) n.—feeling
effect (ə fekt′, i-) n.—result of an action
effect (ə fekt′, i-) v.—to accomplish or to produce a result

all ready adj.—completely prepared
already (ôl red′ ē) adv.—even now; before the given time

any way adj. (any) and n. (way)—in whatever manner
anyway (en′ ē wa′) adv.—regardless

appraise (ə prāz′) v.—to set a value on
apprise (ə prīz′) v.—to inform

bibliography (bib′ lē äg′ rə fē) n.—list of writings on a particular topic
biography (bī äg′ rə fē, bē-) n.—written history of a person's life

bizarre (bi zär′) adj.—odd
bazaar (bə zär′) n.—market, fair

coarse (kôrs) adj.—rough, crude
course (kôrs) n.—route, progression

costume (käs′ tōōm, -tyōōm) n.—special way of dressing
custom (kus′ təm) n.—usual practice or habit

decent (dē′ s'nt) adj.—proper
descent (di sent′) n.—fall, coming down
dissent (di sent′) n.—disagreement; v.—to disagree

desert (dez′ ərt) n.—arid region
desert (di zurt′) v.—to abandon
dessert (di zurt′) n.—sweet course served at the end of a meal

device (di vīs′) n.—a contrivance
devise (di vīz′) v.—to plan

elusive (ə loo′ siv) adj.—hard to catch or understand
illusive (i loo′ siv) adj.—misleading, unreal

emigrate (em′ ə grāt′) v.—to leave a country and take up residence elsewhere
immigrate (im′ ə grāt′) v.—to enter a country to take up residence

farther (fär′ thər) adj.—more distant (refers to space)
further (fur′ thər) adj.—additional (refers to time, quantity, or degree)

flair (fler) n.—natural ability, knack for style
flare (fler) v.—to flame; to erupt; n.—a blaze of light

lay (lā) v.—to set something down or place something
lie (lī) v.—to recline; to tell untruths; n.—an untruth

moral (môr′ əl, mär′-) n.,—lesson; ethic; adj.—relating to right and wrong
morale (mə ral′, mô-) n.—mental state of confidence, enthusiasm

personal (pur′ s'n əl) adj.—private
personnel (pur sə nel′) n.—a body of people, usually employed in an organization

precede (pri sēd′) v.—to go before
proceed (prə sēd′, prō-) v.—to advance; to continue

profit (präf′ it) v. n.—to gain earnings; financial gain on investments
prophet (präf′ it) n.—predictor, fortuneteller

quiet (kwī′ ət) adj.—not noisy; n.—a sense of calm
quit (kwit) v.—to stop
quite (kwīt) adv.—very

step (step) n.—footfall; v.—to move the foot as in walking
steppe (step) n.—large, treeless plain

team (tēm) n.—group of people working together on a project
teem (tēm) v.—to swarm or abound

than (than, then; *unstressed* thən, thən) conj.—word used in comparison
then (then) adv.—at that time, next in order of time

thorough (thur′ ō, -ə) adj.—complete
through (throo) prep.—by means of, from beginning to end; adv.—in one side
and out the other

Glossary

A

abolish (v.) to do away with; to put an end to; p. 151. *Related word*: abolition; p. 157.

absolutely (adv.) positively; completely; p. 100. *Related word*: absolute; p. 106.

abstract (adj.) not easy to understand; theoretical; (n.) summary; (v.) to summarize; p. 160. *Related word*: abstraction; p. 168.

acclaim (n.) praise; approval; (v.) to greet or announce with great approval; p. 62. *Related words*: acclamation, exclamation; p. 68.

acclimate (v.) to get accustomed to a new environment or situation; p. 13.

accommodate (v.) to adjust or adapt to something; to do a favor for; to have space for; p. 62. *Related word*: accommodation; p. 68.

accordingly (adv.) therefore; in a way that is fitting; p. 151. *Related word*: accordance; p. 157.

accustomed (adj.) used to something by regular use or long and repeated experience; customary; habitual; p. 151.

adage (n.) old saying that has been popularly accepted as truth; p. 72.

adapt (v.) to adjust to new circumstances; to make suitable; p. 140. *Related words*: adaptable, adaptation; p. 147.

admirably (adv.) in a manner that deserves praise; p. 62. *Related word*: admire; p. 68.

adorn (v.) to add beauty to; to put decorations on; p. 100. *Related word*: adornment; p. 106.

advocate (v.) to speak in favor of; to defend; (n.) one who argues for a cause; a lawyer; p. 31.

aerial (adj.) of the air; (n.) antenna; p. 72. *Related word*: aerialist; p. 80.

agent (n.) force or substance that produces a result; person or firm that acts for another; p. 140. *Related word*: agency; p. 147.

aggrieved (adj.) troubled; offended; showing grief; p. 119.

agility (n.) ease of movement; p. 72.

ancestral (adj.) pertaining to one's forebears; p. 13. *Related words*: ancestor, ancestry; p. 20.

anticipate (v.) to expect; to realize beforehand; p. 31. *Related word*: anticipation; p. 38.

appall (v.) to shock; to dismay; to horrify; p. 52.

apparently (adv.) seemingly; evidently; according to appearances; p. 52. *Related word*: apparent; p. 59.

apprehend (v.) to capture or arrest; to understand; p. 62. *Related words*: apprehension, comprehension; p. 68.

appropriate (v.) to take for one's own; to set aside for a specific use; (adj.) suitable; proper; p. 109. *Related word*: appropriateness; p. 115.

aspire (v.) to have a great desire; p. 13. *Related word*: aspiration; p. 20.

assemblage (n.) group of persons or things gathered together; p. 100.

assertion (n.) something that is stated positively; declaration; p. 160. *Related word*: assertive; p. 168.

assuage (v.) to ease; to calm; p. 23. *Related word*: assuagement; p. 28.

assume (v.) to take on; to seize; to undertake; to suppose; p. 109. *Related word*: assumption; p. 115.

attribute (n.) characteristic or quality of a person or thing; (v.) to think of as belonging to or resulting from a person or thing; p. 62. *Related word*: attributable; p. 68.

avaricious (adj.) greedy; p. 100. *Related word*: avarice; p. 106.

aversion (n.) distaste; revulsion; loathing; dislike; p. 119. *Related words*: averse, avert; p. 126.

B

befitting (adj.) appropriate; suitable; proper; fitting; p. 119.

brandish (v.) to wave menacingly; p. 23.

buffer (n.) any person or device that serves to prevent a sharp impact between two opposing forces; p. 140.

C

candid (adj.) very honest in speech or writing; informal; p. 151.

characteristic (n.) trait or feature that makes a person or thing different from others; (adj.) distinctive; p. 52. *Related word*: character; p. 59.

circumscribe (v.) to encircle; to limit; p. 31.

circumstance (n.) one of the conditions that determine a course of action; p. 31. *Related word*: circumstantial; p. 38.

collective (adj.) of or pertaining to a group; p. 31. *Related word*: collection; p. 38.

commentary (n.) series of comments or observations; p. 119. *Related word*: comment; p. 126.

competence (n.) ability; fitness; skill; p. 62. *Related word*: competent; p. 68.

component (n.) essential part; element; ingredient; (adj.) serving as one of the parts of a whole; p. 140.

comprise (v.) to consist of; p. 140.

conceal (v.) to hide; to keep secret; p. 72. *Related word*: concealment; p. 80.

conductivity (n.) the property of transmitting heat, electricity, etc.; p. 140. *Related Words with the duc root*: conducive, conduct, deduce; p. 147.

consensus (n.) general agreement; collective opinion; p. 31. *Related word*: consent; p. 38.

constant (adj.) not changing; continual; (n.) anything that does not change; p. 140.

constrain (v.) to force or compel; to hold back by force; p. 151. *Related words with the strain root*: constraint, restrain, restraint; p. 157.

contempt (n.) scorn; disdain; distaste; p.119. *Related word*: contemptible; p. 126.

contrite (adj.) repentent; apologetic; regretful; p. 119. *Related word*: contrition; p. 126.

convert (v.) to change from one form to another; to cause to change from one belief to another; (n.) one who has changed beliefs; p. 140. *Related word*: conversion; p. 147.

crescendo (adj., adv.) gradually increasing in volume or intensity; (n.) gradual increase in volume or intensity; p. 13.

cycle (n.) series of changes or events that repeat themselves in the same order; (v.) to occur in cycles; p. 72. *Related word*: cyclical; p. 80.

cynical (adj.) scornful of the motives of others; p. 23. *Related word*: cynic; p. 28.

D

dandy (n.) man who pays too much attention to his appearance and dress; fop; (adj.) first-rate; p. 119.

dauntless (adj.) fearless; brave; p. 100. *Related word*: undaunted; p. 106.

deadpan (adj.) showing no feelings; expressionless; p. 52.

decade (n.) period of ten years; p. 52.

defiant (adj.) rebellious; provocative; disobedient; p. 119. *Related word*: defy; p. 126.

demoralize (v.) to weaken the spirit; p. 23.

density (n.) number per unit; thickness; p.140. *Related word*: dense; p. 147.

deny (v.) to declare that something is untrue; to contradict; p. 52. *Related word*: denial; p. 59.

dependent (adj.) relying upon something or someone else; (n.) person who relies on another for support; p. 13. *Related word*: independent; p. 20.

deplorable (adj.) regrettable; very bad; wretched; p. 160. *Related word*: deplore; p. 168.

depreciate (v.) to decrease in value; p. 31. *Related word*: depreciation; p. 38.

depress (v.) to press down; to sadden; to decrease the activity of; p. 109. *Related words with the press root*: compression, depression, expression, impression; p. 115.

depth (n.) the quality of being deep; p. 62.

derive (v.) to receive from a source; to get; to obtain; p. 151.

despair (n.) lack of hope; (v.) to lose all hope; p. 23. *Related word*: desperation; p. 28.

despite (prep.) in spite of; p. 13. *Related word*: spite; p. 20.

despotism (n.) rule by someone with absolute power; p. 151. *Related words*: despot, despotic; p. 157.

devotion (n.) loyalty; dedication; p. 160. *Related words*: devote, devotee; p. 168.

dictate (v.) to command or order; to speak or read aloud for someone else to write down; p. 151. *Related word*: dictator; p. 157.

dignify (v.) to add to the prestige of; p.23. *Related word*: dignity; p. 28.

discharge (n.) release; legal order for release; (v.) to release; p. 140.

disfigure (v.) to hurt the appearance or attractiveness of; p. 100. *Related word*: disfigurement; p. 106.

dispose (v.) to make willing; to incline; to prepare; p. 151.

dispute (n.) argument; debate; (v.) to question the truth of; p. 31. *Related word*: disputable; p. 38.

distinctly (adv.) unmistakably; differently; p. 109. *Related words with the* stinct *root*: extinct, instinct; p. 115.

disturb (v.) to break up the quiet of; to annoy; to upset emotionally; p. 100. *Related word*: perturb; p. 106.

E

efficiency (n.) the ability to produce a desired effect with the least effort or waste; p. 62. *Related words*: efficient, inefficient; p. 68.

element (n.) essential part; p. 140. *Related words*: elemental, elementary; p. 147.

enable (v.) to make possible; p. 31.

encompass (v.) to surround or encircle; to include; p. 31.

endow (v.) to provide with some talent or quality; to give money or property; p. 100. *Related word*: endowment; p. 106.

engulf (v.) to overwhelm; to surround totally; p. 23.

ennoble (v.) to add to the honor of; to dignify; p. 23. *Related word*: nobility; p. 28.

enthusiastic (adj.) having intense interest; p. 62. *Related word*: enthusiasm; p. 68

entitle (v.) to give a name or right to; p.151. *Related word*: entitlement; p. 157.

epoch (n.) period of time marked by noteworthy events; p. 109.

evaporation (n.) the process of changing from a liquid or solid to a gas; the process of removing moisture so as to get a concentrated product; p. 140. *Related word*: evaporate; p. 147.

evince (v.) to make clear; p. 151. *Related word with the* vince *root*: invincible; p. 157.

evolve (v.) to develop gradually; to slowly undergo change or transformation; p. 13.

excel (v.) to be or do better than others; to surpass; p. 52. *Related word*: excellent; p.59.

excess (adj.) extra or surplus; (n.) surplus; action or conduct that goes beyond the usual limit; lack of moderation; p. 72. *Related word with the* cede *root*: excessive; p. 80.

exile (n.) a living away from one's country or community because one has been or feels forced to leave; (v.) to force a person to leave his or her country; p. 160.

expanse (n.) large, open area; p. 72.

expediency (n.) the quality of being convenient or advantageous; p. 72. *Related word*: expeditious; p. 80.

exquisite (adj.) beautifully made or designed; p. 13.

extend (v.) to stretch out; to prolong; p. 52. *Related word*: extension; p. 59.

extreme (adj.) farthest in any direction; very intense; radical; (n.) the greatest degree; p. 13. *Related word*: extremity; p. 20.

exuberant (adj.) full of high spirits; p. 13.

F

faculty (n.) skill; the teachers in a school; p. 160.

fervent (adj.) having great emotion; p. 13.

fidelity (n.) loyalty; devotion; p. 160. *Related word*: infidelity; p. 168.

finesse (n.) the ability to handle difficult situations skillfully; p. 62.

flourish (v.) to grow vigorously; (n.) sweeping movement; p. 100.

fluster (v.) to upset; to disconcert; to agitate; to befuddle; p. 52.

forage (v.) to search for food or provisions; (n.) food for animals; p. 72.

foretell (v.) to tell beforehand; to predict; p. 13. *Related words with the* fore- *prefix*: forecast, forerunner, foresight; p. 20.

forethought (n.) prior consideration or thought; anticipation; p. 52.

frayed (adj.) worn; ragged; p. 119. *Related word*: fray; p. 126.

G

gradually (adv.) little by little; p. 109. *Related word*: graduation; p. 115.

gratitude (n.) thankfulness; p. 62. *Related word*: grateful; p. 68.

grotesque (adj.) strange; distorted; p. 23. *Related word*: grotesqueness; p. 28.

H

habitual (adj.) usual; customary; p. 119. *Related word*: habit; p. 126.

humane (adj.) kind; civilized; merciful; p. 160. *Related word*: humanity; p. 168.

I

immaculate (adj.) perfectly clean; perfectly correct; without sin; p. 160.

immense (adj.) huge; limitless; p. 109. *Related word*: immensity; p. 115.

impede (v.) to block; to obstruct the way of; p. 23. *Related word*: impediment; 28.

impel (v.) to compel or urge; to push forward; p. 151. *Related words with the* pel *root*: compel, dispel, expel, repel; p. 157.

impending (adj.) about to take place; menacing; p. 13.

impertinence (n.) bold rudeness; lack of respect; insolence; p. 119. *Related word*: pertinent; p. 126.

implement (n.) tool; utensil; (v.) to accomplish; p. 160. *Related word*: implementation; p. 168.

incognito (adv., adj.) with one's identity concealed; (n.) a person appearing or living with his or her identity concealed; p. 160.

inconspicuous (adj.) attracting little attention; difficult to see; p. 72.

incredible (adj.) unbelievable; p. 13. *Related words with the* cred *root*: credibility, credible, credulous, creed, incredibility; p. 20.

index (n.) ratio of one amount to another; indication; sign; (v.) to make an index; p. 140.

indispensable (adj.) essential; absolutely necessary; p. 119. *Related words*: dispensable, dispense; p. 126.

inert (adj.) unable to move or act; p. 23. *Related word*: inertia; p. 28.

inevitably (adv.) unavoidably; p. 160.

ingenious (adj.) clever; displaying imagination or inventiveness; p. 13. *Related word*: genius; p. 20.

ingratitude (n.) ungratefulness; p. 160. *Related word*: gracious; p. 168.

institute (v.) to set up or establish; to start; (n.) organization or school specializing in the promotion or teaching of art, music, science, technical subjects, or research; established principle or custom; p. 151. *Related word*: institution; p. 157.

intolerable (adj.) unbearable; p. 160. *Related words*: intolerance, tolerable, tolerate; p. 168.

invariably (adv.) uniformly; constantly; p. 151. *Related word*: variable; p. 157.

involuntary (adj.) unwilled; spontaneous; instinctive; p. 119. *Related words*: voluntary, volunteer; p. 126.

irony (n.) occurrence or result that is opposite to what was expected; p. 31. *Related word*: ironical; p. 38.

isolate (v.) to place alone; p. 109. *Related word*: isolation; p. 115.

K

keynote (v.) to give the basic idea or set the dominant tone; (n.) main idea of a speech; (adj.) pertaining to a speech setting forth the principles of a program; p. 72.

L

liable (adj.) responsible; likely; p. 72. *Related word*: liability; p. 80.

lucrative (adj.) profitable; p. 100.

M

magnificent (adj.) outstanding; lavish; p. 23. *Related words*: magnificence, magnify; p. 28

maintenance (n.) upkeep; means of support; p. 72. *Related word*: maintain; p. 80.

majestic (adj.) grand; stately; dignified; p. 72. *Related word*: majesty; p. 80.

meager (adj.) deficient in quantity; scanty; thin; p. 13.

menace (n.) threat; annoying person; (v.) to threaten; p. 23.

metamorphosis (n.) change of form, shape, structure, or substance; p. 109.

militant (adj.) aggressive; (n.) one who is aggressive, especially in politics; p. 31. *Related word*: military; p. 38.

militia (n.) any army composed of citizens rather than professional soldiers; p. 100. *Related words*: militant, military; p. 106.

minimize (v.) to reduce to the smallest possible amount; to lessen; p. 23. *Related word*: minimum; p. 28.

misconception (n.) incorrect understanding; p. 23. *Related word*: concept; p. 28.

misdemeanor (n.) minor offense; misbehavior; misconduct; p. 119. *Related word*: demeanor; p. 126.

monitor (v.) to watch or check on; (n.) one who watches or warns; device used for this purpose; p. 140.

monosyllable (n.) word of one syllable; p. 160.

morality (n.) set of ideas about right and wrong; p. 31. *Related word*: moral; p. 38.

mortal (n.) human being; (adj.) of this world; deadly; p. 62. *Related words*: immortality, mortality; p. 68.

N

native (adj.) related to the place of one's birth; belonging to a locality by birth, production, or growth; (n.) person born in a certain place or country; p. 109. *Related word*: nature; p. 115.

novel (adj.) new; different; fresh; unusual; (n.) a relatively long prose narrative with plot and characters; p. 109. *Related words*: novelist, novelty; p. 115.

O

offensive (adj.) objectionable; disagreeable; annoying; unpleasant; p. 119. *Related word*: inoffensive; p. 126.

ordeal (n.) harsh or trying experience; severe test; nightmare; p. 52.

organism (n.) anything resembling a living thing in its structure or function; p. 140. *Related words*: organ, organic; p. 147.

ostentation (n.) showy display; p. 160. *Related word*: ostentatious; p. 168.

overtake (v.) to take by surprise; to catch up with; p. 23.

P

peerless (adj.) without equal; p. 100. *Related word*: peer; p. 106.

perception (n.) awareness; understanding; p. 160. *Related words*: perceive, perceptible, perceptive; p. 168.

perpetuate (v.) to cause to be remembered for a long time; to preserve from extinction; p. 31. *Related word*: perpetual; p. 38.

perplexity (n.) confusion; bewilderment; p. 119. *Related word*: perplex; p. 126.

precipitate (v.) to cause to happen earlier than expected; to condense and fall as rain, etc.; p. 13. *Related word*: precipitation; p. 20.

predator (n.) one who lives by killing and feeding upon other animals; a person who preys upon other people; p. 72. *Related word*: predacious; p. 80.

prescribe (v.) to order a medicine or treatment; to set down a rule or direction; p. 72. *Related words with the* scribe *root*: prescription, subscription; p. 80.

principality (n.) territory ruled by a prince; p. 100.

procession (n.) a number of persons moving forward in an orderly way; p. 100. *Related word*: proceed; p. 106.

profile (n.) outline; side view of the face; short biographical sketch; (v.) to sketch or write briefly about; p. 109.

profound (adj.) absolute; deep; far-reaching; deep; p. 23. *Related word*: profundity; p. 28.

prominent (adj.) widely known; immediately noticeable; p. 31. *Related word*: prominence; p. 38.

property (n.) characteristic; possessions, especially land or real estate; p. 140. *Related word*: proprietor; p. 147.

prosperous (adj.) well-to-do; successful; p. 100.

provision (n.) something provided for the future; p. 62.

prudence (n.) the quality of being cautious and sensible; careful management; p. 151. *Related word:* prudent; p. 157.

pursuit (n.) a following or seeking of something; career or interest to which one devotes oneself; p. 151. *Related word:* pursuance; p. 157.

R

rancor (n.) bitterness; resentment; hostility; p. 119.

reap (v.) to gather a harvest by cutting; to gain or obtain, as a reward; p. 109.

recognition (n.) acknowledgment; gratitude; p. 72. *Related word:* cognizant; p. 80.

regulation (n.) rule or law; p. 160. *Related word:* regulate; p. 168.

remote (adj.) far off; hidden; slight; p. 109. *Related word:* remoteness; p. 115.

renounce (v.) to give up; to disown; p. 109. *Related words with the* nounce *root:* announce, denounce; p. 115.

reproach (v.) to accuse of a fault; (n.) shame; p. 62. *Related word:* irreproachable; p. 68.

rife (adj.) abundant; well-supplied; p. 100.

routinely (adv.) regularly; frequently; typically; p. 52. *Related word:* routine; p. 59.

S

salinity (n.) amount of salt in something; p. 140. *Related word:* saline; p. 147.

satire (n.) literary work in which wit is used to expose foolishness or wickedness; p. 31. *Related word:* satirize; p. 38.

scrupulously (adv.) in a conscientious and honest manner; p. 62. *Related word:* scruple; p. 68.

seclude (v.) to isolate; to make private; p. 72. *Related word:* seclusion; p. 80.

secretive (adj.) keeping one's thoughts and feelings to oneself; p. 72.

sediment (n.) matter that settles to the bottom of a liquid; p. 140.

self-evident (adj.) needing no proof; obvious; apparent; plain; p. 151.

sensibility (n.) awareness; capacity for physical sensation; p. 160. *Related word:* sensible; p. 168.

sheepishly (adv.) in an embarrassed way; p. 23.

shudder (v.) to shake or tremble; (n.) trembling; spasm; p. 119.

sieve (n.) utensil with many small holes, used for straining; strainer; sifter; colander; p. 160.

simper (v.) to smirk; to snicker; to smile in a silly manner; (n.) a silly, unnatural smile; p. 100.

solitude (n.) isolation; remoteness; p. 100. *Related word:* solitary; p. 106.

sophisticated (adj.) worldly; not simple; complex; p. 62. *Related word:* sophistication; p. 68.

splendor (n.) brilliance; magnificence; p. 23. *Related word:* splendid; p. 28.

staid (adj.) serious or reserved in behavior; p. 23.

stake (n.) money risked; wager; bet; (v.) to mark the boundaries of; to bet; p. 52.

stalwart (adj.) sturdy; well-built; brave; (n.) person who is sturdy or brave; p. 100.

stealth (n.) secret, sneaky, or quiet action; p. 72. *Related word:* stealthy; p. 80.

stereotype (n.) fixed idea or popular conception; (v.) to develop an unvarying idea about something; p. 31.

stolid (adj.) unemotional; unexcitable; impassive; p. 52.

stun (v.) to shock; to astonish; to flabbergast; p. 52. *Related word:* stunning; p. 59.

suave (adj.) smoothly polite or gracious; polished; charming; p. 119.

subject (v.) to cause to experience; to put through; (n.) topic; course of study; p. 52. *Related word:* subjective; p. 59.

sufficient (adj.) as much as is needed; p. 62.

suffrage (n.) right to vote; p. 13. *Related word:* suffragette; p. 20.

suitor (n.) man courting a woman; beau; boyfriend; p. 52.

sunder (v.) to break apart; to split; p. 109. *Related word:* asunder; p. 115.

synopsis (n.) summary; short outline; p. 119.

system (n.) method; set of things that form a whole; p. 140. *Related word:* systematic; p. 147.

T

tact (n.) skill in dealing with people by saying or doing the right thing; p. 62. *Related word*: tactful; p. 68.

technology (n.) the study of industrial arts and applied sciences; p. 140. *Related words*: technician, technological; p. 147.

tedious (adj.) boring; dull; uninteresting; p. 52. *Related word*: tedium; p. 59.

thrive (v.) to prosper; to grow vigorously; p. 13.

thrust (v.) to push; to shove; to force; to drive; p. 109.

transient (adj.) temporary; passing quickly; staying for only a short time; (n.) one who stays for only a short time; p. 151. *Related word*: transition; p. 157.

tyranny (n.) government by an absolute ruler; harsh and unjust government; p. 151. *Related word*: tyrannical; p. 157.

U

unity (n.) the state of being one; singleness; p. 31. *Related words with the* uni *root*: unify, unison, unit; p. 38.

unmercifully (adv.) cruelly; p. 62. *Related word*: mercy; p. 68.

unsung (adj.) not honored, celebrated, or praised; p. 13.

urgency (n.) pressing importance; p. 31. *Related word*: urgent; p. 38.

usurpation (n.) unlawful or violent taking of power; p. 151. *Related word*: usurp; p. 157.

V

vary (v.) to change; to make different; p. 109.

vibrant (adj.) spirited; energetic; vivacious; p. 52. *Related words*: vibrate, vibrato; p. 59.

vigorous (adj.) strong; energetic; p. 100. *Related words*: invigorate, vigor; p. 106.

villa (n.) country estate; p. 109.

virtually (adv.) for all practical purposes; p. 62. *Related word*: virtue; p. 68.

virtue (n.) the quality of moral excellence; a particular beneficial quality; p. 31. *Related word*: virtuous; p. 38.

W

whim (n.) sudden notion; fancy; impulse; p. 52. *Related word*: whimsical; p. 59.

Y

yield (v.) to grant or concede; to surrender in defeat; to give in return; (n.) amount produced; earnings received from an investment; p. 109.

Pronunciation Key

Symbol	Key Words		Symbol	Key Words
a	ask, fat, parrot		b	bed, fable, dub
ā	ape, date, play		d	dip, beadle, had
ä	ah, car, father		f	fall, after, off
			g	get, haggle, dog
e	elf, ten, berry		h	he, ahead, hotel
ē	even, meet, money		j	joy, agile, badge
			k	kill, tackle, bake
i	is, hit, mirror		l	let, yellow, ball
ī	ice, bite, high		m	met, camel, trim
ō	open, tone, go		n	not, flannel, ton
ô	all, horn, law		p	put, apple, tap
o͞o	ooze, tool, crew		r	red, port, dear
oo	look, pull, moor		s	sell, castle, pass
yo͞o	use, cute, few		t	top, cattle, hat
yoo	united, cure, globule		v	vat, hovel, have
			w	will, always, swear
oi	oil, point, toy		y	yet, onion, yard
ou	out, crowd, plow		z	zebra, dazzle, haze
u	up, cut, color		ch	chin, catcher, arch
ʉr	urn, fur, deter		sh	she, cushion, dash
ə	a in ago		th	thin, nothing, truth
	e in agent		zh	azure, leisure
	i in sanity		ŋ	ring, anger, drink
	o in comply		′	able (a′ b'l)
	u in focus		′ ′	expedition (ek′ spə dish′ ən)
ər	perhaps, murder			

Pronunciation key and some glossary entries reprinted from *Webster's New World Dictionary*, Student Edition. Copyright © 1981, 1976 by Simon & Schuster. Used by permission.

Inventory Test

These are all the target words in the book. Why not see how many you think you already know . . . or don't know?

- If you're sure *you know the word, mark the* **Y** *("yes") circle.*
- If you think you *might* know it, mark the **?** *(question mark) circle.*
- If you have no idea *what it means, mark the* **N** *("no") circle.*

Y	?	N	
○	○	○	abolish
○	○	○	absolutely
○	○	○	abstract
○	○	○	acclaim
○	○	○	acclimate
○	○	○	accommodate
○	○	○	accordingly
○	○	○	accustomed
○	○	○	adage
○	○	○	adapt
○	○	○	admirably
○	○	○	adorn
○	○	○	advocate
○	○	○	aerial
○	○	○	agent
○	○	○	aggrieved
○	○	○	agility
○	○	○	ancestral
○	○	○	anticipate
○	○	○	appall
○	○	○	apparently
○	○	○	apprehend
○	○	○	appropriate
○	○	○	aspire
○	○	○	assemblage
○	○	○	assertion
○	○	○	assuage
○	○	○	assume
○	○	○	attribute
○	○	○	avaricious
○	○	○	aversion
○	○	○	befitting
○	○	○	brandish
○	○	○	buffer
○	○	○	candid
○	○	○	characteristic
○	○	○	circumscribe
○	○	○	circumstance
○	○	○	collective
○	○	○	commentary

That's the first 40.

Y	?	N	
○	○	○	competence
○	○	○	component
○	○	○	comprise
○	○	○	conceal
○	○	○	conductivity
○	○	○	consensus
○	○	○	constant
○	○	○	constrain
○	○	○	contempt
○	○	○	contrite
○	○	○	convert
○	○	○	crescendo
○	○	○	cycle
○	○	○	cynical
○	○	○	dandy
○	○	○	dauntless
○	○	○	deadpan
○	○	○	decade
○	○	○	defiant
○	○	○	demoralize

You're making progress.

Y	?	N	
○	○	○	density
○	○	○	deny
○	○	○	dependent
○	○	○	deplorable
○	○	○	depreciate
○	○	○	depress
○	○	○	depth
○	○	○	derive
○	○	○	despair
○	○	○	despite
○	○	○	despotism
○	○	○	devotion
○	○	○	dictate
○	○	○	dignify
○	○	○	discharge
○	○	○	disfigure
○	○	○	dispose
○	○	○	dispute
○	○	○	distinctly
○	○	○	disturb

Y	?	N	
○	○	○	efficiency
○	○	○	element
○	○	○	enable
○	○	○	encompass
○	○	○	endow
○	○	○	engulf
○	○	○	ennoble
○	○	○	enthusiastic
○	○	○	entitle
○	○	○	epoch
○	○	○	evaporation
○	○	○	evince
○	○	○	evolve
○	○	○	excel
○	○	○	excess
○	○	○	exile
○	○	○	expanse
○	○	○	expediency
○	○	○	exquisite
○	○	○	extend
○	○	○	extreme
○	○	○	exuberant
○	○	○	faculty
○	○	○	fervent
○	○	○	fidelity
○	○	○	finesse
○	○	○	flourish
○	○	○	fluster
○	○	○	forage
○	○	○	foretell
○	○	○	forethought
○	○	○	frayed
○	○	○	gradually
○	○	○	gratitude
○	○	○	grotesque
○	○	○	habitual
○	○	○	humane
○	○	○	immaculate
○	○	○	immense
○	○	○	impede

Take a break!

Y	?	N		Y	?	N		Y	?	N	
○	○	○	impel	○	○	○	ordeal	○	○	○	sieve
○	○	○	impending	○	○	○	organism	○	○	○	simper
○	○	○	impertinence	○	○	○	ostentation	○	○	○	solitude
○	○	○	implement	○	○	○	overtake	○	○	○	sophisticated
○	○	○	incognito	○	○	○	peerless	○	○	○	splendor
○	○	○	inconspicuous	○	○	○	perception	○	○	○	staid
○	○	○	incredible	○	○	○	perpetuate	○	○	○	stake
○	○	○	index	○	○	○	perplexity	○	○	○	stalwart
○	○	○	indispensable	○	○	○	precipitate	○	○	○	stealth
○	○	○	inert	○	○	○	predator	○	○	○	stereotype
○	○	○	inevitably	○	○	○	prescribe	○	○	○	stolid
○	○	○	ingenious	○	○	○	principality	○	○	○	stun
○	○	○	ingratitude	○	○	○	procession	○	○	○	suave
○	○	○	institute	○	○	○	profile	○	○	○	subject
○	○	○	intolerable	○	○	○	profound	○	○	○	sufficient
○	○	○	invariably	○	○	○	prominent	○	○	○	suffrage
○	○	○	involuntary	○	○	○	property	○	○	○	suitor
○	○	○	irony	○	○	○	prosperous	○	○	○	sunder
○	○	○	isolate	○	○	○	provision	○	○	○	synopsis
○	○	○	keynote	○	○	○	prudence	○	○	○	system
○	○	○	liable	○	○	○	pursuit				*Only 20 more.*
○	○	○	lucrative	○	○	○	rancor	○	○	○	tact
○	○	○	magnificent	○	○	○	reap	○	○	○	technology
○	○	○	maintenance	○	○	○	recognition	○	○	○	tedious
○	○	○	majestic	○	○	○	regulation	○	○	○	thrive
○	○	○	meager	○	○	○	remote	○	○	○	thrust
○	○	○	menace	○	○	○	renounce	○	○	○	transient
○	○	○	metamorphosis				*This list will end soon.*	○	○	○	tyranny
○	○	○	militant	○	○	○	reproach	○	○	○	unity
○	○	○	militia	○	○	○	rife	○	○	○	unmercifully
○	○	○	minimize	○	○	○	routinely	○	○	○	unsung
○	○	○	misconception	○	○	○	salinity	○	○	○	urgency
○	○	○	misdemeanor	○	○	○	satire	○	○	○	usurpation
○	○	○	monitor	○	○	○	scrupulously	○	○	○	vary
○	○	○	monosyllable	○	○	○	seclude	○	○	○	vibrant
○	○	○	morality	○	○	○	secretive	○	○	○	vigorous
○	○	○	mortal	○	○	○	sediment	○	○	○	villa
			Half the alphabet.	○	○	○	self-evident	○	○	○	virtually
○	○	○	native	○	○	○	sensibility	○	○	○	virtue
○	○	○	novel	○	○	○	sheepishly	○	○	○	whim
○	○	○	offensive	○	○	○	shudder	○	○	○	yield

Congratulations!

That was 240 words. How many of them *don't* you know? Highlight any words you marked **N**, and pay special attention to them as you work through the book. You'll soon know them all!

Strategies for Discovering Word Meaning

Use What You Already Know

There are many ways to get information about what an unfamiliar word might mean.

- It may contain a familiar **whole word**.
- It may be a **compound** of familiar words put together.
- You may recognize the **root**.
- You may recognize a **prefix** or **suffix**.
- There may be **context clues** to the meaning.

Try Everything

When you see an unfamiliar word, use every trick you can think of. You may be surprised to discover how useful what you already know can be. Take a look at how this can work with the word *enfeeblement* in the sentence, "She resented her enfeeblement."

	THOUGHT PROCESS	
enfeeblement	Since *resent* means "to feel hurt about," *enfeeblement* seems to be something bad.	**a context clue**
en • feeble • ment	I see *feeble* in there. Doesn't it mean "weak"?	**a whole word**
en • feeblement	Hmm . . . *en-* like in *endear, enlarge, enrage.* So it means something like "to make" or "to cause."	**a familiar prefix**
enfeeble • ment	That ending is common . . . *enjoy, enjoyment* . . . *measure, measurement.* It creates nouns.	**a familiar suffix**
	Noun. Feeble. To make. . . . So, she resented being made weak!	

Try It Yourself

_____ 1. popularize (think about *popular* and *equalize*)
     a. to succeed   b. to make lived in   c. to make liked by most

_____ 2. overstate (think about *over* and *state*)
     a. to exaggerate   b. to write down   c. to predict

_____ 3. quantify (think about *quantity* and *glorify*)
     a. pour   b. measure   c. send back

_____ 4. discord (think about *disloyalty* and *cordial*)
     a. restlessness   b. disagreement   c. lack of protection

_____ 5. ineffectual (think about *inexact*, *effect*, and *factual*)
     a. useless   b. hopeful   c. accidental

Score Yourself!   *The answers are upside-down on the right.*   Number correct: _____   3. b, 1. c, 5. a, 4. b, 2. a

226

UNIT 1   Test Yourself

Part A   Synonyms

Write the letter of the word that is closest in meaning to the capitalized word.

_____ 1. MEAGER: (A) scanty   (B) main   (B) bad   (C) willing

_____ 2. EVOLVE: (A) relate   (B) decline   (C) replace   (D) develop

_____ 3. EXQUISITE: (A) plain   (B) handmade   (C) gorgeous   (D) decorative

_____ 4. INGENIOUS: (A) intelligent (B) imaginative (C) shy   (D) necessary

_____ 5. EXTREME: (A) rare   (B) intense   (C) rapid   (D) complete

_____ 6. FERVENT: (A) passionate (B) generous   (C) loud   (D) cold-hearted

_____ 7. PRECIPITATE: (A) recall   (B) moisten   (C) trigger   (D) draft

_____ 8. THRIVE: (A) wither   (B) succeed   (C) decay   (D) remain

_____ 9. FORETELL: (A) declare   (B) occur   (C) predict   (D) warn

_____ 10. UNSUNG: (A) ridiculed   (B) silent   (C) downcast   (D) ignored

_____ 11. IMPENDING: (A) approaching (B) unexpected (C) surprising (D) delayed

_____ 12. INCREDIBLE: (A) careless   (B) wrong   (C) unbelievable (D) lucky

Part B   Applying Meaning

Write the letter of the best answer.

_____ 13. To have a picnic <u>despite</u> rainy weather means to have it
a. anyway.   b. later.   c. canceled.   d. because of the rain.

_____ 14. <u>Ancestral</u> traditions are those that came from
a. the imagination.   b. past generations.   c. religious beliefs.   d. other countries.

_____ 15. Generally speaking, all of the following have <u>suffrage</u> in the United States EXCEPT
a. adults.   b. racial minorities.   c. children.   d. citizens.

_____ 16. As orchestra members reach a <u>crescendo</u>, they play more
a. slowly.   b. skillfully.   c. quietly.   d. loudly.

_____ 17. An animal that is usually <u>dependent</u> on human beings is a
a. hornet.   b. cougar.   c. cat.   d. monkey.

_____ 18. The best way to <u>acclimate</u> yourself to a new house is to
a. redecorate it.   b. live in it.   c. get insurance.   d. insulate it.

_____ 19. <u>Exuberant</u> children are likely to
a. cry.   b. be sassy.   c. shout.   d. sigh.

_____ 20. To <u>aspire</u> to something is to
a. want it.   b. accept it.   c. give it up.   d. predict it.

Score Yourself!   *The answers are on page 239.*   Number correct: _____   Part A: _____   Part B: _____

UNIT 2   Test Yourself

Part A   Recognizing Meaning

Write the letter of the word or phrase that is closest in meaning to the word or words in italics.

_____ 1. in complete *despair*
   a. hopelessness   c. exhaustion
   b. discomfort   d. outrage

_____ 2. to *overtake* the leader
   a. check on   c. catch up to
   b. trail behind   d. knock down

_____ 3. a very *cynical* attitude
   a. untrusting   c. sympathetic
   b. easygoing   d. confident

_____ 4. the most *grotesque* mask
   a. delightful   c. cheaply made
   b. handmade   d. horribly odd

_____ 5. to *demoralize* their supporters
   a. encourage   c. be critical of
   b. dishearten   d. express faith in

_____ 6. to *assuage* their concerns
   a. make known   c. take note of
   b. increase   d. relieve

_____ 7. the car was *inert*
   a. hard to move   c. slow-moving
   b. unmoving   d. easily moved

_____ 8. *ennobled by* their deeds
   a. ashamed of   c. made clear by
   b. honored by   d. made rich by

_____ 9. *impeded* on all sides
   a. assisted   c. blocked
   b. developed   d. unreachable

_____ 10. to *minimize* her accomplishment
   a. exaggerate   c. make little of
   b. undo   d. ignore

_____ 11. to *dignify* the proceedings
   a. justify   c. interfere with
   b. lengthen   d. add honor to

_____ 12. a common *misconception*
   a. wrong idea   c. lie
   b. statement   d. evil deed

_____ 13. *engulfed* in troubles
   a. free of   c. used to
   b. drowning in   d. angry about

_____ 14. to *brandish* a sword
   a. mark   c. carry
   b. raise proudly   d. wave threateningly

Part B   Synonyms

Write the letter of the word that is closest in meaning to the capitalized word.

_____ 15. SHEEPISHLY: (A) quietly   (B) embarrassedly   (C) wishfully   (D) warmly

_____ 16. STAID: (A) riotous   (B) growing   (C) serious   (D) angry

_____ 17. MAGNIFICENT: (A) royal   (B) numerous   (C) enlarged   (D) fabulous

_____ 18. SPLENDOR: (A) glory   (B) quantity   (C) impression   (D) truth

_____ 19. PROFOUND: (A) thorough   (B) noticeable   (C) surprising   (D) useful

_____ 20. MENACE: (A) ambition   (B) worry   (C) doubt   (D) danger

---

Score Yourself!   *The answers are on page 239.*   Number correct: _____   Part A: _____   Part B: _____

228

UNIT 3 Test Yourself

Part A Matching Definitions

Match each word on the left with its definition on the right. Write the letter of the definition in the blank.

_____ 1. satire

_____ 2. unity

_____ 3. enable

_____ 4. irony

_____ 5. militant

_____ 6. stereotype

_____ 7. urgency

_____ 8. prominent

_____ 9. perpetuate

_____ 10. depreciate

_____ 11. virtue

_____ 12. collective

a. pressing importance

b. a fixed idea or popular notion

c. to decrease in value

d. the state of being one; oneness

e. the quality of moral excellence; particular positive quality

f. to make possible

g. of or relating to a group

h. aggressive in support of a cause; eager to fight

i. to cause to continue or be remembered for a long time

j. a literary work in which wit is used to expose foolishness

k. widely known; immediately noticeable

l. an occurrence or result that is the opposite of what might be expected

Part B Synonyms

Write the letter of the word that is closest in meaning to the capitalized word.

_____ 13. MORALITY: (A) victory   (B) carefulness (C) patience   (D) goodness

_____ 14. CIRCUMSTANCE: (A) variety   (B) situation   (C) area   (D) posture

_____ 15. CONSENSUS: (A) agreement (B) count   (C) reasoning (D) opposition

_____ 16. ANTICIPATE: (A) understand (B) expect   (C) fear   (D) overlook

_____ 17. DISPUTE: (A) harmony   (B) fame   (C) conflict   (D) goal

_____ 18. ADVOCATE: (A) challenge (B) judge   (C) defend   (D) rule

_____ 19. ENCOMPASS: (A) surround   (B) measure   (C) locate   (D) open

_____ 20. CIRCUMSCRIBE: (A) develop   (B) release   (C) avoid   (D) restrict

---

Score Yourself!   *The answers are on page 239.*   Number correct: _____   Part A: _____   Part B: _____

UNIT 5   Test Yourself

Part A   Applying Meaning
Write the letter of the best answer.

_____ 1. Things that often <u>extend</u> across fences are
    a. backyards.   b. gates.   c. neighbors.   d. tree branches.

_____ 2. A person who is <u>subjected</u> to questioning is one who
    a. is curious.   b. can't answer.   c. must undergo it.   d. likes quizzes.

_____ 3. An example of work that is <u>tedious</u> is
    a. brain surgery.   b. fighting fires.   c. spying.   d. scrubbing floors.

_____ 4. When a friend gives a <u>deadpan</u> reaction, he or she is showing
    a. panic.   b. no expression.   c. great sadness.   d. mild amusement.

_____ 5. Which of the following represents a <u>decade</u>?
    a. 1100-2100   b. 1492-1493   c. 1891-1900   d. the time between elections

_____ 6. If a piece of news <u>stuns</u> you, you are most likely to
    a. gasp.   b. giggle.   c. cheer.   d. yawn.

_____ 7. Actions taken without <u>forethought</u> are always
    a. unplanned.   b. unnecessary.   c. pointless.   d. regrettable.

_____ 8. A statement that is <u>apparently</u> true is one that
    a. is true.   b. is not true.   c. cannot be proven.   d. seems true.

Part B   Recognizing Meaning
Write the letter of the word or phrase that is closest in meaning to the word or words in italics.

_____ 9. to *excel at* math
    a. fail   c. be tops in
    b. do okay at   d. make use of

_____ 10. to *appall* his parents
    a. dismay   c. thrill
    b. satisfy   d. obey

_____ 11. raised the *stake*
    a. profit   c. possibility
    b. bet   d. issue

_____ 12. to *fluster* her opponent
    a. support   c. confuse
    b. deceive   d. praise

_____ 13. turned into *an ordeal*
    a. boredom   c. a huge event
    b. a good time   d. an awful time

_____ 14. efforts to *deny* their claim
    a. prove   c. cover up
    b. contradict   d. disregard

_____ 15. performed *routinely*
    a. quietly   c. in a dull way
    b. as usual   d. spectacularly

_____ 16. a note from her *suitor*
    a. best friend   c. lawyer
    b. dressmaker   d. sweetheart

_____ 17. a *characteristic* complaint
    a. loud   c. bad-tempered
    b. typical   d. humorous

_____ 18. a very *stolid* manner
    a. undisturbed   c. overly proud
    b. unforgiving   d. phony

_____ 19. a rather *vibrant* person
    a. lively   c. memorable
    b. unpleasant   d. disliked

_____ 20. based on a *whim*
    a. command   c. sudden notion
    b. mistake   d. long-time plan

Score Yourself!   *The answers are on page 239.*   Number correct: _____   Part A: _____   Part B: _____

UNIT 6   Test Yourself

Part A   Matching Definitions

Match each word on the left with its definition on the right. Write the letter of the definition in the blank.

_____ 1. unmercifully   a. a human being

_____ 2. enthusiastic   b. cruelly

_____ 3. gratitude   c. having intense interest

_____ 4. attribute   d. intensity; extreme degree

_____ 5. sophisticated   e. thankfulness

_____ 6. depth   f. a quality of a person or thing

_____ 7. mortal   g. worldly; not simple; complex

_____ 8. provision   h. in a careful, exact, and honest manner

_____ 9. efficiency   i. skill in dealing with people without offending them

_____ 10. scrupulously   j. in a manner that deserves praise

_____ 11. admirably   k. something provided for the future

_____ 12. tact   l. the ability to produce a desired effect with the least effort or waste

Part B   Synonyms

Write the letter of the word that is closest in meaning to the capitalized word.

_____ 13. APPREHEND: (A) release   (B) chase   (C) accuse   (D) arrest

_____ 14. SUFFICIENT: (A) unbearable (B) enough   (C) easy   (D) hopeless

_____ 15. REPROACH: (A) scold   (B) forgive   (C) reappear   (D) investigate

_____ 16. ACCOMMODATE: (A) overwhelm   (B) ignore   (C) adjust   (D) approve

_____ 17. COMPETENCE: (A) challenge   (B) opinion   (C) capability (D) training

_____ 18. ACCLAIM: (A) praise   (B) rejection (C) declaration (D) regret

_____ 19. FINESSE: (A) triumph   (B) skillfulness (C) conclusion (D) surface

_____ 20. VIRTUALLY: (A) practically (B) supposedly (C) repeatedly (D) honestly

UNIT 7 Test Yourself

Part A Recognizing Meaning

Write the letter of the word or phrase that is closest in meaning to the word or words in italics.

_____ 1. a familiar *adage*
  a. quotation   c. prayer
  b. folk tale   d. proverb

_____ 2. the *expanse* of the night sky
  a. darkness   c. loneliness
  b. wide extent   d. fascination

_____ 3. the *excess* food
  a. unneeded   c. free
  b. odd-tasting   d. unprepared

_____ 4. an effort to *conceal*
  a. work with   c. show off
  b. hide   d. demonstrate

_____ 5. requires little *maintenance*
  a. upkeep   c. packaging
  b. preparation   d. expense

_____ 6. an endless *cycle*
  a. problem   c. change
  b. dizziness   d. repeated series

_____ 7. a rather *inconspicuous* man
  a. thoughtless   c. extraordinary
  b. unnoticeable d. gigantic

_____ 8. *aerial* attacks
  a. airborne   c. surprise
  b. nighttime   d. televised

_____ 9. *liable* to go off
  a. likely   c. planned
  b. hoping   d. not expected

_____ 10. needed to *forage*
  a. store food   c. steal food
  b. prepare food d. look for food

Part B Matching Definitions

Match each word on the left with its definition on the right. Write the letter of the definition in the blank.

_____ 11. secretive

_____ 12. agility

_____ 13. majestic

_____ 14. stealth

_____ 15. expediency

_____ 16. recognition

_____ 17. seclude

_____ 18. keynote

_____ 19. predator

_____ 20. prescribe

a. acknowledgment

b. to give the basic idea or set the tone

c. to make private or hidden; keep away from others

d. grand; noble; striking

e. ease of movement

f. keeping one's thoughts and feelings to oneself

g. the quality of being convenient

h. to set down a rule or direction

i. secret, sneaky, or quiet action

j. one who lives by killing and feeding upon other animals

Score Yourself! *The answers are on page 239.*   Number correct: _____ Part A: _____ Part B: _____

UNIT 9   Test Yourself

Part A   Synonyms

Write the letter of the word that is closest in meaning to the capitalized word.

_____ 1. ABSOLUTELY: (A) somewhat   (B) always   (C) totally   (D) typically

_____ 2. ADORN: (A) invent   (B) beautify   (C) appear   (D) crush

_____ 3. STALWART: (A) timid   (B) delicate   (C) hardy   (D) overpowering

_____ 4. PROSPEROUS: (A) hardworking (B) successful   (C) dutiful   (D) profitable

_____ 5. PROCESSION: (A) parade   (B) organization   (C) promotion (D) continuation

_____ 6. DISFIGURE: (A) deform   (B) replace   (C) insult   (D) demolish

_____ 7. VIGOROUS: (A) friendly   (B) scary   (C) stiff   (D) strong

_____ 8. ASSEMBLAGE: (A) gathering   (B) construction   (C) factory   (D) display

_____ 9. FLOURISH: (A) rest   (B) succeed   (C) wilt   (D) reappear

_____ 10. DAUNTLESS: (A) untiring   (B) unimaginative (C) weird   (D) courageous

_____ 11. AVARICIOUS: (A) mean-spirited (B) countless   (C) greedy   (D) selfless

_____ 12. PEERLESS: (A) similar   (B) unusual   (C) matchless (D) invisible

Part B   Applying Meaning

Write the letter of the best answer.

_____ 13. If you desire solitude, what you most want is to
a. have company.   b. sleep well.   c. get well.   d. be alone.

_____ 14. To be endowed with a talent is to
a. use it.   b. lack it.   c. have it.   d. be modest about it.

_____ 15. A ruler's principality is his or her
a. territory.   b. throne.   c. crown.   d. palace.

_____ 16. One of the most lucrative professions is that of a
a. lion tamer.   b. truck driver.   c. movie star.   d. bank teller.

_____ 17. A person who simpers is most likely to be considered
a. empty-headed.   b. intelligent.   c. very brave.   d. jealous.

_____ 18. You are most likely to disturb someone by giving him or her
a. a gift.   b. bad news.   c. an invitation.   d. your opinion.

_____ 19. Clowns are most likely to be rife at a
a. birthday party.   b. costume shop.   c. funeral.   d. circus.

_____ 20. The members of a militia are usually all of the following EXCEPT
a. armed.   b. professional.   c. trained.   d. experienced.

Score Yourself!   *The answers are on page 239.*   Number correct: _____   Part A: _____   Part B: _____

UNIT 10 Test Yourself

Part A   Matching Definitions

Match each word on the left with its definition on the right. Write the letter of the definition in the blank.

_____ 1. sunder   a. a country estate

_____ 2. metamorphosis   b. to place alone

_____ 3. vary   c. to press down

_____ 4. villa   d. outline; side view

_____ 5. reap   e. to change; be different

_____ 6. renounce   f. to give up; disown

_____ 7. epoch   g. to push, shove, force, or drive

_____ 8. isolate   h. a change of form, shape, structure, or substance

_____ 9. depress   i. a period of time marked by noteworthy events

_____ 10. appropriate   j. to gather a harvest by cutting

_____ 11. thrust   k. to take for one's own; set aside for a specific use

_____ 12. profile   l. to break apart; split

Part B   Recognizing Meaning

Write the letter of the word or phrase that is closest in meaning to the word or words in italics.

_____ 13. *native to* Kansas City
   a. living in   c. occurring in
   b. born in   d. brought to

_____ 14. the *remote* countryside
   a. distant   c. still
   b. lovely   d. unreachable

_____ 15. that *immense* rock
   a. medium   c. unmoveable
   b. enormous   d. very hard

_____ 16. moved *gradually*
   a. repeatedly   c. step by step
   b. one by one   d. in a showy way

_____ 17. to *assume* control
   a. give up   c. long for
   b. have   d. take on

_____ 18. spoke *distinctly*
   a. quickly   c. clearly
   b. from afar   d. in an accent

_____ 19. this *novel* experience
   a. new   c. recent
   b. ordinary   d. lengthy

_____ 20. to *yield* a fortune
   a. desire   c. require
   b. inherit   d. produce

UNIT 11 Test Yourself

Part A Applying Meaning
Write the letter of the best answer.

_____ 1. An example of an <u>involuntary</u> action is a
a. slap.   b. refusal.   c. handshake.   d. hiccup.

_____ 2. <u>Rancor</u> describes the relationship between two
a. best friends.   b. enemies.   c. siblings.   d. opposites.

_____ 3. Someone who shows <u>impertinence</u> is being
a. rude.   b. playful.   c. creative.   d. threatening.

_____ 4. Which of the following is always meant to be <u>offensive</u>?
a. a bit of gossip   b. a rumor   c. an insult   d. a joke

_____ 5. To show that one feels <u>contrite</u>, a person would say,
a. "Not me."   b. "Please."   c. "You bet!"   d. "I'm sorry."

_____ 6. A <u>frayed</u> garment shows signs of being
a. used.   b. mended.   c. dirty.   d. old-fashioned.

_____ 7. A <u>dandy</u> would be proudest of his
a. work.   b. ideas.   c. looks.   d. jokes.

_____ 8. If you have an <u>aversion</u> to a thing, you
a. hate it.   b. love it.   c. don't care about it.   d. have mixed feelings about it.

Part B Matching Definitions
Match each word on the left with its definition on the right. Write the letter of the definition in the blank.

_____ 9. befitting   a. confusion; bewilderment

_____ 10. shudder   b. scorn; disrespect

_____ 11. commentary   c. rebellious; disobedient

_____ 12. synopsis   d. usual; customary

_____ 13. indispensable   e. suitable; proper; fitting

_____ 14. misdemeanor   f. troubled; offended; showing grief

_____ 15. perplexity   g. essential; completely necessary

_____ 16. defiant   h. a series of comments or observations

_____ 17. suave   i. a minor offense; misbehavior; misconduct

_____ 18. aggrieved   j. smoothly polite or gracious; polished; charming

_____ 19. habitual   k. a summary; short outline

_____ 20. contempt   l. a shiver; trembling; shaking

UNIT 13 Test Yourself

Part A Synonyms

Write the letter of the word that is closest in meaning to the capitalized word

_____ 1. CONVERT: (A) transform   (B) cooperate   (C) replace   (D) eliminate

_____ 2. DISCHARGE: (A) composition (B) exposure   (C) flood   (D) release

_____ 3. INDEX: (A) chapter   (B) brand   (C) indicator   (D) crossroads

_____ 4. AGENT: (A) means   (B) effect   (C) substitute   (D) forerunner

_____ 5. ELEMENT: (A) solid   (B) gas   (C) simplicity   (D) ingredient

_____ 6. COMPRISE: (A) prepare   (B) invent   (C) include   (D) declare

_____ 7. SALINITY: (A) taste   (B) lightness   (C) depth   (D) saltiness

_____ 8. PROPERTY: (A) procedure   (B) usefulness   (C) trait   (D) outcome

_____ 9. SYSTEM: (A) purpose   (B) organization (C) practice   (D) government

_____ 10. MONITOR: (A) observe   (B) reflect   (C) report   (D) enforce

_____ 11. ADAPT: (A) take   (B) succeed   (C) adjust   (D) argue

_____ 12. CONSTANT: (A) useless   (B) opposing   (C) immediate   (D) ongoing

Part B Applying Meaning

Write the letter of the best answer.

_____ 13. One example of an organism is a
a. daisy.   b. mob.   c. bad smell.   d. piano.

_____ 14. Conductivity is the most important feature of a good
a. railroad.   b. roof.   c. musician.   d. lightning rod.

_____ 15. One part of a car that acts as a buffer is a
a. starter.   b. shock absorber.   c. rear-view mirror.   d. headlight.

_____ 16. One component of a car is a
a. driver.   b. gas station.   c. truck.   d. steering wheel.

_____ 17. A common term for the sediment in a river is
a. ice.   b. pollution.   c. mud.   d. current.

_____ 18. Students at a college of technology probably plan to become
a. engineers.   b. writers.   c. athletes.   d. teachers.

_____ 19. Which of the following would you expect to have the lowest density?
a. fog   b. marble   c. foam rubber   d. milk

_____ 20. Evaporation is the process by which water turns into
a. ice.   b. rain or snow.   c. a gas.   d. oceans.

Score Yourself!   *The answers are on page 239.*   Number correct: _____   Part A: _____   Part B: _____

UNIT 14 Test Yourself

Part A Recognizing Meaning

Write the letter of the word or phrase that is closest in meaning to the word or words in italics.

_____ 1. the king's *tyranny*
    a. anger   c. wisdom
    b. harsh rule   d. castle

_____ 2. to *abolish* a law
    a. rewrite   c. get rid of
    b. pass   d. enforce

_____ 3. a very *candid* interview
    a. hurried   c. surprising
    b. comfortable   d. honest

_____ 4. *accustomed* to making do
    a. used to   c. good at
    b. fed up with   d. not capable of

_____ 5. to *derive* satisfaction
    a. give   c. gain
    b. seek   d. demand

_____ 6. to *impel* to action
    a. prod into   c. request
    b. abandon   d. hope for

_____ 7. to *constrain* obedience
    a. desire   c. suggest
    b. offer   d. force

_____ 8. the *pursuit* of rabbits
    a. habits   c. description
    b. living place   d. chasing

Part B Matching Definitions

Match each word on the left with its definition on the right. Write the letter of the definition in the blank.

_____ 9. accordingly

_____ 10. entitle

_____ 11. transient

_____ 12. evince

_____ 13. prudence

_____ 14. dictate

_____ 15. usurpation

_____ 16. self-evident

_____ 17. invariably

_____ 18. despotism

_____ 19. institute

_____ 20. dispose

a. needing no proof; obvious; apparent; plain

b. therefore

c. always; without change; uniformly

d. to make clear; reveal

e. to command or order

f. temporary; passing quickly

g. the quality of being cautious and sensible; careful management

h. rule by someone with complete and total power

i. to set up or establish

j. to give a right, name, or legal title to

k. to make willing; incline; prepare

l. the unlawful or violent taking of power

UNIT 15 Test Yourself

Part A Matching Definitions

Match each word on the left with its definition on the right. Write the letter of the definition in the blank.

_____ 1. perception   a. the capacity for physical feeling; awareness

_____ 2. faculty   b. loyalty; faithfulness

_____ 3. fidelity   c. a hidden identity; one appearing or living in disguise

_____ 4. implement   d. a showy display

_____ 5. ostentation   e. a skill or ability

_____ 6. incognito   f. a utensil with many small holes, used for straining; sifter

_____ 7. exile   g. something that is stated positively; declaration

_____ 8. sensibility   h. a tool; utensil; device

_____ 9. assertion   i. awareness; understanding

_____ 10. sieve   j. the state of living away from one's country because one has been, or feels, forced to leave

Part B Recognizing Meaning

Write the letter of the word or phrase that is closest in meaning to the word or words in italics.

_____ 11. under *deplorable* conditions
a. unavoidable   c. unexpected
b. miserable   d. ordinary

_____ 12. *inevitably* frustrated
a. unavoidably   c. needlessly
b. probably   d. quietly

_____ 13. their *humane* actions
a. practical   c. life-saving
b. good-hearted   d. cruel

_____ 14. with such *devotion*
a. strong desire   c. commitment
b. exaggeration   d. honesty

_____ 15. his *immaculate* shirt
a. spotless   c. well-worn
b. favorite   d. expensive

_____ 16. a fairly *intolerable* delay
a. soothing   c. unbearable
b. well-timed   d. pointless

_____ 17. answered *in monosyllables*
a. at length   c. in a dull voice
b. very quietly   d. very briefly

_____ 18. thinking *in the abstract*
a. in theory   c. practically
b. in a hurry   d. carefully

_____ 19. to follow the *regulations*
a. pattern   c. rules and laws
b. advice   d. usual method

_____ 20. a surprising *ingratitude*
a. memory   c. thanklessness
b. stillness   d. show of support

Score Yourself!

Unit 1	Unit 2	Unit 3	Unit 5	Unit 6	Unit 7
Part A	*Part A*	*Part A*	*Part A*	*Part A*	*Part A*
1. A	1. a	1. j	1. d	1. b	1. d
2. D	2. c	2. d	2. c	2. c	2. b
3. C	3. a	3. f	3. d	3. e	3. a
4. B	4. d	4. l	4. b	4. f	4. b
5. B	5. b	5. h	5. c	5. g	5. a
6. A	6. d	6. b	6. a	6. d	6. d
7. C	7. b	7. a	7. a	7. a	7. b
8. B	8. b	8. k	8. d	8. k	8. a
9. C	9. c	9. i	*Part B*	9. l	9. a
10. D	10. c	10. c	9. c	10. h	10. d
11. A	11. d	11. e	10. a	11. j	*Part B*
12. C	12. a	12. g	11. b	12. i	11. f
Part B	13. b	*Part B*	12. c	*Part B*	12. e
13. a	14. d	13. D	13. d	13. D	13. d
14. b	*Part B*	14. B	14. b	14. B	14. i
15. c	15. B	15. A	15. b	15. A	15. g
16. d	16. C	16. B	16. d	16. C	16. a
17. c	17. D	17. C	17. b	17. C	17. c
18. b	18. A	18. C	18. a	18. A	18. b
19. c	19. A	19. A	19. a	19. B	19. j
20. a	20. D	20. D	20. c	20. A	20. h

Unit 9	Unit 10	Unit 11	Unit 13	Unit 14	Unit 15
Part A	*Part A*	*Part A*	*Part A*	*Part A*	*Part A*
1. C	1. l	1. d	1. A	1. b	1. i
2. B	2. h	2. b	2. D	2. c	2. e
3. C	3. e	3. a	3. C	3. d	3. b
4. B	4. a	4. c	4. A	4. a	4. h
5. A	5. j	5. d	5. D	5. c	5. d
6. A	6. f	6. a	6. C	6. a	6. c
7. D	7. i	7. c	7. D	7. d	7. j
8. A	8. b	8. a	8. C	8. a	8. a
9. B	9. c	*Part B*	9. B	*Part B*	9. g
10. D	10. k	9. e	10. A	9. b	10. f
11. C	11. g	10. l	11. C	10. j	*Part B*
12. C	12. d	11. h	12. D	11. f	11. b
Part B	*Part B*	12. k	*Part B*	12. d	12. a
13. d	13. b	13. g	13. a	13. g	13. b
14. c	14. a	14. i	14. d	14. e	14. c
15. a	15. b	15. a	15. b	15. l	15. a
16. c	16. c	16. c	16. d	16. a	16. c
17. a	17. d	17. j	17. c	17. c	17. d
18. b	18. c	18. f	18. a	18. h	18. a
19. d	19. a	19. d	19. a	19. i	19. c
20. b	20. d	20. b	20. c	20. k	20. c

Acknowledgments

- Mrs. James Thurber: For an excerpt from "The Day the Dam Broke" by James Thurber, from *My Life and Hard Times;* copyright © 1933, 1961 by James Thurber, published by Harper & Row Publishers, Inc.

- Macmillan Publishing Company: For "Story of Indian Humor" by Vine Deloria, Jr., from *Custer Died for Your Sins;* copyright © 1969 by Vine Deloria, Jr.

- Harper & Row Publishers, Inc.: For an excerpt from *An American Childhood* by Annie Dillard; copyright © 1987 to Annie Dillard.

- City News Publishing Company: For "What Makes a Good Police Officer?" by Clarence M. Kelley from *Vital Speeches of the Day,* Vol. XL, April 1, 1974.

- Wyoming Wildlife Game and Fish Department: For "An Owl's Place" by Mike Sawyers, from *Wyoming Wildlife,* September, 1971.

- Random House, Inc.: For the entry for *pale,* from *The Random House Thesaurus, College Edition;* copyright © 1984 by Random House, Inc.

- The New American Library, Inc.: For "California—Character of Population" by Mark Twain, from *Roughing It;* copyright © 1962.

- Simon & Schuster: For an excerpt from *A Week on the Concord and Merrimack Rivers* by Henry David Thoreau; copyright © 1961.

- Simon & Schuster: for definition of *beautiful,* from *Webster's New World Dictionary,* Students Edition; copyright © 1981, 1976.

- International Oceanographic Foundation; For "How Salty Is the Ocean?" by Donald G. Klim, from *Sea Frontiers;* copyright © 1977 by the International Oceanographic Foundation; with permission of the author.

- Doubleday & Company, Inc.: For an excerpt from *Lord Jim* by Joseph Conrad.

Cover Art

Waterfall, 1961, M.C. Escher, Lithograph. National Gallery of Art, Washington, D.C., Cornelius van S. Roosevelt Collection.

Photographs

FPG International: 16; © 1933, 1961 James Thurber, from *My Life and Hard Times,* published by Harper & Row: 25; Dickkehrwald/Black Star: 54; Martin E. Vanderall/DeWys, Inc.: 64; Culver Pictures, Inc.: 102; Peter Vandermark/Stock Boston: 111; © 1988 Bruce Byers/FPG International: 142.

Illustrations

Tom Dunnington: 74; Dan Siculan: 121; George Suyeoka: 153; David Cunningham: 162; Rebecca D. Brown, 180.

Personal Vocabulary Log

Use the following pages to keep track of the unfamiliar words you encounter in your reading. Write brief definitions and pronunciations for each word. This will make the words part of your permanent vocabulary.

Personal Vocabulary Log